THE OTHER SPECIAL RELATIONSHIP:
THE UNITED STATES AND AUSTRALIA
AT THE START OF THE 21st CENTURY

Edited by

Jeffrey D. McCausland
Douglas T. Stuart
William T. Tow
Michael Wesley

February 2007

*****

The views expressed in this report are those of the authors and do not necessarily reflect the official policy or position of the Department of the Army, the Department of Defense, or the U.S. Government. This report is cleared for public release; distribution is unlimited.

*****

Comments pertaining to this report are invited and should be forwarded to: Director, Strategic Studies Institute, U.S. Army War College, 122 Forbes Ave, Carlisle, PA 17013-5244.

*****

All Strategic Studies Institute (SSI) publications are available on the SSI homepage for electronic dissemination. Hard copies of this report also may be ordered from our homepage. SSI's homepage address is: www.StrategicStudiesInstitute.army.mil.

*****

The Strategic Studies Institute publishes a monthly e-mail newsletter to update the national security community on the research of our analysts, recent and forthcoming publications, and upcoming conferences sponsored by the Institute. Each newsletter also provides a strategic commentary by one of our research analysts. If you are interested in receiving this newsletter, please subscribe on our homepage at www.StrategicStudiesInstitute. army.mil/newsletter/.

ISBN 1-58487-276-4

TABLE OF CONTENTS

PREFACE

Jeffrey D. McCausland
Douglas T. Stuart
William T. Tow
Michael Wesley

The idea for this volume grew out of a previous collaboration between Jeffrey McCausland and Douglas Stuart. Arguing that the bilateral relationship between the United States and the United Kingdom was both underappreciated and understudied, they organized a series of conferences in 2005 which brought together a group of well-known American and British academics, journalists, and policymakers to discuss political, military, and economic aspects of the "special relationship." The conference proceedings, published by the Strategic Studies Institute of the U.S. Army War College under the title *U.S.-UK Relations at the Start of the 21st Century,* proved to be extremely popular — requiring a second printing and generating follow-on public discussions on both sides of the Atlantic.[1] Conversation during these public events tended to focus on one basic question and a couple of ancillary questions: Was the U.S.-UK relationship unique? If so, in what respects? And why?

Scholarly inquiry into the "other special relationship" between the United States and Australia flowed logically from these discussions. With the generous financial and administrative assistance of the U.S. Army War College, Dickinson College, the Australian National University, and the Griffith University Asia Institute, and with the indispensable scholarly collaboration of William Tow and Michael Wesley, a series of professional conferences was organized in Carlisle, Pennsylvania, and Washington, DC, on the U.S. side, and in Brisbane and Canberra on the Australian side. A team of American and Australian experts came together in all four locations to discuss issues relating to foreign policy, economics and business, domestic politics and public opinion, and security and defense affairs. The U.S. Army War College also enriched our discussions with panels in Carlisle and Canberra relating to the Global War on Terror.

This volume is designed to summarize the major findings of our fruitful collaboration over the last year. To provide the participants with a common lexicon, all of the contributors to this volume were asked to return to their dog-eared copies of Arnold Wolfers' wise and wide-ranging book, *Discord and Collaboration*.[2] Although Wolfers' book is more than 40 years old, it was selected because of its valuable (and still-valid) insights regarding alliance behavior, the goals and interests of nations, and the interaction of individual, national, and international factors as determinants of foreign policy. Readers will find references to *Discord and Collaboration* throughout this volume.

It came as no surprise when many of the themes that surfaced in the study of U.S.-UK relations resurfaced in our deliberations on U.S.-Australian relations. One recurrent theme was the importance of leadership in both the U.S.-UK and the U.S.-Australian relationships. Both Tony Blair and John Howard have cultivated close personal relationships with George W. Bush, based on the shared "Anglosphere" values of political and economic liberalism and a shared appreciation of the need to act assertively, and globally, in defense of these values.[3] The result has been a level of comfort and mutual trust among the three leaders that has greatly facilitated international cooperation.

In contrast to Prime Minister Blair, who was able to maintain a close friendship with both Bill Clinton and George W. Bush, the personal chemistry between John Howard and Clinton was never strong. President Clinton's oscillations on China policy, his relative lack of interest in Japan, the absence of tangible progress on bilateral free trade negotiations, and Howard's disappointment regarding U.S. support in East Timor, all worked to impose strains on the relationship. This all changed, however, with the arrival of George W. Bush. As Paul Kelly observes in this volume, "Howard and Bush are political soul mates" whose close personal ties have provided the foundation for what Kelly describes as "the new intimacy" between America and Australia.

Beyond the thematic resemblance between this volume and the previous study of U.S.-UK relations, another similarlity is the importance of two events in determining London and Canberra's relations with Washington. The terrorist attacks of September 11, 2001 (9/11) represent the first turning point. The British and Australian governments reacted similarly to these attacks—immediately identifying 9/11 as a transformative moment in international relations. But the Australian Prime Minister's presence in Washington, DC, during the 9/11 terrorist attacks intensified the personal impact of the events, and within a few days his government had invoked the ANZUS Treaty to offer its full support to the United States. This development would have been hard to imagine a half-century before, when the Australians who negotiated the ANZUS Treaty tended to assume that if the alliance were ever called into action, it would be done to apply American power on behalf of Australian security.

The second "big event" dominating both U.S.-UK relations and U.S.-Australia relations has been America's management of the Global War on Terror and, in particular, its leadership of the ongoing operations in Afghanistan and Iraq. Once the Iraq campaign began to look like a quagmire, a growing number of critics in both Britain and Australia began to question the wisdom and the propriety of close collaboration with the American "hyperpower." In Britain, this has taken the form of Tony Blair's "poodle problem," which has contributed to demands from both the British public and Mr. Blair's own Labour Party for the Prime Minister's resignation.

John Howard has confronted his own "poodle problem" (often portrayed in the Australian news media as a "deputy sheriff problem"). To date, Mr. Howard has managed this problem more effectively than his British counterpart. Mr. Howard is nonetheless likely to face increasing domestic criticism about the substantive results he has achieved in his efforts to translate his support for the United States into economic and political benefits. Don Russell addresses one aspect of this cost-benefit issue in his discussion in this volume of the Australia-United States Free Trade Agreement. John Hulsman addresses the same problem at a more general level, arguing that "the U.S. must get away from taking Australia for granted" in its management of foreign affairs.

The Australian Prime Minister will also find it increasingly difficult to manage the vigorous debate which has developed in Australia over what it means to be an ally of a superpower in trouble. Mr. Howard has argued that strong allies do not desert each other when they experience unanticipated difficulties in fulfilling their missions.

> I ask people to contemplate the impact on the authority of the United States, the impact on the west, of a defeat in Iraq . . . If people think that is going to strengthen the West, is going to strengthen America and strengthen Australia, I think they have taken leave of their senses . . . [it] would do great long-term damage to our alliance.[4]

The Prime Minister's increasingly strident critics have responded that a genuinely valuable junior ally would have told its senior partner that its policy was bankrupt, that it needs to change course, and that it would no longer support the current policy with its own manpower and resources.

Mr. Howard also must resolve, or at least effectively manage, a number of difficult strategic decisions concerning when, where, and how to employ Australian military forces in the future. It would have been hard to imagine at the end of the Cold War that Australian-American military collaboration during the first decade of this century would be taking place primarily in areas other than the Asia-Pacific. The deployment of Australian forces in Afghanistan and Iraq in support of America's Global War on Terror triggered a monumental strategic debate in Canberra over how to structure Australia's future military capabilities (to defend Australia or to be part of future expeditionary forces abroad?). Michael Evans describes the two sides of this debate in this volume as the "defender-regionalists" and the "reformer-globalists," concluding that "at the higher policy level, the intellectual uncertainty with regard to Australia's defence posture needs to be filled not by a new Defence White Paper but by an articulated National Security Strategy."

Australia's evolving relationship with China must be at the core of any new national security strategy. Many of the chapters in this volume deal directly or implicitly with the rise of China as a regional and global actor. Some of the contributors have interpreted this issue as a potential source of U.S.-Australian disagreement (or worse!), while others accept the Howard government's assurances that Canberra can manage both an increasingly close relationship with Beijing and continued close strategic ties with Washington.

As the United States and Australia adapt their foreign and defense policies to new regional and global challenges, they can take considerable reassurance from the historical record of each government's handling of the inevitable alliance disputes over the last 55 years. Washington and Canberra have resolved bilateral disputes over accusations of alliance entrapment and abandonment, as well as disagreements over financial and military burden-sharing, in a way that has contributed to the continuous transformation of the ANZUS Alliance. Initially created to protect Australia and New Zealand from an early postwar threat that never materialized—a remilitarized Japan—ANZUS subsequently was rationalized as part of the American global containment architecture directed against international communism. But neither Australia nor New Zealand elected to apply the alliance to U.S. confrontations against China over Taiwan during the 1950s or to go beyond relatively short-lived commitments to fight communism in Indochina over the following decade. Australia kept ANZUS together in the mid-1980s after New Zealand challenged elements of America's nuclear deterrence doctrine. Following the end of the Cold War, Australia enthusiastically endorsed Washington's prescription for a "new world order," while at the same time seeking new links with its northern Asian neighbors as they became more important economic and geopolitical actors. In the wake of the catastrophic events of 9/11, ANZUS has once again taken on a new identity and new missions.

This volume provides valuable insights into the way in which Washington and Canberra have responded to these new missions. It also highlights many of the complexities of "the other special relationship" that are often overlooked in the welter of fiery domestic political rhetoric and media sensationalism. The "politics of intimacy" between close allies is generally more nuanced, less strident, and more resilient than we are led to believe by some politicians and policy analysts. This volume illustrates that this fact is nowhere more true than in the case of the U.S.-Australia relationship.

Many of the contributors to this volume agree with Michael Evans' conclusion that "in the first decade of the new millennium, the Australian-American Alliance is at its strongest since the height of the Vietnam War in the mid-1960s." But if there is one overarching theme to be found in this book, it is that such an intimate alliance relationship cannot be taken for granted. As a general rule, Arnold Wolfers is correct that "their own self-interest will usually suffice to hold allied countries in the alliance."[5] Both governments nonetheless must guard against the danger that international developments will stir concerns in either population which will lead to uncontrollable fluctuations in public opinion. One such concern on the Australian side is abandonment anxiety, often given voice by figures such as former Prime Minister Malcolm Fraser (see William Tow's chapter). If such sentiments are given momentum by a serious U.S.-Australia policy dispute (over China, for example), they could tap into deep Australian sensitivities about reciprocity and gratitude.[6] On the American side, similar political problems could arise as a result of the "loyalty test" (referred to by Tow in his chapter) if Australia were to stand aside from a significant American security commitment.

The key to sustaining and adapting the relationship is a constant dialogue, supported by a network of facilitative institutions, to ensure that both parties understand the other's values, interests, and concerns relating to successive hardships and contingencies. If this is the criterion for enduring ties, the Australian-American relationship clearly stands at the pinnacle of those bilateral relationships that matter most in the world today.

ENDNOTES - PREFACE

1. Public events were organized at the Heritage Foundation in Washington, DC, and at the Chatham House in London.

2. Johns Hopkins University Press, Baltimore, 1962.

3. Regarding "Anglosphere" cooperation, see Douglas Stuart, "NATO and the Wider World: From Regional Collective Defence to Global Coalitions of the Willing," *Australian Journal of International Affairs*, Vol. 58, No. 1, March 2004, pp. 33-46.

3. "Labor Plan would bring defeat—Howard," *The Australian*, October 25, 2006.

4. Arnold Wolfers, *Discord and Collaboration: Essays of International Politics*, Baltimore: The Johns Hopkins Press, 1962, p. 229.

5. One example of this dynamic is recent tensions between Australia and Indonesia over the jailing for 20 years of an Australian woman convicted of smuggling marijuana to Bali, and the freeing after a jail term of 30 months of Jemaah Islamiyah cleric Abu Bakar Bashir, implicated in the October 2002 Bali bombings. In many Australian minds, these episodes have prompted feelings of Indonesia's "ingratitude" for Australia's help after the 2004

Boxing day tsunami, and calls for Australian aid to be returned and for Australians to boycott Indonesia. See Michael Wesley, *The Howard Paradox: Australian Diplomacy in Asia 1996-2007*, Sydney: ABC Books, 2007.

ACKNOWLEDGMENTS

This study of the unique and historic relationship between America and Australia could never have occurred without the dedicated support of many people in addition to our outstanding group of contributors. The effort included conferences in the United States that were held at Dickinson College in Carlisle, Pennsylvania, and in Washington, DC, in the autumn of 2005, as well as subsequent conferences and presentations in Brisbane and Canberra, Australia.

The project greatly depended upon the generous support of the Strategic Studies Institute (SSI) at the U.S. Army War College. We are indebted to Professor Douglas Lovelace, the Director, not only for his advice and assistance but also for his direct participation in our discussions and his support for the participation of key members of the SSI team—Steven Metz, Douglas Macdonald, and Jeffery Sengelman. These participants provided key insights regarding the U.S.-Australia relationship, with special reference to the ongoing Global War on Terror. Dr. Adam Cobb of the Air War College also made a valuable contribution to our discussions relating to the challenges of global terrorism.

The organization/management of our initial conference at Dickinson College, including travel and budgeting, was handled superbly by Ms. Kitzi Chappelle, administrative assistant to the Director of the Leadership Initiative. She was ably assisted by a number of outstanding students from Dickinson College, including Eric Hakanson, Sam Rosmarin, and John Roberts. During our Dickinson conference, all participants benefitted from the contributions of Malcolm Binks (Chairman) and Ms. Jennifer Parser

Re (Vice Chairman) of the American-Australian Association.

We were also fortunate to be hosted by the Institute for National Strategic Studies of the National Defense University in Washington, DC, and wish to express our appreciation to Dr. Steve Flanagan, Director, and Dr. James Schear, Director of Research. Dr. Schear was also an active participant in the conference and prepared the conclusion for this book.

Several people and institutions provided critical support for the Brisbane and Canberra components of the Australian workshops. Ms. Meegan Thorley and Ms. Pearl Lee performed most of the key administrative and logistical tasks in Brisbane. Michael Evans, Russell Parkin, and Amy Chen were the major project facilitators in Canberra. We also must acknowledge the support of the Centre for Defence and Strategic Studies at the Australian Defence College for providing ideal facilities and transportation arrangements during our stay in Canberra. Dr. Peter Londey from the Australian War Memorial gave our U.S. participants the opportunity to explore the historical evolution of the alliance at that unique facility. The Department of International Relations of the Research School of Pacific and Asian Studies (RSPAS) at the Australian National University (ANU) and the Griffith University Asia Institute underwrote the project costs for the Australian component. We wish to thank Professor Christian Reus-Smit, Head of the ANU's Department of International Relations, RSPAS, for authorizing such support on behalf of his institution. ANU also was very well represented by Ms. Shannon Tow, a Ph.D. candidate in International Relations, who served as an insightful respondent on panels in both the United States and Australia.

Finally, the editors must acknowledge the outstanding support we received from the editorial staff of the Strategic Studies Institute at the Army War College. This volume would never have been completed without the expertise and hard work of Ms. Marianne Cowling, Ms. Rita Rummel, and Colonel Lloyd Matthews, USA Retired. In many, many ways, the hard work of the Australians and Americans noted here epitomizes the bonds that exist between these two great countries. We can only hope this relationship will continue to strengthen and grow in the future.

INTRODUCTION

The Honorable Bill Hayden

I am honored to have been invited to address this conference, comprised as it is of key scholars, government officials, representatives of various defense services, and, of course, informed representatives of the general community.

There is a wide canvas of issues to be explored, and all are of sustaining importance to the future of the alliance. The ANZUS Treaty was formally entered into by the three signatories more than half a century ago. In that time, our relationship with the United States has gone through many changes which largely have been unremarked upon as major refinements of the original conceptualization behind the treaty. The treaty document has not changed in 54 years, but it is propelled by a different engine; actually, it probably always was but our politicians were too wiley to tell us.

From the start there was a significant difference of emphasis between the United States and Australia as to the thrust of the treaty. Australia emphasized guarantees of its regional protection by the United States, while the United States was preocccupied with containment of communism in which ANZUS was one link in a chain of global treaties and arrangements. This difference of preoccupation was the continuing cause of perplexity, perhaps even impatience, on the part of some U.S. officials.

In 1962 the Australian government sternly opposed the incorporation of Irian Jaya into Indonesia and sought to invoke U.S. support under ANZUS. The

U.S. rebuff was a severe jolt to Australian domestic confidence in its government's assurances about the nature of the treaty.

President Richard Nixon's so-called Guam doctrine of 1969 announced that the U.S. Government would "furnish military and economic assistance when requested in accordance with our treaty commitments. But we shall look to the nation directly threatened to assume the primary responsibility . . . for its defense." These words again rattled community confidence in the nature of the alliance.

The 1986 defection of New Zealand from the alliance put ANZUS under extreme political stress in Australia, leading to a comprehensive review of it with the United States and a statement which refined and updated its nature. It was more a polishing exercise than a new body job. Nonetheless, as a political exercise, it was extremely successful in managing a potentially difficult domestic political problem in Australia and emphasizing, in association with a number of other foreign policy initiatives taken by the government, the nature of the alliance as one of reassuring closeness yet giving Australia considerable independence of judgment and action.

The end of the Cold War brought a marked and, for the Australian intelligentsia, disturbing, wind-down of the relationship. I will come back to that below. It nonetheless caused some important critical questioning of the durability of the alliance.

The 1999 notice from the U.S. Administration that it would not be putting American troops' boots on the ground in East Timor following an overture by the Australian government, once again shocked many in Australia.

Prime Minister Howard's invoking of ANZUS in 2002, following the terrorist attack on the World

Trade Center in New York, soberly demonstrated to Australians just how globally wide Australia's commitments were under ANZUS.

To all intents and purposes, ANZUS is now a bilaterial agreement although, curiously, still often spoken of as if it had effective trilateral status; it has changed dramatically and is unlikely to revert to what it was.

The alliance treaty, centered on the Cold War ANZUS agreement of 1952, is, in a fundamental sense and for many reasons, an obsolescent document. The concerns of the partners have moved on; the concerns now are terrorism, rogue states, rogue leaders, and new major powers emerging on the scene whose intentions are not exactly clear and whose potential goals may not be entirely benign. Much of this is happening in Australia's broad geostrategic region of interest.

These views of the changed nature of ANZUS are strongly implicit in the recent report of the Australian House of Representatives titled *Australia's Defence Relations with the United States*:

> The future of the ANZUS alliance is a framework under which modernization and policy adjustments can occur between Australia and the U.S. (and preferably New Zealand) in the face of a rapidly evolving strategic reality. Arguably the text of the treaty . . . becomes less important as the years pass. Instead the treaty will continue as a formal declaration of trust between countries that share values and ideals.[1]

The end of the Cold War suddenly found that Australia was, in the words of one American commentator, "relegated to geostrategic marginality notwithstanding its solid alliance with the U.S.-led western alliance."[2] And yet, this happened despite

Australia's having kept its insurance premiums paid up in full. Here, for example, is a view coming from the Heritage Foundation, a respected American think tank.

> Without peer, Australia has been America's most reliable ally and most valuable security partner in the Pacific basin for many years. Australia fought beside the United States in every war during the last century, including the less popular conflicts such as Vietnam, when many of its people objected to its involvement.[3]

We have certainly taken some risks for the alliance. High among them has been hosting key joint bases on Australian soil which would have been, in certain circumstances, critical priority nuclear targets for the former Soviet Union. For instance, Professor Paul Dibb has revealed that joint modeling involving U.S.-Australian defense representatives, when he was with the Defense Department, identified locations in Australia actually targeted by Moscow. In fact, the team estimated that an SS-11 nuclear-armed ballistic missile launched from Svobodny in Siberia was capable of inflicting one million instant deaths and 750,000 delayed radiation deaths in Sydney, not to mention the carnage at other locations also targeted.[4]

Some commentators go so far as to claim that Australia now is the United States' best ally, after Britain, and thus the question many will ask is, "Is that just for now, while we're involved with the United States in Iraq and Afghanistan?" Well, it won't be just an ephemeral interest on our part, because there are some big potential stresses looming in this region of the world — China, in particular, which will be notably tricky challenges for Australia.

Nonetheless the question of how deep and sustainable the U.S. interest in Australia is will continue to be raised. The skill in managing the relationship and its public presentation will determine whether confidence in it is maintained. Opinion polling shows something like 90 percent of the public support the alliance, but that could change in a flash if political management becomes slack, and in particular if stress rises to the point of alarming a public already sceptical as to whether Australia has been exercising the independence it should.

Based on past observations, we know the United States can have difficulty handling displays of independence by allies, as though it expected them, especially smaller ones, to hew to particular roles it notionally has assigned. It is understandable why a superpower, grown now to a hyperpower, reacts like this. Its international agenda of responsibilities is huge, the demands on its attention and energies limitless, but if friendly states are confronted with impatience or worse for engaging in sensible displays of independence, they can drift away.

We should not forget that in the course of exploring these recondite international issues, the ultimate arbiter of it all is public opinion, and skillful political handling of that in a democracy is critical. This situation reminds me of a quotation by the English writer, Hilaire Belloc, favorably commenting on the performance of a guileful politician: "He's like a skillful oarsman. While he resolutely focuses on an objective in front of him he is furiously rowing in the opposite direction." The United States must not assume such an imperial attitude that it makes it impossible for the Australian political leadership to row ultimately to the mutually shared objective.

A notable problem with the relationship is that it is so asymmetrical. Our defense spending is about 1.9 percent of the gross domestic product (GDP) per year, while the United States spends over 4 percent. The United States accounts for 32 percent of world GDP, 43 percent of world military expenditures, half of world arms production, and at least 60 percent of world military research and development (R&D); it is a hyperpower and sometimes an impatient one.[5] These factors, combined with America's strong sense of exceptionalism and manifest destiny plus powerful elements of religious fundamentalism, sometimes incline it to leap out in front, idealizing, moralizing, and incidentally forfeiting international support and respect, as has happened to a large extent in connection with Iraq. It remains the most powerful country in the world, and will remain so for the foreseeable future, but it has isolated itself too sharply from the international community. It desperately needs such ties if it is to formulate an effective and credible exit policy from Iraq.

But even as a hyperpower, it cannot successfully handle some major commitments alone; it must rebuild its international leadership credibility. Let us now discuss in turn several areas of the globe where events have particular salience for both America and Australia.

China.

I mentioned earlier the tricky nature for Australia of handling tensions with China. To be more specific, with respect to tensions between the United States and China over Taiwan, the United States wants our commitment of support. China, however, is stipulating that it expects neutrality from us.

It has been made crystal clear, in a statement by a senior U.S. State Department official at a conference at the University of Sydney, that "we do not consider our relationship with Australia to be a 'regional alliance' in the narrowest sense. Rather, we see our two countries joined in a global partnership."[6] Clearly, the United States has big expectations of the alliance and, in particular, of Australia's role within the alliance. In response to a maladroit comment by the Australian Foreign Minister that the ANZUS treaty would not apply in the case of conflict with China, the United States has made it forcefully clear to the Australian government that ANZUS Treaty Articles IV and V *would* apply. The Foreign Minister is reported to have replied wanly that while the treaty could be invoked if war broke out, "that's a very different thing from saying we would make a decision to go to war."

The minister might rather recall the advice that our best policy on this topic is "calculated ambiguity." About a year ago, China publicly stated that the ANZUS Treaty should be reviewed, warning that the alliance could threaten regional stability if Australia were drawn into a Sino-Taiwan conflict. Now, however, trade and investment here are being grandly underwritten by China. Our surging prosperity and the generous cash dividends the government is lavishing on politically popular domestic programs in each budget — the serendipitous dividend of chronic revenue underestimates — are being pumped up by trade with China to meet its economic requirements.

We can be reasonably sanguine that the Taiwan issue is containable — and indeed it is being contained. U.S. Influence with Taiwan is such that it should be able to discreetly direct Taiwanese conduct into less strident and provocative channels. China could undertake reprisals if we got involved, and the United States could if we didn't; either way we'd be in a bind.

There is another set of reasons for handling this issue cautiously. China's history does not suggest there is an inherent territorially expansionist nature to the country. What its history does show is a tendency toward cycles of strong central government followed by decaying at the center and outer fragmentation and disorder as the writ of government breaks down. China appears as if she may be headed in that direction currently. Unfortunately, popular mythologizing would have us accept that China is a magic dragon that can defy the basic laws of economics and still succeed.

A closer look at China's overall performance should temper this popular view greatly. The economy is overheated; resources are squandered through a combination of bad policy decisions, an inefficient banking system, and the Chinese variety of widespread cronyism and corruption. Economic and social development is occurring at greatly unequal rates between urban areas and countryside, with consequent economic and social inequities and the strong likelihood of political upheavals. Wealth distribution in China is now more regressive than in the United States or Australia. About 0.5 percent of China's population own some 60 percent of the country's wealth.[7]

China should have embarked on a program of economic austerity well before this. The longer it defers action, the worse the economic impact of that action when it finally comes. The political conundrum for China is inescapable: Can she afford the dislocation of several years of economic austerity? Well, scarcely. But can she afford to do nothing? Certainly not. Does she become more repressive and re-erect barriers, as in the not-so-distant past, while she tries to impose economic discipline? That will scarcely wash with her people, and there is some basis for believing that the only legitimacy her government has with the people comes from the economic prosperity it has presided over.

Economic discipline is only part of the solution; she will have to root out a lot of rottenness in the system. The World Bank estimates more than a third of bank-underwritten investment decisions in China between 1991 and 2000 were misguided. The Chinese central bank estimates that politically-directed lending was responsible for 60 percent of bad loans in 2001-02. The banking system costs the Chinese government about 30 percent of annual GDP in bailouts. Minxin Pei, in an illuminating essay on these topics, writes that "China has seen its future leaders, and a disproportionate number of them are on the take."[8] Minxin also reveals the underinvestment in crucial social services, in particular education and public health, and shows the crippling revenue burden that falls on poor peasants. China's main test in the immediate future will be the effort to accommodate the huge gulf between urban wealth and rural squalor.

The task looks to be well nigh impossible. If it proves so, the stability of its large domestic empire will be at stake. In fact, the Indian economy is performing better than that of China, with a published average economic growth rate over 8 percent. Moreover, in the confident words of the *Economist*, "India is producing far more world-class companies than China."[9] The buildup of the Chinese navy has a long way to go before it can hope to match the U.S. Seventh Fleet in the Pacific, but the Seventh Fleet is only one fleet of a very large, global navy.

To match the global U.S. Navy would be prohibitively expensive. The state of the Chinese economy is such that even if the Chinese were foolish and wasteful enough to try to do so at this stage of their development, it would take more than a generation to do.

Japan.

It is difficult to take much of the speculation on the Taiwan issue seriously. What can be taken seriously is the mounting tension between China and Japan. Both are energy-hungry countries. Both are keenly interested in offshore oil and gas deposits under the East China Sea. Each is challenging the other's claims disputing the border defined by the other. China has been provocative, with a submerged nuclear-powered submarine navigating Japanese waters and Chinese military surveillance aircraft intruding into disputed airspace. Japanese legislators and government leaders have been provocative too, preparing bills designed to protect the operations of Japanese drillers and fishermen in disputed waters, by force if necessary. Moreover, Miti has authorized Japanese companies to explore contested ocean areas for natural gas. Prime Minister Koizumi insists on making annual visits to the Yasukuni shrine where Japanese war dead are buried.

China plays these issues up domestically and regionally with marked effect. Japan is still distrusted in much of the region. It seems that all the ingredients for a major clash over resource extraction by two energy-hungry countries are in place. That is a very worrying development. It has clear consequences for the United States, the rest of the region, and, most certainly, for Australia.

North Korea.

Should conflict break out on the Korean peninsula, the United States would expect an Australian commitment, and our Abrams tanks then would have more relevance. They are part of the new and unwise expeditionary force restructure of the Australian Defense Force (ADF). This restructure does not make much sense for defense of Australia in the near regions. It is usually best to proceed on the principle that one's own interests come first, in case the United States is otherwise engaged, or has other priorities, or disagrees with our sense of crisis. Big powers can have an outlook different from that of small states like us.

South Asia.

The only concern about India is the suggestion that we may sell it uranium without it having the de rigueur nuclear safeguards in place. Of course, it is now moving to the status of U.S. ally.

Pakistan is an altogether different case. President Mushariff has been courageous in supporting U.S. actions in Afghanistan, but if he were to be removed from office by Islamic militants and suceeededed by one, then we soon would face an extreme militant Islamic nuclear power. That would be a power not just with nuclear warfighting capability itself, but one able to export nuclear weaponry know-how, components of weapons, and even weapons to like-minded sources. The consequences probably would be calamitous, and Australia would be drawn into the thick of the conseqeunces of this development.

Afghanistan.

Our troop commitment in Afghanistan, particularly in Uruzgan province, carries high risks. Uruzgan province is a recognized danger area, and combat casualties cannot be ruled out. If that happens, it would cause serious public discontent. Afghanistan could unravel before renewed Taliban activity, resurrecting a narco-economy and warlord cruelty and repression, even though they are now nominal allies of President Karzai, who of recent date charmingly appointed 13 such people to senior positions in the police force. These were people, according to a recently leaked United Nations (UN) report, with "links to drug smuggling, organized crime, and illegal militias." The same report names "leading Afghan politicans and officials accused of orchestrating massacres, torture, mass rape, and other war crimes."[10]

As these dreadful acts of government malfeasance become better known, it will be mountingly difficult to keep a public commitment to this engagement in place.

Iraq.

I consistently have believed that the United States and its coalition-of-the-willing partners should not have intervened in Iraq. Secretary of State Colin Powell's justification was overdrawn, based on the facts he alleged. If there had been a little more U.S. patience with UN inspection procedures, the United States and its partners could have been spared the embarrassment of igniting and even "winning" a war there but thus far being unable to keep the peace.

The lessons of history, however, do not provide cause for optimism. The current situation and the hopeful rhetoric accompanying it remind one of Britain's folly entering Iraq in 1922 and being confronted with revolt. Then, in 1927, after empty promises that Iraq was ready to stand on its own feet—all this was well before the 1952 expiry date of the British mandate—Britain removed its troops. There was bloodshed when Britain pulled out, later to be replaced by Sunni repression. Now, in this re-run of that sad experience, the prospect is a balkanization of the country, with the Kurd segment creating major instability in Turkey and Syria.

Nor do the complications end here. Iran aims to use its influence to get control of the southern oil fields. And there will be internal fighting among Iraq's major players to see which dominates the rich Basra fields. Since al-Zarqawi's death, fighting has broken out among Shia factions jockeying for power and future control. At this writing, General George Casey, commander of the coalition forces, has announced "that he may call for more troops to be sent to Baghdad, possibly by increasing the overall U.S. presence in Iraq," in the face of rising bloodshed.[11] This sharp reversal in withdrawal plans contrasts with the earlier announced decision not to replace two brigades of combat troops when they return to the United States in September 2007, and to make big drawdowns of troops by the end of that year It is to be hoped that such backing-and-filling is not a shadow play of the British tactics in 1927. In any case, it would be interesting to learn the views of conference participants about whether Australia's commitment in Iraq is in accord with the contemporary spirit of its alliance with the United States. The great shame is that any hope of a UN option seems to have been squandered from the start.

Southeast Asia.

Australia's major concerns here revolve around our bilateral relationship with Indonesia, one which unfortunately seems to blow hot and cold with regularity. The success with which we deal with this relationship will be seen by other nations as the measure of our skill, maturity, and intellectual depth as a nation in handling international relations.

Our first foray into East Timor was fraught with dangers that could have led to a national humiliation. If Indonesia had supplemented the guerrilla forces with Indonesian troops in mufti, carrying out hit-and-run raids as a tactic of attrition, our relatively small forces would have been pressed over time to the point of exhaustion. We would have found it difficult, perhaps impossible, to sustain the commitment and would have been forced to seek a bailout by the UN, an institution unfairly derided by so-called neoconservatives. U.S. intervention at very high levels ensured that an SOS did not occur. President Habibe misread and acted unwisely in this matter, but our strident, up-front diplomacy did not help either. Indonesia and Malaysia both attributed Australia's interest in East Timor to its oil and gas resources. In short, we were chacterized as neo-colonial resource bandits.

Now we have an issue over West Papua. West Papua is very resource rich, and Indonesia will not give it up. It cannot afford to, and it has legitimacy on its side. Furthermore, no government of Australia, whatever its political complexion, could reasonably challenge that contention. Whatever might be thought of the process, the incorporation of West Papua into Indonesia has UN sanction, and that should be final. It would be most surprising if a Labor government in a similar situation were to conclude otherwise.

The position of President Yudhoyono is tenuous. Indonesia is a new and fragile democracy straining to hold together a widely diverse and potentially fissionable community with the added stresses of a vociferous Islamic fundamentalist movement. At times, President Yudhoyono will have to manage his electorate by massaging popular sentiments carefully. The quality of our own maturity will determine the degree of restraint we can muster in response to such situations.

This sort of diplomatic management is not helped by commentators who sound as though their sole experience with public diplomacy comes from on-the-job learning as an Australian sports writer — loud, boastful, conflictive, and not well thought-through. We should soberly recognize the intense pressure we could be subjected to, and learn to deal with it in measured tones.

Cross-border, hit-and-run incursions in Papua New Guinea by ADF elements, as a retaliation on some pretext or other, could be a major difficulty for Australia. We could not sustain ground forces in a jungle war in Papua New Guinea for any length of time. Yet, there would be a clear expectation that we, as the erstwhile former colonial power, had such an obligation to our former charge.

Oceania Region.

Papua New Guinea is eroding fast. There could be unpleasant fragmentation there. How do we handle such a situation if it happens? Making greedy demands on our limited resources at the same time Vanuatu falls apart, and with us still committed in the Solomon's? Then there is that prickly little mess in East Timor. Some sort of patchup this time cannot guarantee it is finished for the long term. It has the smell of a nasty little internal problem involving ambitions and jealousies in an unsteady micro-state. Our prompt intervention, again, has injected considerable moral hazard in the equation. The East Timorese may adopt an attitude of "don't worry — Australia will come to our rescue." That is not good. All of these untoward events happening at once is unlikely, but is not incredible. Where would we get the military resources for a longer-term commitment in the field? A credible journalist, Fred Benchley, has reported quite recently that Washington, in replying to British complaints about Australia's limited role in Iraq, says "it expects Australia to take the full load managing security problems in its own neighborhood." Benchley concludes: "If the Solomon Islands, Papua New Guinea, or East Timor — Australia's 'arc of instability' — go belly up, don't call Washington."[12] If Benchley is correct, this in turn would raise questions about the wisdom of our defense restructuring, designed more for large-scale operations with the big hitters rather than for defense interests in our immediate region.

CONCLUSION

Australia has quite enough on its plate working out the shape of its contemporary regional and global foreign policy and explaining to a possibly restive public how this fits into the gambit of an old alliance arrangement.

Conferences like this one are essential for the relevant hard think they can elicit and for preparing the public for the sort of engagements Australia might be expected to fight.

ENDNOTES - INTRODUCTION

1. "Australia's Defense Relations with the United States," Canberra, Australia: Joint Standing Committee on Foreign Affairs, Defense and Trade, Parliament of Australia, 2006, p. 21.

2. "Asia's Dawning Multipolar System Increases Australia's Geopolitical Importance," *The Power and Interest News Report*, June 14, 2006, p. 1.

3. "Time to Strengthen U.S.-Australian Relations in Trade and Defense," *The Heritage Foundation Research on Asia and the Pacific*, June 18, 2001, p. 6.

4. P. Dibb, "Our Intelligence Relationship with the US is not "Unprecedented," unpublished paper, p. 2.

5. P. Dibb, "The Consequences for Australia of US Global Dominance" unpublished paper, p. 2.

6. Richard Haass, Director of Policy Planning, U.S. Department of State, Paper presented at "The U.S.-Australian Alliance in an East Asian Context" conference held at the University of Sydney, June 29, 2001.

7. M. Osborne, "China's Blues," *Weekend Australian Review*, June 17-18, 2006.

8. Minxin Pei, "Look Before the Next Great Leap Forward," *AFR*, June 16, 2006. See also Carnegie Foundation website, *www.foreignpolicy.com*, May/June 2006, articles by Roderick McFarquhar, "Rotting from the Inside Out," Bruce Gilley, "If People Lead, Elites Will Follow," and "Hu Attacks 'Rampant' Party Graft." Also see *Far Eastern Economic Review*, Vol. 169, No. 4, May 2006; D. Farrell and S. Lund, "Putting China's Capital to Work," *Weekend Australian*, July 1-2, 2006, pp. 5−10.

9. "Can India Fly?" *The Economist*, June 3, 2006.

10. "Afghan MPs Face Massacre Claim," *Guardian Weekly*, June 16-24, 2006.

11. Ellen Krickmeyer, "More U.S. Troops May Be Iraq-Bound," *Washington Post*, October 25, 2006, pp. A1, A12.

12. Fred Brenchley, "False Sense of Security," *The Diplomat*, June-July 2006.

PANEL I

FOREIGN POLICY:
SETTING THE CONTEXT

CHAPTER 1

PANEL I CHAIRMAN'S INTRODUCTION

Douglas T. Stuart

The first thing that readers will notice when they compare the chapters by John Hulsman and Paul Kelly is that, like the proverbial hedgehog and fox, Hulsman (Chapter 2) focuses on one thing, while Kelly (Chapter 3) focuses on many. Hulsman's essay is a warning to American policymakers about the risks associated with taking a trusted and dependable ally for granted. Kelly's article is a more wide-ranging analysis of the Washington-Canberra relationship from an Australian point of view.

Although the two authors differ in terms of their goals and their styles of argumentation, they exhibit a great deal of similarity in their points of emphasis and, more importantly, their conclusions. Both authors assume that foreign policy in the United States and Australia is a "three-level game," the outcome of which is determined by the personalities and goals of the leaders, national and societal factors, and regional and global forces. Both writers pay tribute to the shared histories and common values which undergird and facilitate U.S.-Australian relations, but in the end they are both realists who assume that the direction and intensity of future bilateral relations will be determined by national interests.

Beginning with the individual level of analysis, Hulsman and Kelly both accord a great deal of importance to the close personal relationship which has developed between President George W. Bush and Prime Minister John Howard. The two leaders are "kindred spirits" (Hulsman's phrase), who share a deep commitment to "Anglosphere" values.[1] Kelly reminds us, however, that the relationship also is based upon a "strategic bond." Howard has sought close cooperation with the United States because he is convinced that a globally dominant America is good for the world, good for the Asia-Pacific region, and very good for Australia. Both authors contrast Howard's decision to accord top priority to the cultivation of a U.S.-Australian bilateral partnership with the more nuanced and conditional policies of his immediate predecessor, Paul Keating. While Mr. Keating was unquestionably pro-American, he tended to place a higher priority on engagement with Australia's Asia-Pacific neighbors.

The contributors to this section survey the most important tests of the U.S.-Australian partnership over the last decade. Mr. Howard's views on the indispensability of American leadership were influenced by his experiences with the East Asian economic crisis of 1997 and the violence which followed the vote for independence in East Timor in 1998. But it was the Prime Minister's immediate and unconditional expression of support for the United States after the September 11, 2001 (9/11), terrorist attacks and his willingness to deliver on that expression of support in Afghanistan and Iraq, which transformed the bilateral relationship into what Kelly describes as "the New Intimacy." Mr. Howard also has taken unilateral actions—including his quick response to the devastating tsunami of 2004 and his deployment of military and police units to the South Pacific and East Timor—which have been applauded warmly by Washington.

With reference to Australia's contributions to the coalition operations in Afghanistan and Iraq, Roy Eccleston has observed: "That Howard has become such a favored US ally with a relatively small military commitment is testament to his political skills. . . ."[2] This assertion is correct, but it should be placed in the context of Australia's limited military capabilities and competing military obligations as well as the effectiveness of the forces which have been deployed. Furthermore, Mr. Howard should be commended for understanding that, in a democratic society, sustaining support for his administration is an indispensable precondition for the success of any controversial long-term strategy. It is a measure of Mr. Howard's skill as a domestic politician that he was elected to a fourth term in 2004.

As noted in the preface to this volume, it is widely assumed that Mr. Howard's active support has been good for America, but there has been a great deal of debate within Australia about the costs and benefits of this policy. Kelly assures readers that the Australian public still values the U.S.-Australia alliance, but criticism of the way that the alliance is managed in Canberra "can be intense." Many of Mr. Howard's domestic critics use the same arguments that have been leveled against British Prime Minister Tony Blair — that he has not been discriminate in his support of Washington, and that he has not been adequately compensated for his loyalty. It can be argued, however, that Mr. Howard already has begun to adjust both the rhetoric and the substance of his foreign policy in order to avoid Mr. Blair's "poodle problem."[3] Since 2005, he has been engaged in a sophisticated campaign to develop a more multifaceted foreign policy, which Maryanne Kelton has described correctly as a "US plus approach."[4] At the core of this strategy is Howard's assertion that ". . . close links to the United States are a plus — not a minus — in forging stronger links in Asia."[5]

Hulsman and Kelly agree that Prime Minister Howard's ability to manage this more flexible foreign policy both at home and abroad will depend on the support he receives from the United States. At the core of Hulsman's chapter is the contention that the Bush administration has placed both the U.S.-Australia relationship and the Howard government in jeopardy by "taking Australia for granted." Hulsman also asserts that even if Mr. Bush were to recognize that Mr. Howard needs and deserves more public support and more substantive rewards for his yeoman service, the American president would be constrained in what he could actually accomplish as a result of his "ongoing political weakness." Indeed, John Mueller has argued that this progressive political paralysis has been felt since early 2005, when public opinion polls indicated that more than half of Americans viewed the U.S. invasion of Iraq as a mistake.[6]

No matter how politically constrained President Bush is during the last 2 years of his presidency, he will still have an obligation, and numerous opportunities, to contribute to peace and prosperity in the Asia-Pacific region. The good news is that the Bush administration already has taken the first essential step by refocusing its attention on the area. The next step should be to take a page from Mr. Howard's play book by treating close ties to Canberra as a "plus . . . in forging stronger links in Asia." An "Australia plus" strategy would involve two progressively more difficult policies for U.S. policymakers. First, the Bush administration should respond to Hulsman's warnings about taking Australia for granted. This should involve more than "public displays of affection." It should utilize the well-developed network of institutional ties between the two governments, in conjunction with high-level consultations, in order to enhance the influence of Australian foreign and defense policymakers within the Washington policy community. On an interpersonal level, this should be a relatively painless adjustment, since, as Kurt Campbell has observed: "It's fair to say that Americans generally like Australians, and it doesn't hurt that senior Australian diplomats and officials are particularly expert at engaging Americans—and even manipulating them on occasion!"[7] The challenge will be for both sides to get beyond comfortable social interaction so that Washington can benefit from Australia's rich foreign policy experience—especially as it relates to the Asia-Pacific region.

The second and more difficult policy which the United States should pursue corresponds to Kelly's "essential truth" that "alliances work better when mutual respect . . . incorporates a margin of difference." As several contributors to this volume have noted, U.S. and Australian interests are likely to diverge on a number of key foreign policy issues in the near future, as the two nations adjust to significant structural changes in the Asia-Pacific region. However, this does not mean, as Doug Bandow has argued, that it is time to scrap the ANZUS alliance so that both nations can pursue more flexible and independent foreign policies. On the contrary, in accordance with my first recommendation, the ANZUS relationship should be strengthened in order to facilitate U.S.-Australia consultation. And to the extent that bilateral consultation is improved, it will make it that much easier for both nations to prepare for situations of foreign policy divergence.

Hulsman and Kelly agree (as do most of the contributors to this volume) that the People's Republic of China (PRC) poses the biggest long-term challenge to the U.S.-Australia relationship. Over the last 5 years, Beijing has been engaged in an extraordinarily successful "friends with everybody" campaign in the Asia-Pacific region. China's success is partly attributable to the fact that the PRC has reached the stage in its economic development where it is able to use financial inducements as a highly effective form of "sticky power."[8] In the case of Australia, this has taken the form of a dramatic increase in Australian exports to China—at a time when Australia faces a serious problem with its overall trade deficit.[9]

The PRC also has been able to challenge, and in some cases displace, the United States as a regional power because Washington's attention was concentrated elsewhere in the wake of the 9/11 terrorist attacks. By the time the Bush administration noticed that China was "eating our lunch" in the Asia-Pacific region, the PRC had established a probably irreversible position of political and economic influence throughout the region.[10] Unfortunately, the Washington policy community has responded to this changed geopolitical situation by tilting toward a posture of anti-Chinese containment. The change of tone is evident in Department of Defense documents such as the *2006 Quadrennial Defense Review* and the *2006 Annual Report to Congress on the Military Power of the People's Republic of China,* and in the *2005 Annual Report of the U.S.-China Economic and Security Review Commission.*

If Washington continues down the path toward explicit anti-Chinese containment, it will undermine not only the U.S.-Australia relationship, but its ties to most of its friends and allies in the Asia-Pacific region. As Hulsman observes, "China will emerge as a great power whether the U.S. objects or not." China's neighbors accept this fact, and have been adapting their policies accordingly. Washington must learn from their example. In some cases, it must also rely upon its most trusted friends to take the lead in what will be a complex process of adjustment. No nation is more deserving of this trust than Australia.

ENDNOTES - CHAPTER 1

1. See the author's discussion of the concept of Anglosphere, in the context of U.S.-Australian relations, in "NATO and the Wider World: From Regional Collective Defense to Global Coalitions of the Willing," *Australian Journal of International Affairs*, Vol. 58, No. 1, March, 2004, pp. 47-68.

2. "Team America," in Nick Cater, ed., *The Howard Factor*, Carlton, Australia: Melbourne University Press, 2006, p. 171.

3. See, for example, "The Poodle's Dilemma," *The Economist*, August 5, 2006, p. 49.

4. "Perspectives on Australian Foreign Policy, 2005," *Australian Journal of International Affairs*, Vol. 60, No. 2, June 2006, p. 231.

5. "Australia in the World," Address by the Prime Minister, the Honorable John Howard MP, to the Lowy Institute for International Policy, Sydney, Australia, March 31, 2005, p. 13. Available on the web at *www.lowyinstitute.org/AustraliaAndTheWorld.asp*.

6. "The Iraq Syndrome," *Foreign Affairs*, November/December 2005, pp. 44-54.

7. Douglas Bandow, Dan Blumenthal, Kurt Campbell, and Peter Brookes, "The Great Britains of Asia," *Alliance, The View from America*, Occasional Paper #96, Centre for Independent Studies, August, 2005, p. 21.

8. Walter Russell Mead, "America's Sticky Power," *Foreign Policy*, March/April 2004, pp. 46-53.

9. See Neal Woolrich, "Australian Trade Defecit Soars," transcript of *PM* radio broadcast, March 3, 2006, available at *www.abc.net.au/pm/content/2006/s1583737.htm*.

10. See David Shambaugh's analysis in "Power Shift: China and Asia's New Dynamism," transcript of a Brookings Institution program, January 12, 2006, available on the web at *www.brook.edu/comm/events/20060112.htm*.

CHAPTER 2

THE FUTURE OF U.S.-AUSTRALIAN RELATIONS AND THE CURSE OF GEORGE HARRISON

John C. Hulsman

The Problems of Being the Third Beatle.

In the late 1960s, the Beatles were at the height of their cultural and creative power. In John Lennon and Paul McCartney, they had the most talented and artful songwriting duo in pop music history. To complement their artistic prowess, the band's ability to fuse catchy pop tunes with profound and moving lyrics made them the rarest of creatures—an artistic and popular success. Seen as the embodiment of 1960s togetherness, most cultural commentators fatuously expected that the band would go on forever.

But all was not well. George Harrison, their superb lead guitar player, had been growing artistically as the 1960s progressed. Yet his increasingly interesting lyrics, showcased in such songs as "While My Guitar Gently Weeps," "Taxman," and "Here Comes the Sun," largely were ignored. After all, with Lennon-McCartney as your primary songwriters, why should the Beatles look elsewhere for material? Over time, Harrison's lament that he had to fight for song slots (and often lost), that the other members of the band took his abilities as "the quiet Beatle" for granted, crystallized into resentment. In his search for artistic fulfillment, neglect had left him with the options of either remaining third wheel in an amazingly successful partnership, or going off on his own. There are many reasons for the Beatles' shattering breakup in 1970, but not the least were the neglect of Harrison's budding talent and the stark choice such neglect had left him.

So it is for U.S.-Australian relations. If Britain is seen as Paul McCartney to America's John Lennon, so Australia under John Howard can be viewed much as George Harrison—quiet, talented, dependable, a vital part of an amazing partnership—but also very much overlooked. As was the case for the Beatles with George Harrison, America ignores its successful relationship with Australia at its peril.

Come Together: The Bush-Howard Years.

Seen simply, Australian foreign policy often has been characterized as a struggle between Asia-leaning and Anglo-leaning tendencies. If former Prime Minister Paul Keating is seen as the embodiment of the former, Prime Minister Howard symbolizes the latter, manifested by Australia's close ties with the United States. Howard often has been denigrated by Australian public policy intellectuals, but his largely successful four-term premiership (characterized by a decade of strong economic growth, budget surpluses, tax cuts, and falling unemployment) underscores the fact that he has remembered and imbibed certain basic home truths that others have deigned to forget.

Howard's closeness to the Bush administration in particular and America in general is founded on the fact that the United States is and will remain the only superpower for the foreseeable future, a fact that gives Australia, with its close cultural ties to America, a competitive advantage in foreign relations. Both Australia and the United States are settler cultures, "better" and more meritocratic offshoots of the

British homeland. Both are more broadly immigrant cultures, beyond their common Anglo roots. Both are enthusiastic capitalist cultures, having relatively low rates of taxation and a deep deference to the rule of law. Both broadly welcome and benefit from globalization; in the last decade Australia and the United States have almost unrivaled growth rates for developed nations. Both, in the 20th century, were reluctant but vital internationalists. These common characteristics, a similar way of looking at the world—economically, socially, politically, diplomatically—have allowed Howard to enjoy the good graces of the sole remaining superpower, while at the same time leading Australia to its status as a leading regional power.

But much as Keating's overly one-sided Asia-centric approach had certain basic problems (it breezily underestimated the effects of living in an increasingly one-superpower world), so Howard's approach is marked by a number of flaws. Don't let the personal intimacy of the Bush-Howard relationship fool you; that era is ending, largely due to the President's political weakness (the most recent AP-IPSOS poll has his approval rating at a lowly 38 percent).[1] Howard saw in George W. Bush a kindred spirit—a tough man disparaged by and disparaging of much of the political establishment, socially conservative, fiscally bound to tax cuts—who has been underestimated much of his political life. Thus the generally close U.S.-Australian ties were enhanced further by the personal closeness of these two conservative leaders. But in the words of George Harrison, "All things must pass."

Completely apart from the fact that the American half of the partnership is in dire political straits (with the Democrats retaking the U.S. House of Representatives and the Senate during the 2006 mid-terms, President Bush's flexibility on the international scene is now constrained even further), there are other factors that limit the chances for the U.S.-Australian relationship to continue as before. Prime Minister Howard himself is unlikely to remain the political colossus he has been for most of the past decade. Though his partnership with Treasurer Peter Costello has been fruitful, increasingly the pair seem to be doing a fairly good impression of Gordon Brown and Tony Blair. As Howard announced his intention to run for a fifth term, Costello confirmed press reports that the Prime Minister privately assured him in far-off 1994 that he would hand over the Liberal Party leadership to the Treasurer one-and-a-half terms into a Liberal-dominated government. Howard has denied this. As was the case in Canada for Jacques Chretien and Paul Martin, as well as for Blair and Brown, it is almost inevitable that the poison of a prolonged succession controversy will come to weaken the present Liberal dominance. Howard's political road ahead is likely to be far more bumpy than it has been up to now.

Further, objective strategic facts limiting America's pull on Australia remain in play. If Prime Minister Keating based his Asia-centric approach on the rise of Asia and especially China and the relative U.S. decline in the region, that process, perhaps interrupted by the Asian financial crisis, continues. For both America and Australia, the great strategic question is whether the two great allies can coordinate their positions concerning the rise of China. Even the halcyon days of the Howard-Bush partnership do not provide a clear answer to this seminal question. It is here that the American strategic response to China must be communicated far more clearly. Above all, as was the case for the Beatles and George Harrison, the United States must avoid a foreign policy towards China that forces Australia and its Asian neighbors to choose between the two; it might not like the answer it gets.

China as Yoko Ono.

As this conference has made crystal clear, though America looks at China as a threat, its Australian ally sees it as a vital economic partner. Paul Kelly (Chapter 3) is correct in asserting that Mr. Howard "purchased a degree of immunity" from U.S. criticisms of its dealings with China, but it is only *temporary* immunity. The longer-term questions about China's rise will not allow this state of affairs to continue. In the neo-conservative Bush administration, the two fundamental questions about China have been as follows: Should the United States oppose China's rise to great power status or seek to shape it? Should the United States focus on carrots or sticks in dealing with the PRC?

As is typical for the neo-conservatives, both these questions largely miss the point. Worse, if they come to define the American relationship with Beijing, they could well imperil Washington's standing throughout the region. Speaking as an ethical realist, my position is that China will emerge as a great power whether the United States objects or not—that horse already has left the stable.[2] With growth rates regularly in excess of 9 percent of gross domestic product (GDP), the largest military force in the world, the third highest level of global defense spending, and a vast trade surplus with the United States, China is by any stretch of the imagination a "rising power."

Worse, futile grandstanding efforts to hinder this process will only strengthen the very anti-American forces in China most likely to urge that Beijing attempt to become a revolutionary power in Asia over the long term. This big question should be substituted for the American neo-conservative's first question: While it is virtually certain that China will emerge as a great power, will it evolve into a status quo or revolutionary power? That is, will it come to be a generally responsible member of the present community of nations, a partner in the Great Capitalist Peace in Asia (though, of course, one that defends its own interests), or will it try to displace the United States as the region's ordering power?

If this should be America's new first question, then we also should adopt a new perspective in answering the second question—carrots or sticks? Instead of either-or, the answer should be *both*. In terms of carrots, the United States should continue to draw China further into the global financial system, to induce it to live up to the World Trade Organization (WTO) fine print and continue to liberalize its economy. Such an approach will lead to the rise of a robust middle class over time, as well as an increase in pluralism. Beyond neo-conservative simplisms, this is the truly subversive approach; it increases the likelihood that China will remain a status quo power, as it enjoys the fruits of the Great Capitalist Peace evolving in Asia. Beijing is unlikely to want to risk its increased standing for highly risky adventurist policies designed to displace the United States as the dominant power in the region. To see the likelihood of the status quo outcome, one need only look at the events in China that have occurred in my lifetime. I was born in the late 1960s, at the height of both the Beatles frenzy and, more insidiously, the Chinese Cultural Revolution. Since that time, the Chinese Communist leadership, particularly that of Deng Xiaphong, has embraced the very notions of capitalism that Mao and the Gang of Four so reviled.

As such, China's middle class has blossomed, a private space has been created beyond government control, and, while remaining far from democratic, China has rejoined the international community, particularly in the economic sphere. The crazy days of dunce caps, defenestrations, mass killings, and bellicose rhetoric seem far away. Surely the carrot has yielded tangible progress.

At the same time, the stick must not be forgotten. The United States presently has the best politico-military ties in its history with both Japan and Australia. It retains close ties to the Association of Southeast Asian Nations (ASEAN) countries, the Philippines, and (though not without problems) South Korea. The Bush administration wisely has seen that closer economic, political, and strategic ties with India are perhaps the highest priority for American diplomacy over the course of the next decade. The United States must continue to push for ever-closer linkages in the region, making it perfectly clear that military ties between Washington and its allies in Asia are defensive and bilateral in nature, and are not overtly anti-Chinese.

Such an approach flies in the face of the North Atlantic Treaty Organization (NATO) paradigm, so close to the hearts of many Americans. But that paradigm does not fit the situation in Asia. For one thing, given Japan's frustrating failure to come to terms publicly with its atrocious war record in the same manner that the Germans have, many likely members of such a multilateral organization, such as South Korea, continue to feel deep psychological alienation from their potential Japanese "allies." Second, the NATO approach would increase greatly the chances that China would choose the revolutionary power option in response to this encirclement. Third, the last thing the countries of the region, as this conference has made clear, want is to be forced to choose between Beijing and Washington. Such an approach ironically could make a permanent rise in tensions in the Asia-Pacific region a self-fulfilling prophecy. Yet, a loosely constructed bilateral concert of powers centered around Washington could make the Chinese leadership hesitate in opting to become a revolutionary power. Having to watch India at its back, with Japan and Taiwan at its front, is likely to bolster those within the Chinese leadership calling for a continued peaceful rise.

We must be under no illusions; ultimately it is the Chinese and not we who will decide China's strategic fate. But a more realistic policy, beyond being compatible with Australian strategic thinking, is likely to tip the Chinese leadership's calculations in a more benign direction. Further, American failure to adopt this approach is certain to strain the U.S.-Australian partnership, perhaps to the breaking point. If not dealt with properly, China could well be the Yoko Ono of the grand strategic partnership formed between the United States and Canberra over the past decade. We must not let this happen.

Conclusion.

First, the good news. The Australian-American relationship could well be a precursor of the way alliances are going to be managed in the new era. For it was due to the endemic close ties between the two peoples that a profoundly new way of working together has begun to evolve. Stung by President Bill Clinton's refusal to send troops to East Timor, Prime Minister Howard went ahead anyway. This is an entirely different model from the simple cliché that

Australia is merely the American Deputy Sheriff in the Asia-Pacific. Rather, Australia acted on what Howard perceived to be its own unique interests; not every operation is dependent on the American calculation of its own specific interests. While America supported the East Timor mission, it did not lead it. Given the failure of the present multilateral system — be it the UN, ANZUS, ASEAN, or NATO — to function effectively as peacemakers, such ad hoc coalitions of the willing are likely to remain a primary tool of international relations. Given their complementary views of the world, this means that Australia and the United States have a head start in creatively working together to solve such problems.

But for this to work, certain psychological hang-ups, which became established in the Cold War, have to come to an end. There are three diplomatic "rules" for dissipating these hangups. First, both the United States and Australia must get used to living in a world where the other says "no"; such an answer does not mean, as Chicken Little would have it, that the sky is falling and that the partnership is at an end. Second, as proved true in the case of East Timor, a lack of agreement about what to do should not necessarily stop the other partner from acting. An alliance where interests are similar, but not the same, can thrive only if this more fluid approach is put into practice.

But this leaves us with the problem of George Harrison, for the third diplomatic rule of the new era is in many ways the most important. The United States must stop taking Australia for granted. It must stop viewing the relationship through the complacent, out-dated lenses of the Keating/Asia-centric or Howard/Anglo-centric alternatives. Rather, America must recognize that an Australia fundamentally engaged in both these realms at the same time is an Australia most profoundly suited to advance American interests in the post-Cold War era. This means not forcing Australia to choose in some either-or fashion between the United States and China. First of all, such a forced choice, with the Australian economy booming largely due to China's insatiable demand for Australian natural resources, is the single greatest threat to the continued centrality of the relationship for both sides. Second, moving closer to Australia's more nuanced view of China, using both economic carrots and military sticks to affect the Chinese leadership's decisionmaking process about its ultimate role in the region, is far more likely to serve American interests well into the future. In moving away from the dead-end zero sum game, the United States can avoid forcing Australia into George Harrison's dilemma. Let it be.

ENDNOTES - CHAPTER 2

1. The AP-IPSOS polling results for October 2006 are available at *www.ipsos-na.com/news/pa/presidential_approval.pdf*.

2. For a fuller discussion of an alternative to present U.S.-China policies, see Anatol Lieven and John Hulsman, *Ethical Realism: A Vision For America's Role In The World*, New York: Pantheon Press, 2006, pp. 169-177.

CHAPTER 3

THE AUSTRALIAN-AMERICAN ALLIANCE: TOWARDS A REVITALIZATION

Paul Kelly

In June 2002, Prime Minister John Howard told the U.S. Congress that "America has no better friend anywhere in the world than Australia."[1] It was an assertion of strategic, political, and personal intimacy. The Australia-New Zealand-U.S. (ANZUS) Treaty, now 55 years old, has enjoyed a revitalization during the era of Howard and President George W. Bush. I call this the New Intimacy. The purpose of this chapter is to assess its meaning and implications.

Australia has drawn closer to the United States at a time when many other nations have kept their distance. Any discussion of the Australia-U.S. relationship must penetrate the fog of mutual self-congratulation that surrounds it. The New Intimacy, however, testifies to the astonishing durability of the spirit that characterizes the relationship and suggests that the ties binding Australians and Americans together may be sturdier and more complex than generally assumed.

This current high tide is driven by the Howard-Bush personal concord, the cathartic impact of the September 11, 2001 (9/11), crisis, and a common strategic view that the alliance has a new relevance. The pivotal question is, What endures from the Howard-Bush era and what disappears?

Such an intimate personal concord probably will disappear. Howard and Bush are political soul mates, united by shared social and cultural values. This interaction between an Australian Liberal leader and an American Republican leader was reinforced by their identity as radical conservatives. The New Intimacy was the creation of this radical conservative political identity. They have enjoyed a special relationship, and that means, by definition, it will not be duplicated by their successors. To take this stance is merely being realistic, not pessimistic, about the ties between future heads of government. This surmise leads directly to the question, How deeply entrenched is the New Intimacy? Can it survive the passing of its political architects?

Any survey of the New Intimacy should begin by noting that it is polarizing, not only in America but in Australia as well. The opposition, the Australian Labor Party, opposed Australia's commitment to Iraq and wants to withdraw all Australia's forces. A majority of Australians dislike the war. Polls show that positive feelings about the United States are down to 58 percent, a low figure by historical norms. This compares with the Australian public's positive feelings towards Europe at 85 percent, towards Japan at 84 percent, and towards China at 69 percent.[2]

In this chapter I will address three issues—the origins of the New Intimacy, the strategic conditions and challenges that underpin the New Intimacy, and the prospects for the New Intimacy's consolidation into a stronger and closer alliance.

The origins of the New Intimacy are more complex than usually recognized. They began with Howard's vision from the time of his 1996 election victory to realign Australia to a position closer to the United States. This was a fascinating aim since bilateral ties in the previous era already were widely and correctly assumed to be close, and there was an effective personal and ideological connection between Prime Minister

Keating and President Clinton, a Labor-Democrat association.

Howard held the unfashionable view that the post-Cold War era would create fresh opportunities for a deeper alliance relationship. Few Australian analysts agreed with such an assessment. Howard and Keating have both conducted successful policies towards the United States, but their approach has been different.

First, Howard put a premium on values with an enthusiasm that Keating did not embrace. Indeed, Howard's entire foreign policy philosophy represents an effort to find a new Australian synthesis between values and *realpolitik*. Howard has shaped Australian foreign policy with a profound sense of cultural traditionalism and the idea that Australia as a nation is immersed deeply in the Western tradition. Keating, more interested in Australia's engagement with Asia, placed less emphasis on its cultural affinity with the West and the United States.

Second, Keating and Howard had different strategic approaches to America. Keating was interested in Asia's regional architecture and crafted an Asia-Pacific Economic Cooperation (APEC) diplomacy, dazzling in scope, that sought to institutionalize the United States in regional institutions. Influenced by the trans-Atlantic strategic ties that had bound America to Europe, Keating obsessed about creating trans-Pacific institutional ties to bind America to Asia. With Clinton's support, the meetings of APEC leaders were Keating's main innovation. Howard, by contrast, did not think in terms of regional architectures, but in terms of bilateral relations. Howard's view of the U.S.-Australian alliance was elemental—that such an asset should be strengthened and enriched. His answer to the question, "What should an Australian leader do with the alliance?" was unhesitatingly simple—you add layers of value. This view was informed by a deep strategic conviction, not widely shared in Australia in 1996, that U.S. power was on the rise and that the 21st century, like the 20th century, would belong to America. This made preservation of the alliance a greater prize than ever.

Third, the differences in the Keating-Howard mindsets arose from the contrasting eras in which they governed. The imprint on Keating's mind was the Asian economic miracle and Australia's participation in that process. The influences for Howard were scepticism about the Asian model, arising from the Asian financial crisis of the late 1990s. This reinforced his belief in the superiority of U.S. power.

Despite Howard's pro-U.S. views, there was little decisive action during the 4 years in which he dealt with the Clinton administration. Howard and Clinton had little personal rapport, though their governments had a strong functional relationship. The turning point was the U.S. 2000 presidential election season, when Australian Foreign Minister Alexander Downer flew to Texas to meet George W. Bush after being advised that Mr. Bush might become the Republican nominee. He reported to Howard that George Bush was "our kind of candidate." Meanwhile, Australia's new ambassador to the United States, Michael Thawley, a Howard confidant and a critical figure in the evolving relationship, had established ties with key Republicans and advised Howard that a bilateral trade deal would be possible with a Bush administration.

In this environment, the Howard cabinet privately cheered Bush along the way to his election win over the Democrats' Al Gore. In anticipation of his victory, the cabinet took a bold decision—to seek a free trade agreement (FTA) with the United States. Expectations within the Howard government about Bush were unrealistically high. Yet Howard's judgment was vindicated in the end.

Howard's motive regarding the FTA transcended trade. For Howard, it was an effort to institutionalize an economic partnership with the United States to match the security partnership represented by ANZUS and to deepen the overall strategic relationship. In this sense, Howard and Bush were fellow travellers. Much to the dismay of free market economists, they saw trade policy in strategic as well as economic and monetary terms.

By 2001, Howard's 5-year-old prime ministership had reached its maturity. At this stage, his foreign and security policy decision of greatest moment had been the assumption of Australian leadership in the UN peace enforcement operation in East Timor after that country's vote for independence from Indonesia in 1999. This operation entailed Australia's most important military deployment since Vietnam. It was the making of Howard as a foreign policy leader— one who negotiated with world leaders, managed a regional crisis, and accepted Australian responsibility for leading and defining the terms of intervention as a strictly UN authorized operation in order to minimize the risk of hostilities between Australia and Indonesia.

Central to the intervention was the military guarantee the Clinton administration gave Australia and the warnings issued by U.S. Defense Secretary William Cohen in Jakarta that if Indonesia's troops challenged the Australia-led forces, they would face U.S. Marines. Howard knew the intervention was underwritten by the U.S. alliance. The Prime Minister, meeting President Bush for the first time in September 2001, then had the confidence of one who had conducted a highly successful military deployment. Moreover, his profound belief in the alliance now had been validated by his own experience.

Howard's September 2001 visit to the United States became the most important of his prime ministership, with the establishment of the Howard-Bush concord falling on September 10. The Bush administration had made its own decision about Howard—he was being inducted into the inner sanctum of valued foreign leaders. The informal barbeque hosted the previous evening by Ambassador Thawley set the scene—all the notables attended, the Cheneys, the Rumsfelds, the Powells. The next day Howard spent 5 hours with Bush, including a welcoming ceremony, a drive, a chat, formal talks, a joint press conference, and lunch. At the press conference, the normally cautious Howard declared that he and Bush were "very close friends." The U.S. side gave its preliminary approval to the FTA negotiations. The Howard-Bush bandwagon was rolling. The emotional and strategic bond was literally sealed in blood the next day. On the morning of 9/11, Howard, from his Willard Hotel window, saw terrorist smoke rising from the Pentagon, where he had met Rumsfeld only 24 hours before.

The 9/11 attack revealed a wellspring of emotional support among Australians for America that Howard instinctively articulated. In the immediate days after 9/11, Howard made some of the most important statements in the history of the alliance. His response fused values and interests. "Of course, it's an attack on all of us," Howard said immediately. It was a startling statement. This interpretation guided his policy for years. The attack, though technically on U.S. territory lying on the other side of the earth from Australia, was actually on "all of us" because of shared values. But Howard could not have been more emphatic. He kept repeating the words like a mantra—the 9/11 attack was also an attack on Australia's values.[3]

At the same time, Howard, aware that this was a defining moment for America, offered strategic assistance. He felt that America would identity its true friends from their responses to this event. Going beyond a mere pro forma declaration of moral support, within 48 hours after the attack, he proclaimed: "I've also indicated that Australia will provide all support that might be requested of us by the United States in relation to any action that might be taken." In response to follow-up questions, Howard said: "We would provide support within our capability.[4]

Bush had made no such request. Howard had no obligation to make such a statement, but he volunteered a military commitment from Australia, and there was no qualification to this core principle. Howard's action was deliberate. This was no rush of blood to the head; he knew exactly what he was saying and he intended to say it. For Howard, this was an exercise in prime ministerial discretion and authority. He chose to stand with America. The origins of Australia's involvement in Afghanistan and Iraq lie in this pledge. In a radio interview, Howard said the attack was "an appalling act of bastardry . . . in some ways worse than Pearl Harbor."[5]

Upon learning that the mutual defense provisions of the North Atlantic Treaty Organization (NATO) alliance had been invoked, Howard and Foreign Minister Downer, after consulting the U.S. side, decided that the ANZUS Treaty also should be invoked. This action was formalized at a special cabinet meeting in

Canberra on September 14. Howard said it was an Australian initiative taken in consultation with the United States.

This action and Howard's statements constituted a significantly broad interpretation of ANZUS, a treaty that legally was limited to the "Pacific area." This interpretation testified to Howard's global view of Australian security policy, an outlook shaped by his Empire and Cold War historical perspectives. Howard, realizing that the international terrorist threat cut across treaty boundaries, saw ANZUS in global as well as regional terms. This was also the view of the Bush administration, an outlook that predated 9/11. The Director of Policy Planning in the State Department, Richard Haass, had stated in mid-2001 that the United States viewed ANZUS not so much as a regional alliance but rather as "two countries joined in a global partnership."[6]

As a consequence, an alliance conceived for the Cold War in Asia and seen by Australians as an insurance guarantee for their nation, now was invoked for the first time as a result of attacks on the U.S. east coast by nonstate actors enacting Islamic terror. Nothing could have been more remote from the 1950s vision of Percy Spender and John Foster Dulles, who negotiated the original treaty. This result was equally remote for an Australian public, psychologically unprepared for such a turn. ANZUS, a Cold War arrangement negotiated against the backdrop of the Chinese revolution and the Korean War, was now being adapted for a new and different threat environment.

The immediate consequence was Australia's military commitment to Afghanistan, announced in October 2001 following talks between Bush and Howard. Bush's aim in deposing the Taliban was not just to pursue al-Qai'da, but to remove the regimes that harbored terrorists. Downer was specific about the war's justification—the U.S. action was validated under the self-defense provision of Article 51 of the UN Charter in addition to the Security Council resolution passed after 9/11. From the standpoint of domestic politics, Australia's support was initially bipartisan, but bipartisanship later evaporated as a result of the Iraq war.

Iraq would become the site of Howard's most contentious actions in support of Bush's "war on terrorism," later branded the Long War. Taken in increments over 2002 and 2003, with the final decision in March 2003, Howard's decisions comprised a traditional Australian response to a nontraditional war. Despite the contentious nature of Bush's war, it was no surprise that Howard went with him. Staying aloof from Iraq would have defied Howard's history, his values, and his strategic instincts, thus violating his political essence. Such was the start and the end of his Iraq decision.

There were, however, important differences of emphasis between Howard and Bush. Howard was pro-American, but, unlike Bush, he was not a foreign policy revolutionary. Howard never subscribed to the desirability of regime change as a justification for the war. Indeed, Howard's own justification was almost cautious, namely, that "disarming Iraq is necessary for the long-term security of the world and is therefore manifestly in the national interest of Australia."[7] Howard lacked British Prime Minister Tony Blair's idealistic enthusiasm for the undertaking and, even in proportionate terms, made nothing rivaling the British military commitment. Howard won Bush's agreement that Australia would be involved in the "sharp end" of the war but would not remain in Iraq for long, a commitment that had to be modified given the subsequent insurgency.

It should be no surprise that Howard has emerged far less politically damaged from the war than either Bush or Blair. As a leader, Howard likes to make decisions but is reluctant to close off options — he presents the decisions as proof of his convictions and the options as proof of his flexibility. In Iraq, Howard committed to the war but had the flexibility to limit that commitment. More than 3 years later, no Australian had been killed in action.[8] Australia's military contribution was designed to maximize Australia's political leverage with the United States and minimize military casualties.

Howard is not a cynic. He believed Saddam Hussein was a threat; he accepted the intelligence assessments about the dictator's weapons of mass destruction (WMD) capability; and he felt after 9/11 that the world's margin for error with such regimes and such weapons had disappeared. But Howard, unlike Bush, did not carry the political responsibility for the intervention. The public knew that Australia was in Iraq as a junior partner, not a principal player. For Australia, Iraq triggered neither the national agony nor strategic trauma that occurred in the United States.

The Iraq war revealed the gap that had opened between the U.S. leadership and UN interventionist sentiments over the years since the First Gulf War. Lack of UN authorization has been pivotal in Australia's domestic politics, with the Labor Party's formal opposition to the Iraq invasion of 2003 resting upon that point. Opposition leader Kim Beazley noted that the Hawke government's 1991 commitment to the First Gulf War had not been under alliance auspices but rather under those of the UN. The distinction was critical. In explaining the decision, Labor's Prime Minister, Bob Hawke, said in 1991: "We are not sending ships to the gulf region to serve our allies; we are going to protect the international rule of law which will be vital to our security however our alliances may develop in the future." Similarly, in Beazley's words some 12 years later, Labor was attracted by the post-Cold War "possibility for a real international community under the United Nations."[9]

In the early 1990s, there was no conflict for the Labor Party between Australia's responsibility under the alliance and its responsibility as a global citizen. But George W. Bush's policies shattered this congruency. In 2003, when Howard chose the U.S. alliance, Labor stayed with the UN and opposed the war.

While Howard's decision reflected his concern over Iraq, his greater concern was the health of the U.S. alliance. Howard saw Iraq as an instrument of deeper purpose. He could have abandoned the Iraq commitment only by abandoning his pre-9/11 strategic objective of realigning his country closer to the United States. Howard, therefore, had much to lose by absenting himself from the war as well as much to risk by attending it. His aim was to maximize his returns while minimizing his risks.

It is wrong to see Iraq as the price Australia paid for its U.S. alliance. It was the price Australia paid for Howard's more ambitious alliance. Howard, ultimately, went to Iraq to seal the New Intimacy, thereby realizing his greater aspiration dating from 1996.

The second issue I wish to address relates to the strategic conditions and challenges that underpin the New Intimacy. They arise in two areas: (1) the Long War against Islamist terrorism; and (2) the rapidly changing power balance in East Asia driven by China's rise, Japan's reaction to it, and future U.S. directions.

Howard is best understood as an agent of synthesis. He seeks a synthesis between Australia's history as a Western multicultural nation on one hand and its geographical position in the Asia-Pacific region on the other. He seeks a strategic synthesis that combines Australia's role as a regional power with its genuinely global interests. And he seeks, above all, to synthesize the U.S. alliance with its East Asian relationships.

Despite the huge value of U.S. intelligence to Australia, it remains an open question whether the Long War will unite U.S. and Australian interests as closely as did the Cold War. Much depends upon the tactics and strategy the United States follows. Since the struggle against Islamist terrorism is likely to be long and unpredictable, there is no easy answer to this question and the answer may change over time in any event.

Australia lives more in an Islamic geographical setting than a Christian one. Its nearest neighbor of moment, Indonesia, is the world's largest Islamic nation and is undergoing active ferment in all of its defining institutional structures, with important implications for its religious, political, economic, and security future. Relations with Indonesia will become more important and probably more difficult for Australia with the passage of time. Australia will need nerve and commitment to maintain an effective relationship with a volatile nationalistic Islamic country.

Each year for the past 5 years, there has been a planned or actual attack on Australians or Australian assets in Indonesia or elsewhere in Southeast Asia. In October 2002, 88 Australians were killed in the Bali bombing, an action perpetrated by the Islamist terrorist group, Jemaah Islamiyah (JI). After the Bali attack, Australia assumed a new regional role in counterterrorist collaboration with Indonesia. The two nations moved closer in police, intelligence, and political cooperation. This was helped by the new Indonesian President, Susilo Bambang Yudhoyono, with whom Howard enjoyed a relationship based on a good measure of mutual trust. Australia began negotiations for a new bilateral security agreement with Jakarta. It also completed counterterrorism agreements with a range of Southeast Asian nations. These initiatives reveal the centrality for Australia of an effective counterterrorism strategy with its Southeast Asian neighbors, a region where both Indonesia and the Philippines pose high risks so far as Australian peace and security are concerned. Australia's challenge is to reconcile such regional interests with its commitment to the U.S. alliance, a task accomplished well to this point.

In this challenge, Australia will be directly affected by future U.S. strategy, the fate of Bush's doctrine of preemption in the post-Iraq world, the outcome of America's inevitable strategic reappraisal, the image and moral authority of the United States in the world at the time, the legitimacy attaching to future U.S. military initatives, and the sentiment towards America among moderate Islamic nations and leaders. Australia will be one of many losers if tensions between Islam and the West are broadly interpreted as part of what Samuel Huntington has called a "clash of civilizations." Given Australia's geography, any further deterioration in relations between America and the Islamic nations would be seriously adverse for those of us "down under." As a junior ally, Australia has a great interest in seeing that U.S. policies are successful.

There is concern within Australia's broad strategic community—its think tanks, retired officials, academics, security specialists, and commentators—that the battle of ideas is not being won. While much of al-Qai'da's structure has been dismantled, the jihadists seem to have a plentiful supply of new recruits. Globalization has helped to create a situation where all Muslims feel sympathy for events adversely affecting other Muslims (witness the Danish cartoon issue and hostility to remarks by Pope Benedict). There would be concern in Australia about any U.S. resort to the military option against Iran, because it would alienate sentiment further in the Islamic world.

The other alliance challenge is different, founded as it is in classic state-to-state *realpolitik*. We are speaking, of course, of the epic interaction between China and America, a story that will shape much of the coming century. The most vital question for Australia is whether U.S.-China relations are defined by shared interests or dangerous rivalry. This question is pivotal because the intellectual and political foundations of the alliance rest upon the idea that Australia's close ties with East Asia and America are mutually reinforcing and not a zero sum game. That is, the alliance is supposed to maximize Australia's options rather than limit them. Prime Ministers from Sir Robert Menzies to John Howard have been able to validate this proposition. Indeed, Howard's major foreign policy achievement is not his realignment with the United States, but his ability to deepen Australia's ties simultaneously with both America and East Asia.

China poses an unprecedented test for this strategy. This huge nation eventually will replace Japan as Australia's major trading partner. But China, unlike the U.S. ally, Japan, is a potential strategic rival of America. For the first time in its history, therefore, Australia will be called upon to reconcile its ties to America as its security partner, with its ties to China as its principal economic partner.

Howard's China policy is one of the hallmarks of his prime ministership, a result that defied prediction in 1996. Nowhere is Howard's transition from novice to veteran more apparent. One of the first lessons that Howard learned is that a successful China policy is essential for a successful Australian prime ministership. As possibly the most pro-U.S. leader in Australia's history, Howard's commitment to the China relationship testifies to the power of this idea in Australia.

In his second most important overseas visit as PM, to China in 1997, Howard and China's President Jiang Zemin defined the basis for the relationship. It would rest upon "the twin pillars of mutual interest and mutual respect." When Howard repeatedly referred to the "national interest," he spoke a language invented by the Chinese.[10] Howard's subtext was that the Australia-China relationship would profit from a mutual acknowledgment that it was between nations with different values.

In 2003, China relations reached a new pinnacle with President Hu Jintao's visit to Australia, including his speech to the Australian Parliament the day after President Bush's own speech. It was the first time a non-U.S. leader had been extended such an honor. For Howard, the message was manifest—that Australia was building successful ties with the two nations of the world likely to dominate the next century.

Howard's policy revealed how much the politics of China played differently in Australia as compared to its reception in the United States. Contrasting public perceptions and strategic outlooks seem to be embedded in the political cultures of Australia and

America vis-à-vis China. Such differences should neither be exaggerated nor ignored. Consider the list. While America often sees China as a "strategic competitor," Howard believes the rise of China is beneficial for Asia and the world. While the United States has a formal commitment to Taiwan, Australia has no such commitment. While America is a global power with a tradition of Wilsonian idealism aspiring to promote democracy around the world, Australia has no such tradition and no such aspiration. While American politics is alert to the threat posed by China's exports, Australia is more influenced by the huge economic complementarity between the nations, and sees China's rise overwhelmingly as an economic opportunity. While America views China from the other side of the world's widest ocean, Australia sees China as a neighbor within the orbit of East Asian regionalism.

There is no doubt that Howard's close ties with the Bush administration has purchased him a degree of immunity in following a more independent approach to China. But Australia's ambivalence over Taiwan was exposed in August 2004 when Downer, in an indiscreet remark, said that ANZUS involvement was not triggered automatically by any war over Taiwan. His mistake was to speculate publicly. But his comment accurately signalled that Australia's political community had little taste for a war over Taiwan. Labor's leader, Kim Beazley, has made a similar point.[11]

These comments offer a revealing insight to Australia's Iraq commitment. Especially with Howard's pro-U.S. stance, there was no overriding national imperative for Australia to remain aloof from the Iraq war. Indeed, Australia had few national interests that were automatically put at risk. The situation over

Taiwan, however, would be the exact opposite—Australia's relations with China would be put at risk, thereby constituting a serious limitation on the scope of Australia's support.

During the period 2004-06, Howard elaborated Australia's strategic position in relation to the United States and China. He rejected any "inevitable" clash between the two giants and refused to frame Australia's policy in terms of any hypothetical requirement to choose between them. Howard told China that Australia was an aligned nation, with the implication that the alliance was immutable and that China should forget any dream about Australia's Finlandization. But he also assured China that the alliance is "not in any way directed against China," a critical qualifier. It prompts the question: "Does the United States agree with Howard in that assessment?" A good measure of U.S. understanding of Australia's predicament was revealed by the two leaders in their joint White House media conference of July 2005, when Bush, referring to China, conceded that Australia "has got to act in her interest."[12]

This may be a prophetic comment. In a region where there are two guiding stars to Australia's future, one star leads to closer economic, political, and regional links with China, enabling it to exert more leverage over Australia's foreign policy. The other star leads Australia into a closer partnership with its traditional friends, America and Japan, in the evolving Asian balance of power. Is there a conflict between the promptings of these two stars? It would be wrong to assume the strategic tensions are irreconcilable. But achieving harmony between these stars presents Australia with unique demands on managing foreign policy.

An intimately related question is how far Australia can support the "normalization" of Japan. Under Howard and Prime Minister Koizumi, the Australia-Japan relationship assumed a strategic dimension. Howard supported Koizumi's more assertive foreign policy. An upgraded ministerial-level security dialogue involving America, Japan, and Australia occurred for the first time in Sydney in early 2006. Downer also raised the prospect of a bilateral security agreement with Japan. A vital issue is whether this Australian support extends to revision of Article 9 of Japan's constitution, now declaring: "The Japanese people forever renounce war as a sovereign right of the nation." Any such revision to the present constitutional declaration is sure to inflame Chinese opinion.

Australian leaders realize full well that their Asia strategy depends heavily on U.S. policy towards China. Their ability to influence the U.S. approach is extremely limited. But Australia has its own strategic decisions to make in the evolving East Asian power balance that concern not just the U.S. alliance but the pivotal relationship between China and Japan. It is entirely possible that Japan-China tensions will outweigh America-China tensions as a potential problem for Australia. The enduring objectives of Australian leaders will be to integrate Australia's East Asian ties with its U.S. alliance and to ensure the changing East Asian power balance does not degenerate into conflict.

The third and final broad issue I want to address is the future outlook for the New Intimacy. A tantalizing crux is the changing nature of alliances and how the United States sees its allies. Former Defense Secretary Donald Rumsfeld gave all U.S. allies a wake-up call when, speaking of future "coalitions of the willing," he explained that "the mission will determine the coalition." Despite America's more accommodating stance towards allies in recent utterances, nobody has forgotten the earlier warning.

In the evolving post-Cold War environment, alliances are more flexible and more linked to improvised ad hoc expeditionary groupings. They also face more unpredictable challenges. Assuming that terrorism, rogue states, WMD proliferation, natural disasters, and health pandemics are the emerging threats, these alliances must adapt further. They will be less static, more supple, and geared to operational initiatives.

While Australia has strengthened its military ties with the United States, the political conditions for alliance cooperation are more fluid than before. In this context, it is worth asking how important it is for Australia to keep fighting in all of America's big wars. This Australia-U.S. tradition, extending from World War I to Iraq, is proud and honorable. But the future will be more than an extension of the past. In the coming century, it may be better for both sides to realize that a strong alliance does not necessarily mean Australia's automatic involvement in every U.S. conflict, particularly if Australia has contravening commitments elsewhere.

This reality leads directly into another challenge — how the alliance adjusts to Australia's new responsibilities within its own region. The Howard era has seen a spreading of Australia's regional as well as global responsibilities. The United States likes to interpret the alliance in "global" terms, yet the pressures on Australia suggest that future strategic priorities will refocus on the region itself. This is likely to be an important strategic event for the alliance. For Australian leaders, the Long War against Islamist terrorism will occur close to home. This is obvious given the

Islamic profile in Southeast Asia. This view is reinforced by regional instability, domestic imperatives, and the permanent task of managing relations with Indonesia.

The Labor Party's main critique of the Iraq venture is the allegation that it has sapped Australia's regional counterterrorism energies. Howard and Downer share Bush's view of the Islamist threat, with Downer having been instrumental in the 2004 White Paper on International Terrorism describing a global ideological challenge in which "we are engaged in a battle of ideas, a struggle to the death over values."[13] Having said this, Howard and Downer are drawn increasingly to the region where Australia must live and must address a combination of weak nations, poor economies, and struggling leaderships. This is a long-run challenge, and the Long War indeed is aptly named.

Since its decision to participate in the Iraq war, Australia has intervened on request in the Solomon Islands, a de facto failed state, and returned on request to East Timor to help curb residual violence in that nation, one of the poorest in Asia. Australia's further concern is that Papua New Guinea's decline will become systemic, precipitating Australian intervention there. The South Pacific includes several potentially failing states, thus presenting Australia and New Zealand with a joint management task. Howard has terminated the neocolonial mindset of the past generation that shunned Australian paternalism, and implemented instead a new realism based upon acceptance of regional responsibility. Recent decisions to expand the Australian Defence Force and the Australian Federal Police reflect concerns over the deepening regional instability and an acceptance that Australia must shoulder a greater responsibility in its geographical neighborhood. The success of this policy remains an open question and probably will vary from country to country.

The United States should not be alarmed about this trend. Australian policy always pivots around a balancing point between global and regional commitments. Each Australian prime minister is called upon in turn to judge this balance. Howard is a classic study—he made the most extensive global military commitments (Iraq and Afghanistan) since Vietnam, yet he also launched Australia's most interventionist military and police policy in the region.

The defining feature of Howard's regional policy is that of Australia operating as an initiator and leader. This stance is the opposite of the U.S. "deputy sheriff" role widely used to characterize Howard's policy. From the 1999 East Timor intervention onwards, the United States, in effect, has assisted Australia to achieve its regional goals. This suggests that the alliance is best seen as a compact under which Australia safeguards regional interests with U.S. support, as well as operating beyond its immediate region, depending upon capability and interests, in support of U.S. global objectives.

For Howard, commitments to Afghanistan and Iraq were not inconsistent with regional priorities. And meeting regional priorities did not exclude wider global commitments. Yet priorities must be set—and the balance is likely to shift back towards the regional. This will be accentuated if Labor comes to office in the near future, and if the Iraq intervention is seen by Australians to be a failure.

For all Howard's national security profile, defense spending has been kept to just under 2 percent of GDP. When he came to power in 1996, Howard exempted the defense portfolio from his steep spending cuts, producing the fiscal surplus that is such an embedded feature of his governance. He subsequently initiated a long-term basis for defense spending and programs. Cost overruns and expanding commitments may see the defense budget running at a higher level than projected. The point, however, is that Howard has not used the heightened national security climate post-9/11 to justify a significant increase in defense spending as a proportion of GDP. This is a reminder of a reality too little observed — that the alliance subsidizes Australia's security policy, thus permitting a level of social spending that otherwise would be required for the defense budget.

The New Intimacy has bequeathed a stronger institutional framework. The most obvious is the Australia-America FTA designed to secure increased economic, investment, and corporate links. Howard had high hopes for the FTA. In a few years, the balance sheet will be drawn: Was the FTA a sound judgment on Australia's part or did Australia delude itself about the benefits? The answer will play into the wider economic relationship as well as political attitudes.

Another strengthened institutional link is at the military-security-intelligence level. Australia-U.S. intelligence ties are closer than before. Military and equipment interoperability have assumed a new saliency from the momentum of Afghanistan and Iraq. The Howard era has seen an even greater emphasis in defense procurement for integration with U.S. forces. These changes, of course, are essential in a meaningful alliance.

A mjor test for the alliance's future is the verdict of public opinion. Australia's public supports the alliance, and the wellsprings of that support run deep. Criticism of the alliance in Australia is confined overwhelmingly to how it operates and not whether it should exist. But that criticism can be intense, driven by views about presidential popularity and U.S. foreign policy. Australia's public has never been enthusiastic about the Iraq war, yet it is realistic about the threat posed by Islamist terrorism.

Australia's political mind was formed in the context of a relatively small population holding sovereignty over a relatively large continent. The strategic culture of working within an empire or grand alliance is engrained in the majority but disputed by a noisy minority.

One lesson from Howard's alliance experience is reinforcement of an ancient verity—the Australian public likes to see independent Australian discretion exercized within the alliance. It wants to know there is an independent Australian mind in the partnership. The people know the reality of alliances—that nations support each other and enter wars for each other. Yet the public grasps an essential truth—that alliances work better when mutual respect is apparent, and such respect incorporates a margin for difference. The Howard government has not emphasized sufficiently the essentiality of such discretion.

Australia, like all U.S. allies, is affected deeply by the quality of U.S. global leadership. Australians evaluate American presidents. They want an American leadership that is tough yet persuasive, that uses both hard power and soft power, properly proportioned and modulated. It is in Australia's interest for the United States to exercise multilateral leadership, not just unilateral leadership.

Americans might reflect on what Australia brings to the table as an ally: it is prepared to fight; it is a country on the rim of East Asia with standing in the region; it is the metropolitan power within its own immediate and unstable region; it is a global player in trade, security, governance, and environmental issues; and it is an independent partner with shared values and a capacity to provide informed private counsel to assist the United States.

ENDNOTES - CHAPTER 3

1. John Howard, speech to the U.S. Congress, June 12, 2002.

2. Lowy Institute poll, "Australians Speak 2005," Lowy Institute, Sydney, 2005.

3. John Howard, interview with John Laws, September 12, 2001; interview with Mike Munro, *A Current Affair*, September 12, 2001; and press conference, Canberra, September 14, 2001.

4. John Howard, press conference, September 11-12, 2001, Washington, DC.

5. Howard, interview with John Laws.

6. Richard N. Haass, "The US-Australia Alliance in an East Asian Context," in Henry Albinski and Rawdon Dalrymple, eds., *The United States-Australia Alliance in an East Asian Context*, Conference Proceedings, The University of Sydney, June 29-30, 2001.

7. John Howard, House of Representatives, Hansard, March 18, 2003.

8. As of October 2006, there have been two Australian casualties associated with the Iraq campaign. Both have been attributed to accidents.

9. Kim Beazley, *Foreign Affairs and Defence in the Hawke Government*, Susan Ryan and Troy Bramston, eds., Melbourne: Pluto Press, 2003, pp. 363-364.

10. John Howard, press conference, Beijing, China, April 1, 1997.

11. For an analysis of Downer's remarks and their significance, refer to Paul Kelly, *The Australian*, August 25, 2004.

12. Joint Press Conference, The White House, July 19, 2005.

13. Alexander Downer, National Press Club speech, July 15, 2004.

PANEL II:

FOREIGN POLICY:
THE ALLIANCE IN THE ASIA-PACIFIC REGION

CHAPTER 4

PANEL II CHAIRMAN'S INTRODUCTION

William T. Tow

A major finding of the workshops related to the present project was that the global and regional dimensions of Australia-U.S. alliance politics are becoming increasingly amalgamated. The forces of international terrorism can strike in any Asian city, precipitating extensive adjustments in the homeland security policies of Australia, the United States, and other states worldwide. Proliferating weapons of mass destruction (WMD), coupled with modern delivery systems, can hit Australian or American targets from great distances within or beyond Asia. Nontraditional security threats such as pandemics originating in southern China and Africa, or the forced movement of peoples in the aftermath of natural disasters or human security contingencies, can quickly overwhelm developed societies and economies. Emerging security challenges in the Asia-Pacific region merely reflect the larger global challenges that promise to be even more severe than those that the Australia-New Zealand-U.S. (ANZUS) alliance confronted and prevailed against during the Cold War. The ultimate alliance objective, however, whether applied regionally or globally, has not changed: as Andrew Scobell correctly observes at the outset of Chapter 5, it is stability.

Several important themes emerge from Scobell's and Robert Ayson's chapters that deal with the American outlook and the Australian outlook, respectively, on how ANZUS relates to the Asia-Pacific region.

While the region has undergone a historic structural transformation over the past decade, the Australian-American alliance has held up well as a relevant component of U.S. grand strategy. However, the authors warn that both allies face the danger of policy miscalculation in this new and uncertain regional security environment, and must therefore work assiduously to avoid it. Another theme of both authors is that weak states can be as lethal to ANZUS alliance objectives as strong ones. Weak or failing states, and substate threats such as terrorist groups, can test the alliance as sharply as a rising China (the ultimate powderkeg state according to Scobell), an awakening India, or a more normal Japan. Finally, they posit that alliance expectations must be constantly monitored and adjusted by both Canberra and Washington.

U.S. Strategy: Reconciling Australia's Regional and Global Role.

As Robert Ayson (Chapter 6) observes, Australia's extra-regional commitments to Afghanistan and Iran have earned it a special place of honor in the George W. Bush administration's alliance politics. Australia is a prominent member in what Kurt Campbell has termed "a new international cohort" of core allies that work closely with the United States in the global war on terrorism and that rank highly on the loyalty index that the administration has relied upon to build its coalitions of the willing.[1] Prominent Australian defense analyst Paul Dibb has gone even further, claiming that "Australia is America's closest ally in the [Asia-Pacific] region and the second most important U.S. ally in the world after the United Kingdom."[2] In part, this may be due to a resurgence of Anglosphere solidarity in the aftermath of the September 11, 2001 (9/11), international terrorist threat.[3] Perhaps even more important, Australia has developed and deployed diplomatic and military niche capabilities that constitute nice fits in U.S. global strategy: Australian Special Air Service Regiment (SAS) forces adeptly clearing points of advance for coalition forces in Afghanistan and Iraq; Australian Federal Police (AFP) units mediating in internecine conflict in South Pacific failed-state environments; and envoys executing and managing middle power diplomacy with respect to arms control and human security.

This global role notwithstanding, Australia's regional position and its potential ability to facilitate what American policy-planners regard as a stable regional balance is probably more important to U.S. global strategic planning. Critics have, however, labeled Australian support for controversial Bush administration postures, and its own intervention actions in East Timor and the South Pacific, as nothing more than the sycophantic behavior of a U.S. strategic proxy or "deputy sheriff."[4] An alternative view is that if Australian regional security interests do not mesh with U.S. interests, abandonment by Washington would become a distinct possibility. Former Australian Prime Minister Malcolm Fraser, now a frequent alliance detractor, has encapsulated this view: "When there have been concerns in our region, the United States has made it plain they didn't really want to be involved. . . . We should not allow the American relationship to blind ourselves."[5]

Supporters of a more coordinated Australian-American strategic role in the Asia-Pacific region such as Scobell, however, view Australia as a critical linchpin state whose "formidable" and "viable" democracy can serve effectively as outposts in behalf of both Australian and American objectives in Asian settings and institutions, especially where U.S. power may be less directly assertable. At his confirmation hearing in January 2001, Secretary of State-designate Colin Power graphically encouraged a strong Australian regional identity in recognition of the close affinity between Australian regional security interests and those of the United States. "In the Pacific," he stated, "we are very, very pleased that Australia, our firm ally, has displayed a keen interest in what has been happening in Indonesia. So we will coordinate our policies. But let our ally, Australia, take the lead as they have done so well in that troubled country."[6]

Who is right between those who oppose Australia integrating more closely with U.S. global strategy, and those who support it? To employ the old adage, "the truth is probably somewhere in between." U.S. global preoccupations continue to oscillate between addressing strategic threats that are clearly extra-regional in nature, and applying traditional balancing strategies toward the Asia-Pacific region's rising powers. As a Western industrialized democracy, Australia undoubtedly has a stake in supporting Washington's predisposition to lead the quest against counterterrorism and WMD proliferation. Yet, it has a primary interest in staking out an independent regional identity in diplomatic and strategic terms. That identity should not be subject to an American loyalty test as a measure of alliance durability in the event that Australian and American interests diverge on one or more critical regional security issues.

Avoiding Misguided Policy Expectations.

There is a need to avoid policy miscalculations within this other "special relationship." Such miscalculations can be engendered by false expectations or ambiguous communications about what are each ally's actual national security interests. Robert Ayson alludes to past instances where miscalculations have prevailed in Asia-Pacific strategic settings: U.S. differences with Labor governments in the 1980s over missile testing and South Pacific nuclear-free zone politics; Australian-American differences over the value of regional multilateral security dialogues and institutions; and the perception, within various Australian circles, of a lack of American material support for Australia's 1999 intervention in East Timor. This litany is cited often by alliance critics such as Fraser when raising the fundamental question about ANZUS: "There were a number of leaders throughout Asia that believed that ANZUS reinforced American involvement in the region . . . they believed that this provided some assurance of American support in times of crisis. In retrospect, however, how much support did we get?"[7] Andrew Scobell correctly argues that good alliance management often does not flow easily from the course of events; policymakers need to work hard at it. In general, however, ANZUS officials have risen to the task, and the history of alliance collaboration that has spanned over half a century is a generally positive one. Although less central than NATO during the Cold War, of course, ANZUS helped contain Soviet power in Asia and in the wider Pacific. It contributed to the planning and resources applied by the Western powers to defeat Chinese-backed Communist political or military insurgency movements in a number of Southeast Asian countries. Australia and New Zealand (even after the latter country's de facto exit from the ANZUS Council in August 1986) largely were successful in preventing Cold War politics from entering the South

Pacific region. ANZUS became an invaluable conduit for exchanges of intelligence relevant to the area's strategic balance.

As the post-Cold War regional security order evolves, however, the emerging challenges to Asia-Pacific stability are laden with potential for intra-alliance miscalculations. The rise of China is the most significant of these developments. Both chapter contributors in this subsection of the volume emphasize that China will affect alliance politics in highly diverse ways. Scobell acknowledges that the United States, by its engagement policies toward China, can affect significantly what type of power that country eventually becomes. Australia also can contribute to a positive outcome by encouraging successive U.S. administrations to stay the course in cultivating stronger economic and diplomatic ties with Beijing. It can counsel against U.S. support for any increased separatist tendencies on the part of Taiwan, urging that such support would work against U.S. core national security interests. If such counseling is deemed necessary but proves to be unsuccessful, Australia risks confronting what Ayson terms the stuff of nightmares — having to choose between a regionally dominant China and an American superpower serving notice that it expects Australia to adhere to the loyalty criteria of alliance politics.

The recent deterioration of relations between China and Japan presents a similar dilemma for Australia, especially if U.S.-Japan security cooperation continues to grow along the lines of the May 2006 roadmap agreement that effectively integrates the command structure of U.S. forces operating in Okinawa and other parts of Northeast Asia far more closely with that of Japan's Self Defense Force (SDF).[8] Australia recently has announced its own intentions to move toward a more formal security relationship with Japan, although this relationship will not be as encompassing as the ANZUS alliance.[9] How will Australia interact with a Japan that is clearly shifting toward the status of a military power in Northeast Asia without inciting Chinese apprehensions that it is working in league with the United States and Japan to curb any Chinese move toward hegemony? Balancing its increasingly comprehensive economic and political ties with China against a more explicit security relationship with Japan will sharply test Australian policymakers' communications and diplomatic skills.

Coordinating Responses to Asymmetrical Threats and Powderkegs.

With regard to how emerging asymmetrical threats such as terrorism and rogue states affect alliance politics, two countervailing interpretations emerge. One is that such threats are so diverse and numerous that alliance managers will have no choice but to become more risk tolerant in formulating policies and applying resources to meet them. Rod Lyon has argued that globalization, the "demassification" of military forces into smaller units, and technological proliferation have created a new generation of "raiders" (i.e., terrorists) that are redefining the classical battlefield for international dominance. He states that Australia's

future security partnership with the US [therefore] needs to address a new security environment characterized by technological diffusion and the rise of smaller war-making units able to exploit global networks. It also needs to address a broader set of security challenges, and to think through the logic of interdependency that is needed if [ANZUS is] to offset new adversaries.[10]

An opposing perspective is conveyed by John Ikenberry, who believes that the postwar international order and the alliances that underwrite it are sufficient to withstand emerging asymmetrical threats:

> The Bush administration is launching its war on terrorism from a foundation of stable and cooperative relations built over many decades . . . . Certainly the terrorist events present the United States, Europe, and other states with an opportunity to renew and expand the political bargains on which the current international order rests.[11]

Australian Prime Minister John Howard activated Article IV of the ANZUS alliance — an existing but previously unused alliance mechanism — immediately following the 9/11 terrorist attacks in New York and Washington. Five years later, Australia is regarded by U.S. leaders as an ally sharing core U.S. values, pursuing common strategic objectives, and willing to share common political and military risks. Indeed, one of America's most authoritative experts on international terrorism has predicted that Australia will incur a major terrorist strike in the near future.[12]

To date, the arguments of both Lyon and Ikenberry are correct. Alliance preoccupations with state-centric threats that were dominant in the Cold War are now giving way to concerns about weak actors compensating for their lack of conventional power with creative and lethal strategies of high risk. Suicide bombers, limited and rudimentary Iranian or North Korean nuclear weapons capabilities, and criminal gangs holding South Pacific microstate governments at bay are all illustrative. Yet state-centric power and competition persist in our international system, and Scobell's concern with powderkeg states validates this reality.

A future Sino-American conflict, a Sino-Japanese confrontation, or a renewed Korean War would have immense repercussions for Asian-Pacific prosperity and for Australia's own physical and economic security. Over half of Australia's trade is with Northeast Asia, and increasingly strained American military forces cannot patrol the wider Pacific in any such contingencies. The challenge for alliance managers is to identify and implement a carefully balanced set of strategies that can respond to both state and nonstate threats. That can be done only if Australian policymakers work with their American counterparts to decide wisely and proactively which contingencies should be assigned priority in their strategic planning.

Multilateral Security Involvement.

Ayson considers to what extent growing multilateralism in Asia is a bus which Australia has to get on, and to what extent American participation is desired or required to facilitate regional security community-building. The existing international order, as envisioned by Ikenberry and others, remains shaped by an American hegemon projecting hard power, but whose values are increasingly under attack by radical jihadists, ardent nationalists, and other dissident contenders. Asian countries, like the United States and Australia, are striving to find the middle ground to accommodate the most reasonable grievances of these dissenters within existing international processes and structures without relinquishing the benefits of globalization and liberalization.

A consensus is developing on which approach to multilateral security politics is best suited to achieve that middle ground. The Bush administration has remained wedded to the hub-and-spokes formula, with America at the center, for managing its security relationships in Asia. Although Scobell insists that this architecture "continues to function with great relevance," it nevertheless is viewed by many of America's friends in the region as too lopsided. After initially concurring with the American approach and arguing that the predecessor government had slighted traditional Australian friendships in favor of a too rapid move toward Asia, the Howard government now has come to endorse much of the policy it previously condemned. It has struck a judicious balance between alliance cultivation and regional affiliation.

This has been a hard learning experience for an Australian prime minister, who is an unmitigated Anglophile by background and by emotional inclination. It is one that, at least in part, has led to Canberra's ultimate rejection of the logic of Colin Powell's mechanistic "sphere of national influence" concept alluded to above. Later, when U.S. Secretary of State Condoleezza Rice failed to attend a key ministerial meeting in Southeast Asia, Australian interests as well as American ones were affected adversely.[13] This incident, and others like it, tends to drive Australia toward making a choice between appearing as Washington's regional proxy or appearing as an increasingly soft American ally that gradually can be weaned away from the American orbit by a China that cleverly leverages the regionalist angle.

Both of the succeeding chapters tender policy prescriptions for avoiding either outcome, supporting these prescriptions with in-depth and highly valuable empirical analysis in support of their conclusions. As ANZUS has become more global in scope since 9/11, it also has remained a key element in the Asia-Pacific region's future security equation. Part II of this volume thus is intended to provide a coherent explanation of how America's other special relationship can influence Asia's future security environment in a constructive and mutually beneficial fashion.

ENDNOTES - CHAPTER 4

1. Kurt Campbell, "The End of Alliances? Not So Fast," *The Washington Quarterly*, Vol. 27, No. 2, 2004, p. 157.

2. Paul Dibb, *Australia's Alliance With America*, Melbourne Asia Policy Papers No. 1, March 2003, p. 1, accessed at *www.asialink. unimelb.edu.au/cpp/policypapers/pauldibb.pdf*.

3. James C. Bennett, "The Emerging Anglosphere," *ORBIS*, Vol. 46, Winter 2002, pp. 111-126; and Douglas Stuart, "NATO's Anglosphere Option: Closing the Distance Between Mars and Venus," *International Journal*, Vol. 60, Winter 2005, pp. 171-187. Stuart, however, identifies Australia as an "outlier" relative to a British-American core in the Anglosphere community.

4. Background on this debate is provided by Richard Leaver, "The Meaning, Origins, and Implications of the Howard Doctrine," *The Pacific Review*, Vol. 14, No. 1, March 2001, pp. 15-34; and William T. Tow, "'Deputy Sheriff' Or Independent Ally? Evolving Australian-American Ties in an Ambiguous World Order," *The Pacific Review*, Vol. 17, No. 2, June 2004, pp. 271-290.

5. Fraser, "An Australian Critique," *Australian Journal of International Affairs*, Vol. 55, No. 2, July 2001, p. 235.

6. U.S. Department of State, "Confirmation Hearing by Secretary-Designate Colin L. Powell," Washington, DC, January 2001, at *www.state.gov/s/index.cfm?docid=443*.

7. Fraser, "An Australian Critique," p. 226.

8. The Ministry of Foreign Affairs of Japan, "United States Japan Security Consultative Committee Document — United States–Japan Roadmap for Realignment Implementation," May 1, 2006, at *www.mofa.go.jp/region/n-america/us/security/scc/doc0605. html*.

9. Paul Kelly, "Warming up to Tokyo," *The Australian*, August 12, 2006.

10. Rod Lyon, *Alliance Unleashed: Australia and the U.S. in a New Strategic Age*, ASPI Strategy Paper, Canberra: Australian Strategic Policy Institute, pp. 19-20, 22 (the quotation is found on p. 22).

11. John Ikenberry, "American Grand Strategy in the Age of Terror," *Survival*, Vol. 43, No. 4, Winter 2001-2001, p. 31.

12. Natalie O'Brien, "Melbourne the Terror Target," *The Australian*, September 8, 2006, who cites a briefing by the University of Chicago's eminent political scientist Robert Pape for Australia's Attorney-General's Department. On the dividends Australia has received in the aftermath of invoking ANZUS in response to 9/11, consult Greg Sheridan, "Canberra Push Reaps Rich Rewards," *The Australian*, August 3, 2006.

13. See Joel Brinkley, "Rice, in Asia, Takes Heat for Avoiding ASEAN Trip," *International Herald Tribune*, July 12, 2005. She was the first American Secretary of State in more than 20 years to miss the annual ASEAN Ministerial Meeting. Asian critics observed that "lots of people were offended by this decision" and considered it a "statement of her priorities."

CHAPTER 5

THE ALLIANCE AND THE ASIA-PACIFIC REGION: AN AMERICAN PERSPECTIVE

Andrew Scobell

This chapter assesses U.S. interests in the Asia-Pacific region and the principal threats to those interests for the next 20 years, focussing especially on the role of the U.S.-Australian alliance in promoting such interests.[1] It will conclude with recommendations for future U.S. strategy in the region. In this chapter, the term "Asia-Pacific region" refers to the area that stretches from Hawaii to Pakistan and from the Aleutian Islands to Australia.

U.S. INTERESTS

The United States has a number of vital interests in the Asia-Pacific region. Paramount among these is the continued peace and prosperity of the region. This often is abbreviated to a single word — "stability." Peace cannot be said to be simply the absence of war; peace should be defined rather in robust terms. "Enduring peace" can be defined as the presence of thriving regional and subregional cooperation mechanisms in the arenas of politics, economics, security, and environment.

Other critical U.S. interests include the prevention of attacks against the U.S. homeland or its forces deployed in the Asia-Pacific region, the quelling of terrorist movements (especially in Southeast Asia), access to regional markets, and the promotion of democratic political systems there.[2] Recent concerns about Chinese and North Korean ballistic missile capabilities, the intensification of terrorist problems in the Philippines and southern Thailand, the growth of ASEAN + 3 following the Asian financial crisis, and the defense of robust democracies in South Korea and Taiwan all impact upon these interests. U.S. alliances with key regional allies such as Australia are designed to realize key U.S. regional security objectives.

WHERE THE MILITARY FITS IN

A fundamental assumption of this chapter is that a U.S.-oriented security architecture, underscored by regional alliances, and a U.S. military forward presence, in some form or another, are essential for peace and prosperity in the Asia-Pacific. The particular shape and substance of this security architecture should be adaptable since it will likely need to evolve over time. The U.S. bilateral alliance architecture shaped around a hub-and-spokes concept has served American strategic interests well in the region throughout the postwar time frame, and it continues to function with great relevance in a post-September 11, 2001 (9/11), context.

While the precise positioning, size, and mix of forces will depend on specific threats and conditions, it is vital that such a forward presence include a significant land power component. In a region as vast and ocean-dominated as the Asia-Pacific, naval and air forces are extremely important. Nevertheless, the Army is the ultimate symbol of an enduring U.S. commitment to peace and prosperity of the region. The Army is the core service in the labor-intensive business of peacetime security cooperation.[3] Continued U.S. land force deployments on the Korean peninsula and recent arrangements to integrate U.S. Army components more closely with the operations of counterpart Japanese Self Defense Forces in Okinawa are cases in point. They serve as effective deterrents to conflict escalation in Northeast Asia and as flexible components of a U.S. global strategy that is evolving to neutralize asymmetrical threats in Asia and in other regions.

It should be remembered, of course, that the military is but one component of American national power.[4] To ensure peace and prosperity in the Asia-Pacific region, the United States must employ the full array of both hard power and soft power instruments at its disposal: economic, diplomatic, and informational. These must be employed in a coordinated and coherent fashion and, again, in close conjunction with the interests and strategic support of U.S. allies in the Pacific.

In this context, the Australian-American alliance (still most commonly known by the acronym, ANZUS) fits well with U.S. regional politico-security and economic interests. Along with Britain, Australia perhaps is viewed as Washington's most loyal global security partner on counterterrorism, anti-proliferation and other key international security issues. As one of the Asia-Pacific's most advanced industrialized democracies, it plays a key role in such regional institutions such as the Asia-Pacific Economic Cooperation (APEC), the Association of Southeast Asian Nations (ASEAN), and the ASEAN Regional Forum (ARF) in advancing values and interests highly commensurate with those of the United States. Along with Japan and perhaps Singapore, it is the only defense actor in the region capable of operating in a high-tempo, cutting-edge combat environment shaped by U.S. military power and led by U.S. forces.

Yet Australia also maintains workable, even cordial trade and political relations with China and formal diplomatic ties with North Korea, affording it a measure of diplomatic leverage as a middle power in an increasingly competitive Asian geopolitical environment that is disproportionate to its own modest (if highly proficient) defense capabilities. In many ways, Australia might be deemed as an ideal American ally.[5]

KEY THREATS AND CHALLENGES TO THE STABILITY OF THE ASIA-PACIFIC

Over the next 20 years, the stability of the Asia-Pacific is likely to face complex threats from four key geographic hot spots. Moreover, the United States and its regional allies will be faced with four fundamental strategic challenges. The four threats emanate from Korea, the Taiwan Strait, South and Central Asia, and Southeast Asia. If current trends continue, the threats posed on the Korean peninsula and in the Taiwan Strait are likely to become permanent, remaining the most serious flashpoints in the region. South and Central Asia, meanwhile, are subregions of significant instability and are increasingly likely to cause complex and multidimensional threats to the stability of the entire Asia-Pacific region. In contrast, trends in Southeast Asia seem to be more positive, although significant security threats could emerge to undermine stability in this subregion as well.

The four fundamental challenges likely to confront the United States in the Asia-Pacific region during the first quarter of the 21st century are (1) managing relations with allies and friends in the region (aka "linchpin states"); (2) shaping countries at risk (aka "powder keg states"); (3) maintaining a credible forward presence; and (4) managing and deterring the flashpoints identified above. These threats and challenges are addressed below.

Key Flashpoints.

Korea. The situation on the Korean Peninsula appears to be a principal challenge to peace and prosperity in the Asia-Pacific, and without a fundamental reorientation of the eroding totalitarian regime in Pyongyang, tensions are unlikely to dissipate in the foreseeable future.[6] North Korea's July 2006 missile launches and October 2006 nuclear test have underscored how quickly an erosion of diplomatic negotiations and confidence-building can occur as the so-called Six Party Talks now appear stymied in the aftermath of United Nations (UN) Resolutions that condemn North Korean strategic behavior and Pyongyang's absolute transigence in the face of worldwide condemnation of its missile and nuclear testing.

Although President Roh Moo Hyun of South Korea has been supportive of the U.S.-Republic of Korea (ROK) alliance and Chairman Kim of North Korea reportedly has indicated a willingness to accept a U.S. military presence on the Korean Peninsula even after a posited unification, this does not represent any firm commitment by either government.[7] On the other hand, it reflects their distrust of other foreign powers and can be a point of great U.S. leverage.[8] The Perry Commission concluded 7 years ago that the status quo on the Korean Peninsula did not appear to be "sustainable."[9] Yet, in 2006 the Pyongyang regime seems stable and sustainable enough to last for perhaps another 10 to 15 years.[10] The leaders of both North and South Korea desire at least some limited form of reconciliation. However, while in general accord on the concept of unification, they both seem to believe that the process should move forward gradually. Both sides, each for its own reasons, want to see the continued existence of the two separate Korean regimes and steady progress toward some kind of confederation. Seoul is concerned about shouldering the staggering costs incident to unification, while Pyongyang is fearful that unification will mean the end of the regime.[11]

The current relationship between North and South Korea appears highly skewed. The ROK had initiated the vast majority of positive inducements to reduce protracted tensions with the North. The Democratic People's Republic of Korea's (DPRK) posture appears to be one of presumed entitlement for nothing conceded in return. Certainly, unification on the peninsula is possible in the next 2 decades, but it would require a Korean peace agreement, a framework for regular trade, travel, and communication between North and South, and an intensive, continuing dialogue leading up to the event itself.[12] Reconciliation would be a drawn-out and graduated process.

Hence the United States must remain vigilant and continue to work hand in glove with its allies, including the ROK and Japan, to ensure it is prepared for any eventuality. The Australian connection also is important here. Australia has undertaken a leading role in the Proliferation Security Initiative (PSI) that originated in 2003, largely in response to alleged North Korean shipments of materials for weapons of mass destruction (WMD) on the high seas. It also has assumed a higher profile in regional security coordination via the Trilateral Strategic Dialogue, the ministerial-level consultations between Australia, Japan, and the

United States to manage joint strategy toward North Korea and, more indirectly, toward China's rise. As part of an initial diplomatic response to North Korea's mid-2006 missile tests, Australian diplomats reportedly queried their North Korean counterparts about a "secure energy deal, probably coal shipments, if the rogue state returned to peace talks as part of an attempt to solve the missile crisis."[13] Yet, along with Japan, Australia continues to engage in advanced missile defense technology research with the United States that, when deployed, is intended to intercept limited missile strikes of the type that North Korea may well be able to launch over the next decade. Australian alliance cooperation with the United States and Japan thus is targeted discriminatingly to generate maximum benefits while sufficiently multifaceted to respond effectively to North Korean oscillations in strategic behavior. The DPRK's October 2006 detonation of an actual nuclear device, of course, adds an enormously ominous complication to the Korean problem, one that all players, including even the UN, are scrambling to deal with as this chapter goes to press.

Taiwan Strait. In the first decade of the 21st century, tensions in the Taiwan Strait appear moderate and manageable but chronic. Strait tensions seem likely to remain a principal threat to peace and prosperity in the Asia-Pacific for the foreseeable future. Reconciliation between Beijing and Taipei is certain to be very difficult to attain, and unification probably is unachievable in the short term. This situation will constitute a major challenge to ANZUS because Australia and the United States often entertain different perspectives on the meaning of China's rise to regional security. We shall discuss this topic in greater depth in the pages to follow.

American perceptions are shaped more by the specter of an intensifying Chinese military threat in the East China Sea and beyond. Currently, China appears wary, even if momentarily satisfied, over perceived trends in the Taiwan Strait. But Beijing, and especially the People's Liberation Army (PLA), has been increasingly frustrated over the lack of tangible progress toward Taiwan's political assimilation by the Chinese mainland.

Before discussing this flashpoint's implications for ANZUS, it may be useful to offer a brief review of its evolution. Unification with Taiwan has been a core Chinese national security objective for half a century. More than 25 years after the moderate and pragmatic "one country, two systems" policy was formulated by the late Deng Xiaoping, it has yet to bear tangible fruit. This is all the more disappointing in Beijing's view when measured by the successful returns of the former British colony of Hong Kong in mid-1997 and former Portuguese enclave of Macao in late 1999. Beijing's expectations also were heightened by a dramatic Sino-Taiwanese rapprochement of the late 1980s and early 1990s when cross-Strait trade and investment developed and travel for family reunions, business, and tourism expanded virtually overnight.[14] Most noteworthy was the significant diplomatic groundwork: the establishment of quasi-official organizations in Beijing and Taipei to manage bilateral relations. The high point was the summit held in 1993 in Singapore between the chiefs of these two organizations.

The goodwill and progress evaporated in mid-1995 when Taiwan President Lee Teng-hui was granted a visa to visit the United States. Lee's rhetoric during the visit, combined with other initiatives launched by Taipei, led Chinese leaders to conclude that Taiwan was embarked down a path toward independence. China's missile tests off the Taiwan coast and naval exercises near the Taiwan Strait during late 1995 and during Taiwan's first contested presidential election in early 1996 were orchestrated to persuade the Taiwanese to rethink the advisability of such a course of action.[15]

For several years China's saber-rattling appeared to have had its intended effect: Taiwan cooled its rhetoric and gestures. But in mid-1999 Taiwan's President Lee suggested that relations between China and Taiwan should be treated as "state to state." This triggered a further round of vitriolic rhetoric and threats from China, culminating in the Taiwan White Paper of February 2000.[16] This official Chinese government document added a third justification for the use of force against Taiwan: lack of progress on negotiations directed at unification. Further statements issued in the lead-up to Taiwan's presidential elections of March 2000 admonished the island's electorate not to vote for long-time pro-independence candidate Chen Shui-bian. The attempt at intimidation seemed to backfire when Chen won the election.

Tensions cooled following Chen's 2000 inauguration, with China reverting to a wait-and-see policy.[17] Despite periodic tensions, the climate of cross-Strait relations has remained relatively calm during the past 6 years. Beijing has tended to be restrained in its rhetoric and reactions to events in Taipei, including the March 2004 reelection of Chen Shui-bian. More recently, some Chinese officials have issued stern warnings over Chen's plans for constitutional reform on the island. But the visits in 2005 of several prominent Taiwanese politicians to the mainland appear to have helped to reassure Beijing that the trends are working in China's favor.[18]

This episode represented the first testing of how ANZUS might respond to a scenario involving possible Sino-American confrontation over Taiwan. From Washington's perspective, newly elected Prime Minister John Howard passed this test with flying colors, as Australia was the only state in the region that openly supported the United States' deployment of two aircraft carrier task forces adjacent to the East China Sea as a signal to China that further conflict escalation could have dire consequences for Beijing's own security. However, Australia paid a steep price for such support: China effectively severed commercial and political ties with the Howard government for about a year. Howard was forced to visit Beijing and reassure the Chinese leadership that Australia still adhered to a one-China policy and that it would not deal on an official basis with Taiwanese representatives.

By 1999, Sino-Australian relations had warmed to the point that respected American policy observers such as Richard Armitage (later to become Deputy Secretary of State in the George W. Bush administration) felt obliged to speak out. Participating at an Australia-American Dialogue session convened in Sydney during August 1999, Armitage warned his hosts that the United States would expect Australia to provide meaningful military support to the United States in order to carry out "dirty, hard, and dangerous" work. He insisted that Canberra's interests as well as those of the United States directly related to the outcome of such a confrontation, and that the future of ANZUS could hinge on whether such Australian support was forthcoming. The Australian government responded merely that it could not speculate on specific outcomes to hypothetical contingencies, but Armitage's warning aggravated already raw nerves over the nightmare of Australia having to choose between China and the United States over Taiwan.

The ensuing years witnessed the Howard government's pursuit of an adroit dual strategy of cultivating strong economic and diplomatic ties with Beijing by insisting that no such choice needed to be made. Australia could deal with Beijing as a growing and respectable regional power, counting on the Chinese to understand the imperative of Australia continuing to sustain and strengthen its natural alliance with the United States. Because the so-called global war on terror (now labeled "The Long War") had defused Sino-American tensions early in the Bush administration, this strategy proved to be a workable one from Canberra's perspective. At various intervals the Chinese attempted to test this Australian proposition, most notably following the PRC's adoption of an anti-secession law directed at Taiwan in early 2005. At least one Chinese official recommended that Australia might reconsider the ANZUS commitments, formally exempting a Taiwan contingency from any alliance application. This suggestion was politely and firmly refused by Australian officials. The Chinese probe in this instance may have been prompted by the musings of Australian Foreign Minister Alexander Downer when visiting Beijing the previous year, to the effect that ANZUS might be exempted from a defense of U.S. forces in a Taiwan conflict depending on the circumstances that arose. But Downer was immediately enjoined to deny this supposition by his own Prime Minister and by forceful admonishments of U.S. State Department officials who interpreted any attack on American forces in the Pacific region as an automatic trigger for ANZUS activation.

Tensions in the East China Sea could flare up again at any time. As of December 2004, the PRC officially characterized the situation in the Taiwan Strait as "grim."[19] It is important to note that the PRC government has never renounced the use of force to achieve unification with Taiwan (or to prevent the island from gaining independence). Moreover, the Taiwan Strait conflict remains the PLA's dominant war scenario. The Chinese military believes it has been entrusted with the sacred mission of unifying Taiwan with the Chinese mainland.[20] There is significant potential for miscalculation or misperception in the coercive diplomacy and calculated risk-taking that China is in the habit of pursuing.[21] In some future round of saber-rattling, a missile launched simply to intimidate Taiwan could veer off its intended course and hit a civilian target. Or a massive military exercise in the Taiwan Strait could be misinterpreted by Taipei as the prelude for an imminent attack. A deliberate decision by Beijing to launch a military operation against Taiwan also cannot be ruled out. The issue of unification with Taiwan is sensitive, emotive, and, most importantly, a core element of the Chinese Communist Party's political legitimacy. With that being the case, many of China's elites appear to believe that the party-state might not be able to survive the righteous indignation of the masses should the regime not fight to keep Taiwan. Thus, under certain circumstances, the PLA might be ordered to launch an operation against Taiwan even if it were thought to have little or no chance of success.[22] The bottom line is that political expediency — not military feasibility — will be the paramount determinant of whether or not China uses armed force.[23]

PLA war planning appears to be focused on either of two options: a sudden whirlwind military campaign to subdue Taiwan so rapidly as to present the United

States with a fait accompli; or a more gradual and carefully calibrated campaign targeting selected key military, political, or infrastructural targets that would produce maximum psychological pressure but minimal casualties. In the first scenario, PLA planners would assume that the United States had too little time to marshal forces to defend Taiwan and therefore almost certainly would be forced to accept the situation. In the second scenario, Beijing would do its best not to cross the threshold that would trigger U.S. military intervention.[24] In either case, in the context of deterring U.S. military support for Taiwan, Chinese military modernization focuses on operations against Taiwan and the United States. An outright invasion scenario with maximum-effort amphibious landings is highly unlikely but cannot be ruled out.[25]

If ANZUS were to be activated in a future Taiwan conflict, how would a posited Australian role play out? As an integral part of the U.S.-allied global intelligence network, the Australian signals installation at Geraldton in Western Australia links up with the Taiwan National Security Bureau's signal intelligence base at Pingtung Lee on the Yangmingshan Mountain north of Taipei to provide information on Chinese satellite communications.[26] Australian maritime elements such as the extraordinarily quiet *Collins*-class submarine fleet could be introduced into the waters of the Taiwan Strait in an interdiction role. It is more likely, however, that they would join Australian surface elements to monitor patrolling lanes normally assigned to the U.S. Seventh Fleet if the latter were to be diverted to Northeast Asia. Land and sea elements of the Australian Defence Force (ADF) also would be preoccupied with securing rear areas of maritime Southeast Asia and the South Pacific to ensure unconstrained passage of U.S. forces from

CONUS bases into the Northeast Asian and East Asian theaters of operation.

With regard to any future Asia-Pacific security vision, Australia has a keen interest in furthering the declared U.S. strategy of swaying China to embrace the role of "responsible stakeholder," in the words of former U.S. Deputy Secretary of State Robert Zoellick. Thus engagement should be the dominant strategic frame of reference rather than containment. Given Taiwan's extensive involvement in China's own trade and investment sectors, the engagement approach promises to be the best long-term chance of sustaining some form of Taiwanese autonomy vis-à-vis the mainland until the forces of political change can work within China to bring about greater political liberalization.

South and Central Asia. Much attention in both the United States and Australia has focused on the Asian subcontinent since the nuclear tests by India and Pakistan in the spring of 1998. Considerable attention also has been given to the upheaval in the disputed region of Jammu and Kashmir, the turbulence in neighboring Afghanistan, and Nepal's ongoing political crisis and protracted insurgency.[27] But the most dramatic events have unfolded in Afghanistan in late 2001 and early 2002 with the U.S.-led intervention in Operation ENDURING FREEDOM (in which Australian forces played a key role). This operation triggered in quick succession the overthrow of the Taliban regime and expulsion of Osama Bin Laden and al-Qai'da.

While trends in Afghanistan appear generally positive, numerous challenges continue to confront the administration of President Hamid Karzai and NATO forces assisting the Kabul government. Recent increases in the size of both Australian and British force commitments testify to the always delicate balance between building stability and contesting anarchy in this beleaguered country.

Afghanistan's continued travails reflect conditions throughout the entire Central/South Asian subregions. The prime threats to the stability of these areas are major interstate war, WMD, terrorism, and persistent ethnic conflict and insurgency.

The most plausible scenario is a war between India and Pakistan over Kashmir. The historical record is sobering: to date, the two countries have fought serial conflicts. There have been three major wars, in 1947, 1965, and 1971, and most recently a smaller war in the remote Kargil region in 1999 and the threat of war in several other crises.[28] Given the level of distrust and animosity between Islamabad and New Delhi as well as the roller coaster experience of bilateral relations in recent years, the situation must be considered volatile. In the past 2 years, there has been a modest but significant rapprochement between Islamabad and New Delhi, including summitry and cricket diplomacy. Yet, the status of Kashmir remains a major point of contention between the two countries, with no potential resolution in sight.[29]

Moreover, if Pakistan appeared on the verge of disintegrating or exploding into civil war, India would be tempted to intervene.[30] Such a chain of events could escalate the conflict dramatically. There also is the potential for a conflict between India and China, although this is far less likely than another Indo-Pakistani war.[31] An outcome along any of these lines would confront ANZUS strategic planners with immense problems: How could the alliance stay strategically neutral in such a conflict involving a primary ally in the war against terror (Pakistan), a major and democratic Commonwealth power (India), and the region's rising hegemon (China)? How would it ensure continued access to regional markets and key littorals under such conditions?

The threat of WMD also must be taken very seriously by the United States and Australia (spearhead powers in the Pacific Security Iniative or PSI), particularly nuclear proliferation or a nuclear conflict between India and Pakistan.[32] The proliferation exploits of Pakistan's A. Q. Khan network are now infamous. Although the full extent of the nuclear materiel and technology sold to various regimes around the world remains unclear (along with exact role of the Pakistani government), these activities highlight the dangers of poor control over a country's nuclear facilities and the absence of proliferation controls. Moreover, in both India and Pakistan, the command and control mechanisms are dubious at best. This increases the potential for mistakes with horrendous strategic implications.[33] But the greatest cause for alarm is the political instability in Pakistan. This point is underscored by fact that Pakistan is the only nuclear power to have experienced a successful military coup (in October 1999).[34] While the current military regime arguably provides more stability for Pakistan than did its civilian predecessor, the domestic political scene is far from settled, particularly in view of the assassination attempt against President Mushariff.[35] Without a doubt, the military is the most important national institution in the country. If the military were to fragment, so too would the country. If nuclear devices or materials were to fall into the hands of extremists, the outcome could be catastrophic.

India's nuclear program has come under international scrutiny recently with the signing of the controversial March 2005 nuclear agreement between

New Delhi and Washington. The agreement covers civilian nuclear energy cooperation. But experts question whether India's civilian and military programs can be disentangled readily and express concern about the implications for nuclear proliferation.[36] The nuclear deal is but one element of the larger rapprochement between New Delhi and Washington. However, if the deal flounders or self-destructs, this blooming partnership could wither swiftly.[37]

Terrorism. The threat of terrorism from extremists in Central and South Asia is all too evident, as witnessed by the recent train bombing in Mumbai.[38] The terrorism problem in this subregion is magnified further by ethnic and clan conflict. Insurgencies continue to afflict many countries, including India and, more severely, Nepal.

The threats of major interstate war, use and proliferation of WMD, terrorism, and ethnic conflict and insurgency produce chronic turmoil in an arc of instability running across South and Central Asia. Australian and U.S. officials have been less focused jointly on these issues than on those emanating from further to the northeast (China, Japan, and the Korean peninsula). As the boundaries separating "global" challenges from "regional" blur more noticeably, however, the Central/South Asian imbroglios inevitably will capture a greater level of attention within ANZUS policy circles. Moreover, these challenges continue to test whether America's alliance with Australia is indeed global in scope as stated in the 2006 U.S. *National Security Strategy.*

Southeast Asia. The Southeast Asia subregion, though it has always been in Australia's "front yard," is very likely to require greater attention from the United States in the future. Despite experiencing dynamic economic growth, unprecedented prosperity, and significant democratization, it remains at risk.[39] While there are significant territorial disputes among Southeast Asian neighbors, the underlying causes of the instability are not interstate tensions but intrastate and transnational threats. Certainly the simmering disputes over islands, reefs, and territorial waters in the South China Sea—including claims by China to virtually the entire area—are worrisome, but these issues are unlikely to erupt into a major conflict. For the foreseeable future, none of the disputants, including even China, has the capability to seize outright direct control of the area through military force.[40] This reality contributes to the region's overall stability and saves ANZUS resources from being stretched even further than they already are.

Moreover, a basic level of trust and understanding has been fostered through entities such as the 10-member Association for Southeast Asian Nations (ASEAN) and the ASEAN Regional Forum (ARF). While ASEAN and the ARF have proved to be disappointments to many observers, they have endured and provide useful mechanisms to ensure a basic level of dialogue and modest regional confidence-building initiatives.[41]

Of greater concern are the threats emanating from within Southeast Asian states, which, like their Central/South Asian counterparts, include ethnic and religious conflicts, terrorism, and insurgency. More distinct, nonmilitary threats include contagious diseases, transnational crimes (including piracy),[42] narcotics, and environmental pollution, all of which have spread throughout the subregion without regard to national borders. These nontraditional security threats pose the greatest danger to the subregion. Moreover, lurking in many Southeast Asian countries is an underlying political instability or fragility.

The severity of these threats varies from country to country. In Thailand, for example, major security threats come from narcotics and the AIDS virus, while a Muslim insurgency simmers in the southern part of the country. The forced resignation of Prime Minister Thaksin Shinawatra in the spring of 2006 following a concerted campaign to force him from office, raises questions about the durability of the democratic system, there.[43] In countries such as the Philippines and Indonesia, political turmoil, ethnic conflict, and terrorism are the major security threats. The Philippines appears to be in a chronic state of instability. President Gloria Arroyo survives in the middle of a perpetual political storm as Manila continues under torment by Islamic ethno-secessionist movements in the south. In Indonesia, meanwhile, problems persist, but conditions appear to be slowly improving under democratically elected President Susilio Bambang Yudhoyono (who assumed office in 2004). Despite natural disasters such as the devastating tsunami of December 2004 and successive natural disasters in Java throughout 2006, the country continues to thrive. While secessionism remains serious, with regions throughout the archipelago seeking independence, the situation appears to be stabilizing in some locations, such as Aceh. In 2006, East Timor was racked by violence, apparently pitting different elements of the security apparatus against each other. Such turmoil prompted some observers to label it a "failing state" and triggered intervention by Australian military forces.[44] Terrorism has been directed against Australians and Americans—tourists, entrepreneurs, and diplomats—notably the October 2002 Bali bombings and the August 2003 bombing at the Jakarta Marriott Hotel. On top of such chronic instability, there is potential for terrorism expanding to neighboring countries and beyond.

Key Challenges.

The U.S. Department of Defense and its Australian counterpart naturally tend to be preoccupied with military matters, and their thinking inevitably hovers at the operational level—working to ensure that their countries' forces are positioned, postured, trained, and equipped to undertake core military missions. Warfighting and other operational challenges, however, involve critical strategic-level issues such as alliance management and engagement with other states to deter, prevent, and manage conflict. These matters require greater attention to alliance grand strategy and security policy.

In the face of budgetary and resource constraints and global U.S. commitments, an American grand strategy for the Asia-Pacific that is focused on pivotal states makes good sense. A pivotal states strategy explicitly recognizes the simple truth that some countries are more important than others and directs the lion's share of limited resources and attention to these states. What are pivotal states? These are key countries that by dint of population size, territorial expanse, geographic location, political cohesion, and economic strength (or weakness) play the most influential role in determining a region's degree of stability. Thus they are the critical actors in determining the security environment of neighboring states.

It is useful to divide pivotal states into two varieties: those that are linchpin states and those that are powder keg states. The former are stable countries that ensure the peace and prosperity of a region or subregion, while the latter are "volatile countries upon which the stability . . . of the region or subregion hinges."[45] Significantly, linchpin states tend to be "established and staunch democracies" that are "favorably disposed toward the United States."[46] For each subregion of the Asia-Pacific, it is relatively easy to find a linchpin state and a powder keg state. For the entire region, the country that constitutes its linchpin state is, predictably, the United States. Similarly, identifying the potential powder keg state for the entire region is simple: it is China (see Figure 1).

(Sub)Region	Linchpin	Powder Keg
Northeast Asia	Japan	North Korea
Southeast Asia/South Pacific	Australia	Indonesia
South Asia	India	Pakistan
Asia-Pacific	United States	China

Figure 1. Strategic/Pivotal States.

LINCHPIN STATES: EFFECTIVE ALLIANCE MANAGEMENT

Linchpin states tend to be staunch allies or at least close friends of the United States. A top U.S. priority should be given to the strategic-level matter of alliance management.[47] Cultivating relations with our allies and friends (i.e., linchpin states) has not received the priority it deserves.[48] Ongoing, dramatic developments on the Korean Peninsula have resulted in closer cooperation and coordination between South Korea, Japan, and the United States through the Trilateral Coordination and Oversight Group. As noted previously, a commensurate Trilateral Strategic Dialogue between Australia, Japan, and the United States also has emerged. Yet, alliance management requires constant attention and adjustment to rapid changes in the strategic environment. There must be greater recognition of the importance of public relations efforts and matters of protocol and culture.

Such symbolism is important, of course, but following up substantively is the truly essential part. Moreover, U.S. relations with its allies and friends in Southeast Asia and Australasia require sustained and concerted attention.[49]

Good chemistry and close ties between leaders at the highest levels of government can be a huge asset. The current top political leaders in Canberra and Washington, Prime Minister John Howard and President George W. Bush, have had an excellent personal relationship. Howard happened to be visiting Washington in the aftermath of the 9/11 attacks and promptly and publicly stressed his country's support for U.S. efforts to counter the terrorist threat. This rhetoric was backed by action. Australia has demonstrated its commitment by activating ANZUS and by dispatching troops to serve in Afghanistan and Iraq. If the successors to Howard and Bush make the effort to build a good person-to-person relationship, this asset will keep the alliance vibrant.

SHAPING POWDER KEG STATES

There are at least four powder keg states in the Asia-Pacific: China, North Korea, Indonesia, and Pakistan. Much of ANZUS's future success will be measured by how well alliance policy planners deal with these potentially volatile regional security actors.

China is the key powder keg state for the entire region—some would say the world—and will require sustained attention. While a stronger China could become a revisionist or aggressive state and disrupt the stability of the region from a position of strength, perhaps a more likely challenge to regional stability could come from a weak regime in Beijing that is coming unraveled. In any event, U.S. action can influence China's future trajectory significantly. Often overlooked are the notable results of the U.S. policy of engagement with China, for example, the entry of China in a strategic dialogue, expansion of China's involvement in multilateral forums, and her increasing transparency. A modest but significant milestone was the release in December 2004 of China's latest White Paper on National Defense, Beijing's most detailed and forthcoming to date.[50]

While the challenge of China in 2006 is probably best portrayed by picturing the country as a powder keg state, China is potentially a linchpin state for the Asia-Pacific region in the longer term. Indeed, Beijing can be a major force for stability rather than instability, a confident and mature power with a more viable political system that is more accountable to the Chinese people. Washington's desire to see Beijing assume this kind of role is exemplified by Deputy Secretary Zoellick's aforementioned invitation for China to become a "responsible stakeholder."

North Korea, now with tested nuclear and missile programs and the world's fourth largest armed forces, is the powder keg state in Northeast Asia and will require the most immediate attention. Indonesia, with the world's fourth largest population inhabiting an area about three times the size of Texas, is the powder keg state in Southeast Asia and one that will require more American and Australian efforts in coming decades. The specter of chronic instability in the Indonesian archipelago threatens to destabilize the entire subregion. The daunting challenges associated with Indonesia's size and economic disparities are further complicated by significant ethnic and religious fault lines. Meanwhile, Pakistan, a nuclear state with the world's sixth largest population living in an area approximately twice the size of California and with the world's seventh largest armed forces, is the powder keg state for South and Central Asia. Addressing such areas will be politically sensitive since all the states mentioned have poor human rights records and large militaries. Three of them (China, North Korea, and Pakistan) pose serious threats to U.S. proliferation policy, and three (Indonesia, North Korea, and Pakistan) have had a history of significant ties to and/ or as breeding grounds for terrorist groups, or a record of state-sponsored terrorism.

MAINTAINING A U.S. FORWARD PRESENCE

The more specific security challenge for the United States in the Asia-Pacific over the next 20 years is likely to be the mere maintenance of our strong alliance structure and a robust forward presence in coordination with allied forces.[51] In particular, America's alliances with Japan, the ROK, and Australia are critical to U.S. national interests in the region. Political trends on the Korean Peninsula and in Japan strongly suggest that the United States might be faced with increasing pressures to reduce or curtail its military presence. However, a greatly reduced presence or complete withdrawal from Northeast Asia would bring into question the extent of the U.S. commitment to the security of the entire region and to maintaining its overall balance of power.

U.S. OBJECTIVES IN THE ASIA-PACIFIC

Baseline U.S. objectives in the Asia-Pacific should be pursued along several lines. First, the United States should sustain and nurture relations with its allies and friends (linchpin states). American priorities should be in working with South Korea and Japan to improve not only cooperation and coordination with the armed forces of these countries but also relations with their governments and people.[52] Again, the recent roadmap agreement with Japan is an apt example as is the January 2006 Strategic Implementation Agreement with South Korea. U.S. alliances with Australia, Thailand, and the Philippines also need attention.

Second, Washington should move forthrightly to influence regional powder keg states like China, North Korea, Pakistan, Indonesia, etc., with particular attention to military-to-military relations. Military cooperation — both bilateral and multilateral — can foster cooperation, develop trust, and provide basic building blocks for regional stability and security architecture. The United States should encourage real reconciliation and rapprochement between North and South Korea, recognizing that North Korea's new semi-nuclear status vastly complicates the problem. The United States also should promote confidence-building measures between India and Pakistan.

Third, and perhaps most importantly, the United States needs to maintain a forward presence in the region. This is imperative if conflict in the Taiwan Strait is to be deterred, and tensions on the Korean Peninsula are to be managed.

After remaining vibrant and functional for over a half century, the Australian-American relationship is still a key facilitator of regional stability in the Asia-Pacific. Remarkably, the alliance has withstood major challenges during the Cold War and the post-9/11 time frame, becoming stronger in the process. Although a country of modest population, Australia has emerged in this century as one of the world's formidable economies and vibrant democracies. It has an impeccable track record as a loyal U.S. ally through successive crises where it could as easily have avoided involvement. As an embodiment of western values and a hallmark for regional development, this alliance is a testimonial to effective security policy management. It will need to draw upon all of its substantial attributes, however, if it is to sustain its successful legacy in the face of the threats and challenges now emerging in the region.

ENDNOTES - CHAPTER 5

1. The author would like to thank conference participants for helpful comments. In particular I would like to thank Robert Ayson and Michael Wesley their valuable feedback. The author would also like to express his sincere thanks to Bill Tow for incisive input and expert editing.

2. For a recent authoritative articulation of this idea, see *The National Security Strategy of the United States of America*, Washington, DC: The White House, March 2006. For discussion of goals in South Asia, Central Asia, Southeast Asia, and Northeast Asia, see pp. 39-42.

3. The Marines would also have a key role to play. On the general point, see Brigadier General Huba Wass De Czege (USA Ret.) and Lieutenant Colonel Antulio J. Echevarria, "Precision Decisions," *Armed Forces Journal International*, October 2000, p. 58.

4. This point is made in the *Quadrennial Defense Review Report*, Washington, DC: Department of Defense, February 6, 2006, p. 92.

5. While this certainly has not been explicitly stated anywhere, it can be inferred from the statements of senior U.S. officials and texts of key policy documents. For example, on May 16, 2006, President Bush told visiting Prime Minister Howard: ". . . you and I stood together here at the White House the day before September the 11th, 2001. And our nations have stood together on every day afterwards. The American people know that Australia is a strong ally. We admire your courage, and we appreciate your sacrifice." "Remarks by President Bush and Australian Prime Minister John Howard in Arrival Ceremony," available at *www.state.gov/p/eap/*

rls/ot/66295.htm, accessed August 20, 2006. Further, according to the 2006 U.S. *National Security Strategy*, "With Australia, our alliance is global in scope. From Iraq and Afghanistan to our historic FTA, we are working jointly to ensure security, prosperity, and expanding freedom" (p. 40).

6. Andrew Scobell, *Kim Jong Il and North Korea: The Leader and the System,* Carlisle Barracks, PA: U.S. Army War College, Strategic Studies Institute, March 2006.

7. For more on the alliance, see, for example, Donald W. Boose, Jr., Balbina Y. Hwang, Patrick Morgan, and Andrew Scobell, eds., *Recalibrating the U.S.-Republic of Korea Alliance*, Carlisle Barracks, PA: U.S. Army War College, Strategic Studies Institute, 2003.

8. Indeed, this concern about the intentions of other powers is clearly evident in the exchange between the two Korean leaders. Kim Dae Jung reportedly told Kim Jong Il: "The peninsula is surrounded by big countries, and if the American military presence were to withdraw, that would create a huge vacuum that would draw these big countries into a fight over hegemony." The North Korean leader is said to have responded: "Yes, we are surrounded by big powers–Russia, China, and Japan, and so therefore it is desirable that the American troops continue to stay." See Doug Struck, "South Korean Says North Wants U.S. Troops to Stay," *Washington Post*, August 30, 2000.

9. "Review of United States Policy Toward North Korea: Findings and Recommendations," Unclassified Report by Dr. William J. Perry, October 12, 1999, available at *www.fas.org/new/dprk/1999/991012_northkorea_rpt.htm*, accessed December 6, 1999.

10. Scobell, *Kim Jong Il and North Korea.*

11. On North Korea's thinking, see Andrew Scobell, *North Korea's Strategic Intentions*, Carlisle Barracks, PA: U.S. Army War College, Strategic Studies Institute, March 2005; and Scobell, *Kim Jong Il and North Korea.*

12. The distinction between reconciliation and unification is an important one, having been recognized by General Henry Shelton, former Chairman of the Joint Chiefs of Staff. See Richard Halloran, "Ground Forces in Japan, S. Korea Under Review," *Washington Times*, September 29, 2000.

13. Dennis Shanahan and Mark Dodd, "Howard in Secret North Korean Mission," *The Australian*, July 8, 2006.

14. Ralph N. Clough, *Reaching Across the Taiwan Strait: People to People Diplomacy*, Boulder, CO: Westview Press, 1993.

15. See, for example, Andrew Scobell, *China's Use of Military Force: Beyond the Great Wall and the Long March,* New York: Cambridge University Press, 2003, chap. 8.

16. See Jean-Pierre Cabestan, "'State to State' Tension Rises Again Across the Taiwan Strait," *China Perspectives*, No. 25, October 1999, pp. 4-13; and "The One China Principle and the Taiwan Issue," Xinhua News Agency, February 21, 2000.

17. Andrew Scobell, *Chinese Army Building in the Era of Jiang Zemin*, Carlisle Barracks, PA: U.S. Army War College, Strategic Studies Institute, September 2000, p. 21; and author's interviews with civilian and military researchers in Beijing and other Chinese cities, February-March 2000, September 2000, May 2002, September 2003, June 2004, May 2005, and March 2006 [hereafter "Authors interviews in China"].

18. See, for example, Edward Cody, "China Easing Its Stance on Taiwan: Tolerance Grows for Status Quo," *Washington Post*, June 15, 2006.

19. *China's National Defense in 2004*, Beijing: State Council Information Office, December 2004.

20. Scobell, *China's Use of Military Force,* pp. 185, 189-190.

21. *Ibid.*, chap. 8; Andrew Scobell, "Is There a Chinese Way of War?" *Parameters*, Vol. XXXV, No. 1, Spring 2005, pp. 118-122.

22. Author's interviews in China; Scobell, *Chinese Army Building in the Era of Jiang Zemin*, p. 26.

23. Author's interviews in China. See also Mark Burles and Abram N. Shulsky, *Patterns in China's Use of Force: Evidence From History and Doctrinal Writings*, Santa Monica, CA: RAND, 2000.

24. Author's interviews in China; Andrew Scobell, "China's Military Threat to Taiwan: Coercion or Capture?" *Taiwan Defense Affairs*, Vol. 4, No. 2, Winter 2003/04, pp. 18-35.

25. This is the most commonly discussed scenario. For a study assessing the likelihood of success for an amphibious invasion of Taiwan, see David A. Shlapak, David T. Orletsky, and Barry A. Wilson, *Dire Strait?: Military Aspects of the China-Taiwan Confrontation and Options for U.S. Policy*, Santa Monica, CA: Rand, 2000. All three scenarios are discussed in the Department of

Defense's "Report to Congress Pursuant to Public Law 106-113" made public on December 18, 2000. See Scobell, "China's Military Threat to Taiwan"; and Steve Tsang, ed., *If China Attacks Taiwan: Military Strategy, Politics, and Economics*, New York and Abingdon, UK: Routledge, 2006.

26. *Asia Times Online*, March 6, 2003.

27. Recent events give cause for cautious optimism, but the challenges to achieving a peaceful, negotiated solution are significant. See, for example, Somini Sengupta, "Nepal Rebel Vows Not to Disarm Before Charter Vote," *New York Times* (Washington Edition), May 21, 2006.

28. Sumit Ganguly, "Wars Without End: The Indo-Pakistani Conflict," *The Annals of the Academy of Political and Social Sciences*, No. 542, September 1995, pp. 167-178; Eric S. Margolis, *War at the Top of the World: The Struggle for Afghanistan, Kashmir, and Tibet*, New York, Routledge, 2000, pp. viii-ix, 139-140.

29. Somini Sengupta, "As India Premier Calls for Treaty, Pakistan Says Kashmir is the Key," *New York Times* (Washington Edition), March 25, 2006.

30. Margolis, *War at the Top of the World*, p. 172.

31. For an analysis making the case that a China-India war is all but inevitable, see Margolis, *War at the Top of the World*.

32. Judith Miller and James Risen, "A Nuclear War Feared Possible over Kashmir," *New York Times* (Washington Edition), August 8, 2000.

33. On the general problem, see Paul Bracken, *Fire in the East: The Rise of Asian Military Power and the Second Nuclear Age*, New York: HarperCollins, 1999, pp. 117-120. On India and Pakistan, see Dibb, "The Strategic Environment in the Asia-Pacific," p. 10. On India, see George Perkovich, *India's Nuclear Bomb*, Berkeley and Los Angeles: University of California Press, 1999, chap. 15.

34. Of course, since the 1960s, there have been unsuccessful military coup attempts or at least rumors of these in nuclear states, notably France, China, Russia, and North Korea.

35. Ahmed Rashid, "Pakistan's Coup: Planting the Seeds of Democracy?" *Current History*, Vol. 198, No. 632, December 1999, pp. 409-414.

36. See, for example, "India and America: Joining the nuclear family," *Economist*, March 4, 2006, pp. 37-38.

37. For more on the extent of the relationship, see Sumit Ganguly and Andrew Scobell, "India and the United States: A Security Partnership?" *World Policy Journal*, Vol. XXII, No. 2, Summer 2005, pp. 37-44.

38. John Lancaster, "U.S. Study Finds Terrorist Shift to South Asia," *Washington Post*, May 2, 2000.

39. See, for example, "South-East Asia: All Serene," *Economist*, February 25, 2006, pp. 47-48; Alan Dupont, "Southeast Asian Stability At Risk," *International Herald Tribune*, September 28, 2000.

40. Andrew Scobell, "China's Strategy Toward the South China Sea," in Martin Edmonds and Michael R. Tsai, eds., *Taiwan's Maritime Security*, New York and London, RoutledgeCurzon, 2003, pp. 40-51.

41. See, inter alia, James Cotton, "The 'Haze' Over Southeast Asia: Challenging the ASEAN Mode of Regional Engagement," *Pacific Affairs*, Vol. 72, No. 3, Fall 1999, pp. 331-352; John Garofano, "Flexibility or Irrelevance?: Ways Forward For the ARF," *Contemporary Southeast Asia*, Vol. 21, No. 1, April 1999, pp. 74-94; Carlyle A. Thayer, *Multilateral Institutions in Asia: The ASEAN Regional Forum*, Honolulu, HI: Asia-Pacific Center for Security Studies, October 2000.

42. According to the International Maritime Organization, the South China Sea was the most active zone in the world for piracy (and the Straits of Malacca ranked fifth on the list). See the figures cited in "Piracy Insurance: For those in peril," *Economist*, April 22, 2006, p. 73.

43. "Thailand: Goodbye . . . or au Revoir?" *Economist*, April 8, 2006, pp. 41-42.

44. Jane Perlez, "Australian Forces Intervene to Halt Fighting in East Timor," *New York Times* (Washington Edition), May 26, 2006; Jane Perlez, "Poverty and Violence Sink Grand Plans for East Timor," *New York Times* (Washington Edition), May 31, 2006; Yang Razali Kassim, "Timor as a Failed State," *PacNet*, Vol. 29, June 22, 2006, received via electronic mail from Pacific Forum on June 22, 2006.

45. For more on the concept of pivotal states, see Robert Chase, Emily Hill, and Paul Kennedy, eds., *The Pivotal States: A New Framework for U.S. Policy in the Developing World*, New York: W.W. Norton, 1999. The definition of a powder keg state comes from

Andrew Scobell and Larry Wortzel, *The Asia-Pacific in the U.S. National Security Calculus for a New Millennium,* Carlisle Barracks, PA: U.S. Army War College, Strategic Studies Institute, 2000, p. 24.

46. Andrew Scobell, "An Orderly Pacific Asia or Asia-Pacific Powder Keg?" *Issues and Studies,* Vol. 41, No. 1, March 2005, p. 246.

47. This is a key theme in the 2006 U.S. *National Security Strategy.*

48. Philip Zelikow, "American Engagement is Asia," in Robert D. Blackwill and Paul Dibb, eds., *America's Asian Alliances,* Cambridge, MA: MIT Press, 2000, p. 25.

49. Zelikow, "American Engagement in Asia," pp. 29-30; on the U.S-Australia alliance, see John Baker and Douglas H. Paal, "The US-Australia Alliance," in Blackwill and Dibb, *America's Asian Alliances,* pp. 87-109.

50. *China's National Defense in 2004.*

51. See, for example, the discussion in Andrew Scobell, *The U.S. Army and the Asia-Pacific,* Carlisle Barracks, PA: U.S. Army War College, Strategic Studies Institute, April 2001.

52. *The United States and Japan: Advancing Toward a Mature Partnership,* Special Report, Washington, DC: Institute for National Strategic Studies, National Defense University, October 11, 2000; Kurt M. Campbell, "Energizing the U.S.-Japan Security Relationship," *Washington Quarterly,* Vol. 23, No. 4, Autumn 2000, pp. 125-134; William E. Rapp, *Paths Diverging?: The Next Decade in the U.S.-Japan Security Alliance,* Carlisle Barracks, PA: U.S. Army War College, Strategic Studies Institute, January 2004.

CHAPTER 6

THE ALLIANCE AND THE ASIA-PACIFIC REGION: AN AUSTRALIAN PERSPECTIVE

Robert Ayson

In 1968, political scientist P. J. Boyce from the University of Tasmania made two summary observations about the Australian-U.S. alliance in the context of Asia-Pacific security:

> Firstly, the Australian commitment in Vietnam has not alienated Asian governments or Asian pressmen to anywhere near the extent that was feared (and is still sometimes easily assumed) by the Asia-oriented left-wing critics of Australian policy. Secondly, there seems to be growing conviction among many sensitive Australians of all political parties, that their government should occasionally strike a different public posture from the United States in foreign policy matters—if only to give the appearance of independent thinking in Canberra and willingness to seize the initiative.[1]

The broader arguments underlying this quotation might just as easily have been made today by an Australian commentator on the regional implications of Australia's close alliance relationship with the United States. On the one hand, Australia's active participation in U.S.-led coalitions of the willing beginning with the war on terror, including its original commitment in 2003 to the war in Iraq, have not been met with stampedes of protest in Asia's capitals. On the other hand, analysts in Canberra have still tended to seek a degree of policy differentiation in the Asia-Pacific between Australia and the United States. That said, they continue to regard the alliance relationship as a fundamental contributor to Australia's strategic interests in the region. The intimate links it allows between Australian leaders, officials, and defense personnel and their U.S. counterparts give it some unique characteristics in comparison to many other Australian relationships. But the alliance still needs to be understood as part of a wider array of relationships, including those with rising Asian countries, through which Australia pursues its national interests.

This chapter deals with a number of Australian perspectives on the role of the alliance in Canberra's Asia-Pacific regional engagement. It begins by examining the importance of Asian strategic issues in the formation and evolution of ANZUS. Close cooperation between the two allies outside the region since the September 11, 2001 (9/11), terrorist attacks is then considered alongside contemporary challenges in a changing Asian regional balance. Particular attention is devoted here to the respective positions of Washington and Canberra on relations with a re-emerging China. Consideration also is given to the alliance implications of weak state issues in the Asia-Pacific, many of which lie in close proximity to Australia.

The Asia-Pacific Dimension of an Evolving Alliance.

The Asian regional security dimension looms large in the history of U.S.-Australia alliance relations. Disagreement may continue over when that relationship really began, but the Asian balance comes to the forefront for both sides of the debate. For those who date the alliance from the 1951 ANZUS Treaty, signed during the Menzies era, attention is drawn to Australian and New Zealand participation in the Korean War, to their concern about the possibility of a remilitarized Japan, and to American worries about increasing Soviet and Chinese communist influence in Asia. For those who date the alliance's beginning earlier, from the Australia-U.S. cooperation in World War II, with Australia under a Labor Prime Minister, that wartime relationship centered on combined efforts to halt Japan's advance in the Asia-Pacific, to win the Pacific theater of the global contest, and to ensure a favorable postwar regional balance.[2] As with many debates, the answer probably lies in a mixture of these two positions, but any combination of them whatsoever ends up highlighting American and Australian interests in Asian security. It also reveals, however, that while these interests overlapped significantly, they were not identical.

Asian security issues also got top billing in the subsequent evolution of U.S.-Australian alliance relations as the competition of the Cold War spread to Asia. With a strategy of forward defense, Australia (and New Zealand, the third signatory of ANZUS) positioned their forces forward in Southeast Asia in a series of overlapping commitments under American and/or British leadership.[3] These commitments included standing arrangements such as the Commonwealth Strategic Reserve and the Southeast Asia Treaty Organization (SEATO). They also included actual deployments of forces such as the assistance provided in the 1960s to Malaysia in the face of the konfrontasi campaign launched by Indonesia's President Sukarno, and to South Vietnam as part of the U.S.-led effort to prevent a North Vietnamese takeover.

The United States also played a strongly influential role in Australia's shift away from forward defense.

Alongside a declining Britain's decision to remove its forces from East of Suez, the Nixon administration's Guam Doctrine spelled the end of such a forward defense philosophy guiding Australia's regional security commitments. By the early 1970s, Australia was moving to a strategy of defense self-reliance which focused rather more on meeting possible challenges in its own regional neighborhood, and which was advanced in a series of important policy documents, including the 1972 *Defence Review*, the 1976 *Defence White Paper*, and Paul Dibb's influential report of 1986,[4] often regarded as the leading distillation of Australia's defense logic.

Rather than emphasizing the contributions that Australia might make to U.S.-led engagements in Asia—which seemed far less likely in a post-Vietnam era—increasing emphasis was placed on Australia's need to develop the capacity for independent operations in its nearer neighborhood should these be required. In this endeavor, there was a rather earlier period in Australian-U.S. alliance relations regarding Asian security to draw on. As early as 1959, the Defence Committee of Cabinet was considering advice (including that from Arthur Tange, who was to become Secretary of Defence in 1970) that if Australia found itself in an armed conflict with Indonesia (including over what is now called West Papua), it could not assume that its allies would be there to help. This advice called for a correspondingly greater emphasis on the development of Australia's ability to conduct operations independently.[5]

The change in Australia's regional strategy in the early 1970s did not usurp the alliance with the United States, however. ANZUS remained a cornerstone in Australia's approach, but from perhaps a somewhat different angle. The alliance with the United States offered the sort of networks, training, intelligence, and equipment access around which a greater capacity for defense self-reliance could be erected. Common approaches to regional affairs continued, including the blind eye turned by the three ANZUS partners towards Indonesia's invasion of East Timor in 1975, reflecting a joint appreciation of the stabilizing power which a resolutely anticommunist Suharto regime in Jakarta seemed to offer. There were advantages for Washington as well — as a southern anchor of the San Francisco alliance system, Australia could be relied upon as a security sub-contractor in its own security neighborhood. This role came to the fore after the Soviet invasion of Afghanistan in 1979 and the extension of such Soviet influence as its Southeast Asian presence in Vietnam's Cam Ranh Bay. As a close partner with a significant role in Pacific security, Australia thereby contributed to strategic denial in its own neck of the woods.

There were still difference in the views from Washington and Canberra. While Australia continued to host the joint facilities — vital components in the U.S. network — Labor governments of the 1980s were unconvinced regarding the value of U.S. MX missile testing in the Pacific and helped establish the South Pacific Nuclear Free Zone, which the United States steadfastly declined to sign. Unlike New Zealand, however, Australia did not let such antinuclear sentiment get in the way of its overall relationship with the United States. Washington's suspension of New Zealand from active ANZUS security relations actually increased the importance of the Australia-U.S. leg of the alliance, with the annual AUSMIN talks (between the U.S. Secretary of State and the Australian Minister for Foreign Affairs) taking the place of formerly trilateral meetings.

A close strategic relationship with Washington remained a high priority for Canberra as it watched the changing Asian regional balance in the post-Cold War period. Alongside Japan, Australia encouraged the emergence of Asia-Pacific Economic Cooperation (APEC) as a means of reminding Washington of the value of its Asian relationships and embedding the United States in any future regional order. It must be admitted that Canberra was rather more enthusiastic than Washington about other emerging multilateral forums in the region, including the Association of Southeast Asian Nation's (ASEAN) Regional Forum (ARF) which came into being in 1994 to provide an annual venue for security dialogue. Australian policymakers nonetheless continued to view these arrangements as complements to, rather than replacements for, traditional alliance relationships.

The first foreign policy challenge faced by John Howard's government after its defeat of Labor in the 1996 general election confirmed the centrality of the U.S. alliance in the new leadership's view of Asian security affairs. Canberra sided with Washington in the Taiwan Strait crisis, a position which may have reinforced suspicions in Beijing that China was being squeezed between the twin alliance relations the United States was enjoying with Japan and Australia.

Concerned as he was about being left behind in an era of dramatic East Asian economic expansion,[6] Prime Minister Howard attached continuing importance to Australia's links with the world's superpower as a central pillar in his strategy. But developments in Indonesia which followed in the wake of the 1997 financial crisis taught Mr. Howard another lesson. The Prime Minister placed a high value on the diplomatic and logistical support offered by the Clinton administration during the crisis over East Timor in 1999 — and the positioning offshore of the USS *Belleau Woods* was similarly appreciated for its deterrence value.[7] It was left largely to the Australian government, however, to coordinate and man the main deployment of forces on the ground. This confirmed the necessity for Australia to pay attention to its own independent capacity to manage and lead local operations in a part of the world some leading analysts were regarding as an "arc of instability."[8]

Such a capacity was also put to the test in Australia's next major deployment in its own neighborhood — the 2003 Regional Assistance Mission to Solomon Islands (RAMSI) which also featured contributions by New Zealand and a number of other Pacific Island Forum countries. Here, the alliance connection was philosophical rather than material. In justifying this commitment, Prime Minister Howard portrayed the Solomon Islands as a failed state in the making. The absence of effective governance in the Solomon Islands, it was argued, might allow a base from which transnational threats including drug running and terrorism could materialize with potential adverse implications for Australia's own security.[9] Here there was a discernible link to the Bush administration's argument that "America is now threatened less by conquering states than we are by failing ones."[10] There was also a philosophical link to Australia's combat participation further afield in U.S.-led missions which had followed the September 2001 terrorist attacks.

The Alliance Today: Towards West Asia?

At the start of the Australian Prime Minister's seventh visit to Washington during the George W. Bush incumbency, the President noted that "the American people know that Australia is a strong ally. . . . Our two nations are closer than ever, and Americans admire Australia's strong leader. Prime Minister John Howard has affirmed our common values. He's strengthened our alliance."[11] In official documentation, the chorus of approval is, if anything, even stronger. The 2006 *Quadrennial Defense Review* (QDR) has placed Australia on a pedestal shared only by one other country—the United Kingdom. According to the QDR, the unique relations the United States enjoyed with these two fellow members of the Anglosphere, were "models for the breadth and depth of cooperation that the United States seeks to foster with other allies and partners around the world."[12]

But it is not so much cooperation with Washington in Asian security affairs that has earned Canberra its current position in the American sun. Instead, the Bush administration seems especially to have valued its antipodean alliance partner's extraregional commitment of forces in the post-9/11 period. The first such commitment was the deployment of Australian Defense Force (ADF) units to Afghanistan and its environs, which included a special forces detachment, maritime patrol and F/A-18 aircraft, and a naval task force.[13] This substantive contribution followed the first-ever invoking of ANZUS itself: had pundits in the early 1950s been asked to predict the first-ever such use of the Treaty, this scenario is most unlikely to have figured high in their probability rankings.

The second such commitment was Australia's agreement to participate in the war against Iraq. Canberra's presence in the very select coalition of the willing which invaded Saddam Hussein's country in 2003, and its continued active support of the American role there, have warmed the cockles of important hearts within the Beltway. It is clear that when the Howard government indicates that it is committed to Iraq "for the duration," the actual timetable has a strong connection with the anticipated length of stay for U.S. forces. By the middle of 2006, earlier hopes that the U.S. commitment could be scaled back had been replaced by a sober resolve to reinforce the Pentagon's support for the increasingly at-risk Iraqi capital. For its part, Australia had transferred (not withdrawn) its forces based in al Muthanna province (where they had been providing protection for Japan's detachment of engineers) to Dhi Qar province, and retained in theater other ADF units including transport and maritime aircraft detachments, a frigate, an army training team, and a joint task force headquarters.[14] Canberra also increased its force commitment to Afghanistan in response to the deteriorating provincial security situation facing the Karzai government.[15]

Sino-Australian and Sino-U.S. Strategic Relations.

When one turns to Australia's view of Asia, it is the reemergence of China rather than the alliance relationship with United States that occupies center stage—although, of course, the two concerns can intersect in very interesting ways. This is an Asia preoccupied most of all with the maintenance of economic expansion driven by the impressive locomotive of China's demand for goods, capital, and natural resources. For Australian voters, the Middle Kingdom's vast appetite is a key factor in the reduction of taxes which the Howard government has been able to deliver.[16] This mutually beneficial relationship can only be expected to continue and will extend into new areas such as uranium exports.

Mr. Howard's campaign of economic engagement with China has deep roots. As far back as 1997, senior members of the first coalition ministry under Howard's leadership, including the Prime Minister himself, were speaking of an economic strategic partnership with China.[17] In 2004, the Prime Minister cited progress towards an Australia-China Free Trade Agreement in declaring that his "Government has clearly signalled its interest in forging a strategic economic partnership with China based on far-reaching economic complementarities."[18] The annual report of the Department of Foreign Affairs and Trade at that time refers to "Australia's strategic partnership with China in energy and resources."[19]

If we consider this strategic relationship solely in economic terms, there seems no obvious connection to, or conflict with, Australia's security relations with the United States. But the situation changes if one takes a wider view: a strategic partnership with China may imply that Australia will bear in mind that country's interests when making significant decisions on issues in which Beijing has a major stake. In this context, it is fascinating to consider Foreign Minister Alexander Downer's reinterpretation of Australia's obligations under ANZUS in the event of a Taiwan conflict, which he made during a news media interview in Beijing in August 2004. Mr. Downer said, "The ANZUS Treaty is invoked in the event of one of our two countries, Australia or the United States, being attacked. So some other military activity elsewhere in the world, be it in Iraq or anywhere else for that matter, does not automatically invoke the ANZUS Treaty."[20] What is doubly fascinating about this attempt to gain Australia some wriggle room in entertaining the prospect of a China-U.S. crisis, is the fact that Mr. Downer began the media conference by stating that he and Premier Wen Jiabao had "agreed that Australia and China would build up a bilateral strategic relationship that would strengthen our economic relationship, and we would work closely together on Asia-Pacific issues, be they economic or security issues." Lending point to his words is the fact that he was responding specifically to a question as to how the "strategic partnership" with China related to Australia's ANZUS obligations.[21]

This tale reminds us that Asia, in addition to its role as a venue of economic dynamism, remains an arena of significant interstate competition. Traditionally, there has been a tendency to emphasize what have become rather standard flashpoints—the Korean peninsula, Kashmir, the South China Sea, and especially the Taiwan Strait. To the potential relief of the United States and Australia, there seem to be reasonable prospects that China and Taiwan will find ways to manage their family squabble, or at least to avoid a major armed conflict. But this should not encourage us to relax. Not far away in the great power game reserve known as North Asia, the relationship between traditional rivals Japan and China has been deteriorating significantly. This is the region's real hotspot, and its consequences are potentially very grave. The simultaneous intensification of U.S.-Japan strategic cooperation only enhances the prospects that if there is to be a war between China and the United States, it may well start in a crisis or exchange of blows involving China and Japan. And the possibility of such a China-Japan dustup certainly cannot be ruled out.[22]

For Australian strategic analysts, such an eventuality—a U.S.-China clash started over other issues—is the stuff of nightmares. Should the United States get into such a difficult situation, it is likely that

Australian assistance would be expected. And Canberra would face an awful choice. Saying yes (on balance still the more likely response) would cause serious harm to its burgeoning relationship with China. Saying no (for now perhaps the less likely response) would please Beijing but could cause irreparable harm to Australia's security relationship with the United States.[23] In 2001, responding to questions about his previous comments on a Taiwan scenario, then Deputy Secretary of State Richard Armitage (known as one of Australia's closest friends in the Bush administration) said that "if the Australian Government made a decision — in the terrible event the United States was involved in a conflict — that it was not in their interest to participate at some level, then we would have to take a look at where we are after the dust had settled."[24] In 2005, having left office, Mr. Armitage added this thought: "I do believe that if America was ever involved in a military contingency in the Pacific, that we would hope and pray that Australians were alongside us."[25]

Of course such a choice between the United States and China may never have to be made. That would be the good news of the future. But the good news of today, at least, is that Canberra's extraregional commitments in the Middle East and Central Asia are allowing Australia to pay tribute to Washington in a part of the world some distance from the main points of contention between the United States and China. And as this security relationship with the world's preeminent power flourishes outside of Australia's traditional Asia-Pacific bailiwick, the smaller ally also is able to enjoy the fruits of its expanding, mainly economic relationship with the Middle Kingdom. Hence the war on terror has not only been good for U.S.-China relations: the Long War also has been good for two of Australia's most important bilateral relationships.

Australia's Interests in U.S. Regional Engagement.

The point of this discussion has not been to suggest that Australia's alliance relationship with the United States has been deprived of its Asian dimension completely. Several elements are important to note in that regard. First, it remains strongly in Australia's interests for the United States to continue to play a significant balancing role in East Asia in the process of promoting peace and stability. Securing the ongoing presence of substantial U.S. forces in North Asia in particular remains one of the core objectives behind Australia's commitment to its own part of the hub-and-spokes system. The 2005 Defence Update states that "U.S. engagement in the Asia-Pacific region has been the foundation of the region's strategic stability and security since World War II, and is no less relevant 60 years on."[26] Australia's close relations with the U.S. Pacific Command, and that Command's interest in Australia's neck of the regional woods, also remain highly valued in Canberra, including the regular Pacific rim exercises which involve the ADF alongside forces from the U.S. and a number of other regional countries.[27]

Second, the Long War has a significant Asian regional dimension in which Australian and U.S. interests converge. Both have had significant concerns about jihadist terrorism in Southeast Asia and are keen to cooperate with major regional countries in helping them to address this challenge. Paramount here is cooperation with Indonesia—although Canberra may find that its own direct bilateral relationship with Jakarta is the best way forward here. The initial and more catastrophic Bali bombing (October 2002) provided Australia with a very direct stake in the future management of the terrorist challenge in Indonesia. In the successful police-led cooperation with Indonesia that followed, it also provided Canberra with the opportunity to further enhance bilateral relations which had been so strained in 1999, and which will continue to be challenging to manage. Notwithstanding the terrorism issue, however, one possible role here for Australia is to encourage Washington to view Indonesia's internal circumstances in all of their complexity. It also should be noted here that Australia has increased its counterterrorism cooperation with the Philippines,[28] whose struggles with a southern insurgency also have been a major concern for the United States.

Third, Canberra welcomes Washington's endorsement of Australia's leading role in addressing state fragility in its nearer neighborhood. For the United States and its partners (including Australia), reminders of the difficulties associated with nation-building have come not only from Afghanistan and Iraq. They also have been evident in the disappointing return of violence in 2006 to the streets of both Dili in East Timor and Honiara in the Solomon Islands, which precipitated the reentry of Australian forces in both instances. These instances raise the question of both countries' reliance on the military option in their responses to complex internal political challenges. For some, it also recalls criticisms after the initial 1999 intervention in East Timor that Australia tends to act as Washington's regional deputy. But this perception probably has less relevance in the Pacific than in parts of Southeast Asia, and even there one would have to consider P.J. Boyce's valid disclaimer of Asian alienation over Australian participation in the Vietnam war, which begins this chapter.[29] But the validity of his second point — the need for policy differentiation between Australia and the United States — also needs to be considered.[30]

Fourth, Australia has played an important role in U.S.-led efforts to neutralize potential weapons of mass destruction (WMD) challenges in East Asia. Canberra has been a prominent supporter and participant in the Proliferation Security Initiative (PSI) — ostensibly designed to intercept shipments of WMD-related materials wherever they occur but in reality designed principally with North Korea in mind. On this latter score, Canberra also has been an active supporter of the Six Party Talks process in which the United States is a direct participant, and Cranberra has been a vocal critic of North Korea's provocative missile tests of July 2006. The Howard government also has signed a Memorandum of Understanding with the United States on missile defense cooperation,[31] an issue prefaced by the 2005 *Defense Update* containing the significant clause, "Australia will continue to look for ways to support the United States in the Asia-Pacific region."[32]

Fifth, Canberra continues to be a strong supporter of Washington's engagement in East Asian multilateral and regional forums including APEC, ARF, and more recent initiatives such as the Shangri-La dialogue hosted in Singapore by the International Institute for Strategic Studies. There is a challenge here to the extent that the United States is not involved in this latest talkfest — the East Asian Summit, whose inaugural meeting was held in Malaysia in December 2005. It is quite possible that the inclusion of three non-East Asian countries, Australia, New Zealand, and India, has persuaded China that this is not a bus it wants to board. This may in turn allow Washington and Canberra to relax about the implications of Washington's absence. But it was still a bus Canberra felt it had to ride, and the United

States and Australia need to consider whether this is a sign of things to come in terms of opportunities for Washington's future regional participation.

Sixth, Australia has welcomed the U.S. discovery (or rediscovery) of India as an emerging great power with the potential to be one of Washington's most valuable bilateral partners. While its own relations with New Delhi have never really raced along, especially after India's 1998 nuclear tests, Canberra also is keen to see India play a significant role in wider Asian security affairs. Moreover, taking the lead somewhat from the Bush administration's plans to cooperate on civilian nuclear technology with India, Mr. Howard has left the door ajar on the prospect that Australia might one day sell uranium to Asia's second most significant rising power.[33] Even so, Canberra might usefully suggest to Washington that any ideas of India fitting in neatly as a regional balancer to China will work only so far as a very independent-minded New Delhi will want to perform this role.

Seventh, Australia has worked with Japan and the United States in the development of a growing trilateral strategic relationship. In early 2006, the trilateral strategic dialogue between the three countries was elevated to Foreign Minister level as Secretary of State Condolezza Rice and Foreign Minister Aso joined Alexander Downer for talks in Sydney. For Australia, the results of this meeting were satisfactory. For reasons already discussed in this chapter, Canberra would not have wanted a trilateral version of the early 2005 2+2 meeting between the United States and Japan in Tokyo where Taiwan was mentioned in dispatches for the first time, much to China's dismay.[34] Instead, the 2006 Sydney trilateral meeting produced a reassuringly benign statement which "welcomed China's constructive engagement in the region."[35]

Managing Regional Perceptions of the Alliance.

Such an approach ties in well with former Deputy Secretary of State Robert Zoellick's September 2005 speech in which he suggested that the United States could help "encourage China to become a responsible stakeholder in the international system,"[36] a sentiment which goes down well in Canberra. And it was certainly consistent with Mr. Downer's repeated and very public insistence that it would be a mistake to seek to contain China.[37] These comments were also picked up by the Chinese news media,[38] which also noted Secretary Rice's rejection of containment as a strategy for dealing with a modern China.[39] But some of the other reporting reflects mixed messages, which are all too easily generated on this issue. Observing differences in the Rice and Downer approaches, *The International Herald Tribune* ran the headline "Rice Assails China on Australia Trip."[40] And a few days before the meeting, a report from the *Sydney Morning Herald*'s Washington correspondent ran under the banner, "Rice and Downer in Talks on How to Contain China."[41]

This colorful variation in reporting illustrates the potentially complicating impact of diverse news media responses to any development in alliance relations. But it also illustrates Canberra's challenge in generating the right impression of the message it is busy sending to the United States, China, and other East Asian countries on its views and interests in the changing regional balance. Of course, what a country says can sometimes be rather less important to attend than what it does. But even this does not remove the possible dilemma for Canberra. Despite its repeated commitments to American-led operations outside of East Asia, can Canberra signal effectively that its answer to calls for help may be more qualified in the case of a North Asian crisis—especially where the strategic interests of the rising Asian powers are involved?[42] And can Canberra do this without harming its own interests in a long-term alliance relationship with the United States? How much wriggle room in turn is Washington prepared to give its antipodean alliance partner?

Conclusion.

It is tempting to take a triumphal approach to U.S.-Australian strategic relations at the start of the 21st century. The view from Canberra seems very heartening—Australia has enjoyed an enviable profile within the Washington Beltway during the war on terror. This may encourage the refrain, "all power to the Long War and the Bush-Howard partnership."

It also is tempting to downplay the importance of the Asia-Pacific dimension of the U.S.-Australian alliance. But the demands of the Asia-Pacific security environment not only explain the origins of this alliance, those demands also will be the alliance's future testing ground and the venue where its value may be best realized.

Looking north into the Asia-Pacific region from Australia, one is struck by two leading security themes. The first (and, for Australia, the closest) is the range of countries challenged by problems of weakness—which face significant problems in maintaining internal security and stability. The second is the group of Asian countries (mainly in North Asia) which are growing stronger and/or more assertive and whose rising power is potentially a challenge for each other.[43]

In the longer term, the United States is likely to be most welcoming of support from its Australian ally as it deals with the second category—the great power relations which will shape the future East Asia. But for a range of reasons discussed above, Australia's cooperation in times of relative peace may not always translate into an automatic commitment in times of crisis or war. For its part, there also will be times when Australia will be preoccupied with the problems arising from the first category in its own immediate neighborhood. Experience suggests that it will be wise to plan for the need to deal with these more or less independently, but in ways which will still generate Washington's seal of approval.

This comparison suggests that there are limits to the commitment that either country can expect realistically from the other in particular Asia-Pacific scenarios in coming years. The challenge may be to accommodate these limitations in a healthy alliance relationship based on continuing cooperation, which still serves their respective interests. This may seem odd in an era of "you're either for or against us" dichotomies. But the bargain of limited commitments may help make for an especially resilient alliance. This might just be a model for other alliance relationships in a reshaped San Francisco system.

ENDNOTES - CHAPTER 6

1. P. J. Boyce, "Australian Attitudes to Security," in T. B. Millar, ed., *Australian-New Zealand Defence Co-operation*, Canberra: Australian National University Press, 1968, p. 29.

2. Australian concerns that its voice might not be heard in forthcoming considerations of its own regional environment, however, encouraged the signing of the bilateral Canberra Pact with New Zealand in 1944. See J. A. Nockels, "Australian-New Zealand Defence Cooperation in the Asia-Pacific Region," in Desmond Ball, ed., *The ANZAC Connection*, Sydney: George Allen & Unwin, p. 83.

3. See Peter Edwards, *Crises and Commitments: The Politics and Diplomacy of Australia's Involvement in Southeast Asian Conflicts, 1948-1965*, Sydney: Allen & Unwin, 1992.

4. *Review of Australia's Defence Capabilities: Report to the Minister for Defence by Mr. Paul Dibb,* Canberra: Australian Government Publishing Service, March 1986.

5. See Peter Edwards, *Arthur Tange: Last of the Mandarins*, Crows Nest, New South Wales: Allen & Unwin, 2006, pp. 124-125.

6. See, for example, Australian Department of Defence, *Australia's Strategic Policy*, Commonwealth of Australia, Canberra, 1997.

7. Rod Lyon and William T. Tow, *The Future of the Australian-U.S. Security Relationship,* Carlisle, PA: U.S. Army War College, Strategic Studies Institute, December 2003, p. 6.

8. Paul Dibb, David H. Hale, and Peter Prince, "Asia's Insecurity," *Survival*, Vol. 41, No. 3, Autumn 1999, p. 18.

9. "Transcript of the Prime Minister, The Hon. John Howard, MP, Interview with Kerry O'Brien, The 7:30 Report, ABC," June 23, 2003, at *www.pm.gov.au/news/interviews/Interview194.html*, accessed August 9, 2006.

10. The White House, *National Security Strategy of the United States of America,* Washington, September 2002, p. 1.

11. The White House, "President Bush Welcomes Prime Minister Howard of Australia in Arrival Ceremony at the White House," Press Release May 16, 2006, at *www.whitehouse.gov/news/releases/2006/05/20060516.html*, accessed June 22, 2006. Also see "Howard, Bush Reaffirm Ties," *ABC News Online*, May 17, 2006, at *www.abc.net.au/news/newsitems/200605/s1640172.htm*, accessed June 10, 2006.

12. U.S. Department of Defense, *Quadrennial Defense Review Report*, February 6, 2006, p. 7.

13. Prime Minister of Australia, John Howard, "Force Deployment," Media Release, October 17, 2001, at *www.pm.gov.au/news/media_releases/2001/media_release1342.htm*, accessed June 27, 2006.

14. Australian Department of Defence, "Rehabilitation of Iraq: Operation Catalyst," July 27, 2006, at *www.defence.gov.au/opcatalyst/*, accessed August 9, 2006.

15. "400 Aussia Troops Take on Taliban," *The Australian,* August 9, 2006, p. 1.

16. See Paul Kelly, "Costello's Golden Egg," *The Australian,* May 13, 2006, at *www.theaustralian.news.com.au/story/0,20867,19116653-12250,00.html,* accessed June 10, 2006.

17. "A Twenty Five Year Partnership Between Australia and China," Address by The Hon. Tim Fischer, MP, Deputy Prime Minister, Leader of the National Party, Minister for Trade, to the Australia-China Forum, Beijing, September 8, 1997, at *www.dfat.gov.au/media/speeches/trade/1997/a-c_forum8sept97.html,* accessed June 22, 2006.

18. "Transcript of the Prime Minister the Hon. John Howard, MP Address to the Australian Strategic Policy Institute," Westin Hotel, Sydney, June 18, 2004, at *www.pm.gov.au/news/speeches/speech921.html,* accessed June 22, 2006.

19. Department of Foreign Affairs and Trade, *Annual Report 2003-2004,* p. 30.

20. The Hon. Alexander Downer, MP, Transcript, Media Conference, Beijing, August 17, 2004, at *www.foreignminister.gov.au/transcripts/2004/040817_ds_beijing.html,* accessed June 22, 2006.

21. *Ibid.*

22. Denny Roy, "The Sources and Limits of Sino-Japanese Tensions," *Survival,* Vol. 47, No. 2, Summer 2005, pp. 191-214.

23. For the same logic in an important earlier study, see William T. Tow and Leisa Hay, "Australia, the United States and a 'China Growing Strong': Managing Conflict Avoidance," *Australian Journal of International Affairs,* Vol. 55, No. 1, April 2001, p. 39.

24. "Armitage Reaffirms U.S.-Australian Ties," Transcript of Sydney media roundtable with Deputy Secretary of State Richard Armitage, U.S. Consulate General Sydney, August 17, 2001, at *canberra.usembassy.gov/anzus/2001-08-17_Armitage.html,* accessed June 22, 2006.

25. "Govt Sparing No Effort to Find Wood: Armitage," Transcript of Television Interview of Richard Armitage by Tony Jones, Australian Broadcasting Corporation Lateline, December 5, 2005, at *www.abc.net.au/lateline/content/2005/s1367465.htm,* accessed June 22, 2006.

26. Australian Department of Defence, *Australia's National Security: A Defence Update 2005,* p. 6.

27. Australian Department of Defence, "Australia to Participate in Largest Maritime Exercise," Media Release, CPA140/06, June 26, 2006, at *www.defence.gov.au/media/DepartmentalTpl.cfm?CurrentId=5766*, accessed June 27, 2006.

28. See Minister for Foreign Affairs and Minister for Trade, "Inaugural Philippines-Australia Ministerial Meeting: Joint Ministerial Statement," Joint Media Release, Sydney, August 11-12, 2005, at *www.foreignminister.gov.au/releases/2005/joint_philippines_120805.html*, accessed June 23, 2006.

29. See Boyce, "Australian Attitudes to Security."

30. *Ibid.*

31. "Hill commits Australia to US missile defence," *The Age*, June 24, 2004, at www.theage.com.au/articles/2004/06/19/1087595777243.html?from=storylhs, accessed June 10, 2006.

32. *Defence Update 2005*, p. 14.

33. ABC Radio AM, "Howard Reviews Policy on Uranium Trade to India," March 6, 2006, at *www.abc.net.au/am/content/2006/s1584571.html*, accessed June 23, 2006.

34. U.S. Department of State, "Joint Statement of the U.S.-Japan Security Consultative Committee," February 19, 2005, at *www.state.gov/r/pa/prs/ps/2005/42490.htm*, accessed June 22, 2006. On Beijing's reaction, see "US, Japan: Taiwan a Common Security Issue," *China Daily*, February 20, 2005, at *www.chinadaily.com.cn/english/doc/2005-02/20/content_417697.htm*, accessed June 22, 2006.

35. The Hon. Alexander Downer, MP, Minister for Foreign Affairs, Australia, "Trilateral Strategic Dialogue: Joint Statement Australia-Japan-United States," Sydney, March 18, 2006, at *www.foreignminister.gov.au/releases/2006/joint_statement-aus-japan_usa_180306.html*, accessed June 22, 2006.

36. Robert B. Zoellick, Deputy Secretary of State, "Whither China: From Membership to Responsibility?," Remarks to National Committee on U.S-China Relations, New York City, September 21, 2005, at *www.state.gov/s/d/rem/53682*, accessed June 22, 2006.

37. See "Containing China a Big Mistake," *The Australian*, March 16, 2006, at *www.theaustralian.news.com.au/story/0,20867,18482800-31477,00.html*, accessed June 23, 2006.

38. See "Rice Says Iraq Transition Will Take Time," *China Daily*, March 16, 2006, at *www.chinadaily.com.cn/english/doc/2006-03/16/content_541427.htm*, accessed June 23, 2006.

39. See "US Has No Policy of Containment against China: Rice," *China View*, March 17, 2006, at *news.xinhuanet.com/English/2006-03/17/content_4311717.htm*, accessed June 22, 2006.

40. "Rice Assails China on Australia Trip," *International Herald Tribune*, March 16, 2006, at *www.iht.com/articles/2006/03/16/news/rice.php*, accessed June 23, 2006.

41. See "Rice and Downer in talks on how to contain China," *Sydney Morning Herald*, March 11, 2006, at *www.smh.com.au/news/world/rice-and-downer-in-talks-on-how-to-contain-china/2006/03/10/1141701692756.html*, accessed June 23, 2006.

42. On this and other dilemmas facing Australian strategic policymakers, see Robert Ayson, "Understanding Australia's Defence Dilemmas," *Security Challenges*, Vol. 2, No. 2, July 2006, pp. 25-42.

43. On this combination in Australian thinking, see Robert Ayson, "A Shift in Focus? Australia and Stability in East Asia," Australian Strategic Policy Institute, *Strategic Insights*, No. 17, June 2005.

PANEL III

POLITICAL AND LEGAL ASPECTS
OF THE SPECIAL RELATIONSHIP

CHAPTER 7

PANEL III CHAIRMAN'S INTRODUCTION

Michael Wesley

Surveying the alignments and commitments of the United States at the height of the Cold War, Arnold Wolfers observed that "solidarity, even among close allies, has usually proved to be a perishable asset."[1] Had Wolfers been given the chance to look back on an Australian-American alliance that has endured for over half a century, he may have added a footnoted caveat. The remarkable constancy of the U.S. "other special relationship" requires the word "solidarity" to be measured on two distinct levels.

On one level, that of official alliance relations, the alliance has shown remarkable constancy. In the words of Charles Krauthammer, one of the most enthusiastic American supporters of the alliance, "Australia is the only country that has fought with the United States in every one of its major conflicts since 1914, the good and the bad, the winning and the losing."[2] According to John Higley (Chapter 8), "Military and intelligence cooperation is close to seamless." Finally, as another observer of the alliance argues, both Washington and Canberra continue to devote substantial bureaucratic and political resources to maintaining the solidarity of the relationship:

> The American Secretaries of State and Defense . . . plan their days in 15-minute segments, and literally hundreds of ambassadors and officials of comparable status in Washington would sacrifice much for one of those 15-minute sessions. To have unrestricted access to both

Secretaries and the Chairman of the Joint Chiefs of Staff for an entire day, as Australians have at regular AUSMIN talks, is an extraordinary boon.[3]

However, as John Higley (Chapter 8) and Brendon O'Connor (Chapter 9) demonstrate, "solidarity" also should be discussed on the level of political dynamics and public opinion within each country. At the end of 2006, the political dynamics underlying the Australian-American relationship appeared to have reached a cyclical high point, which by its nature cannot be sustained at the current level of intimacy. George W. Bush and John Howard share very similar approaches to international relations. The Howard government had identified Bush as a possible future President and begun building a relationship with him long before the 2000 Presidential elections in the United States, and was delighted when Bush scraped home.

Howard and Bush developed a close friendship based on shared conservative values and a common contractualist, interest-based approach to international affairs.[4] Most crucial, however, was Australia's support for the United States after the September 11, 2001 (9/11), attacks and during the war in Iraq. Canberra's solidarity in the face of opposition, especially as the enunciated prewar case for invasion unravelled, was a gesture that resonated strongly in Washington. As Tom Schieffer, the American Ambassador to Australia, described it, "You had a deepening of the relationship. Adversity creates a bond. And particularly with George Bush, he is a person who responds to people who are friends when it is harder to be a friend, because he knows there's more friendship there."[5]

The Howard government realized quickly that in the minds of the Bush administration, 9/11 would become "a purifier of alliances"[6] after which America's defense relationships would no longer be seen as defensive assets to be maintained and deferred to, but as potentially perishable arrangements that needed to be justified according to their usefulness. Australia's small but high-profile contributions in Afghanistan and Iraq, its initiative in leading state-building operations in what Washington sees as Australia's patch in Southeast Asia and the South Pacific, and its early actions against North Korean vessels in support of the nascent Proliferation Security Initiative, all earned substantial political capital in Washington.[7] Canberra has lost no time in locking in the payoffs: the Australia-U.S. Free Trade Agreement; visa-free entry for Australians to the United States (remarkable at a time of greater American sensitivity about the integrity of its borders); and, by way of a Presidential decree in September 2005, a level of access to American intelligence matched only by that of the United Kingdom.[8] But as both John Higley and Brendon O'Connor observe, it is worth asking how evolutions in political dynamics and public opinion, respectively, may affect this greater level of official intimacy between the two allies.

Political Dynamics.

As Higley observes, the second half of the second Bush term will see the energy and momentum sapped from the U.S. Government. Preoccupation with seemingly intractable and worsening conflicts in Afghanistan, Iraq, and possibly Israel-Palestine will suck the oxygen of relevance and resources from Washington's ability to tend its alliance relationships and attend to other parts of its global interests. With the superpower lapsing into ever deeper attention deficit disorder, its allies such as Australia are likely to be expected to an even greater extent to take the lead within their respective regions and to contribute globally as well. Higley predicts alarming adverse ripple effects of the Iraq war on U.S. military prowess and resolve, seeing even the Vietnam syndrome as too optimistic a parallel to draw. He argues, convincingly, that in the coming years the United States and Australia will come to see their respective nation-building tasks to be Sisyphean in their endlessness, and that both the drain on the exchequer and the ever-receding exit benchmarks for these operations will be deeply corrosive of public support. The result will be to accept the permanent presence on the international security stage of "bandits and anarchists," and for alliances such as ANZUS to lapse back into defensive arrangements—but defense against a new type of transnational threat.

In addition to the foregoing attenuative forces, political dynamics in the United States also will act to drain the Bush administration's energy and resolve. The loss of control in both the House of Representatives and the Senate in the mid-term elections, combined with the resignation of key foreign policy officials such as Robert Zoellick, will lead, if not to policy paralysis, at least to slackened initiative. U.S. allies such as Australia will find it harder to gain traction within a distracted and deflated Washington bureaucracy. As Republicans look ahead to the 2008 elections, they will try to shore up their key "red state" constituencies by getting tough on agricultural trade, a perennial irritant in Australian-American relations, even with a newly-minted free trade agreement.

It is within this context that Australian officials have two pressing tasks. One is to preserve the access and goodwill built up during the periodic upswing in Australia-American relations. The new and newly strengthened strands of the relationship must be tended carefully, and every effort should be made to resist the inevitable attempts by distracted and time-pressed American officials to downgrade new forums, such as the U.S.-Japan-Australia Trilateral Security Dialogue. The second pressing task lies in not permitting issues such as agricultural protectionism to erode the goodwill which is at the core of the relationship. The United States has too many allies that come to Washington with demands; Australia needs to be mindful that it is one of the few American allies perceived in Washington as a source of fresh and constructive ideas and perspectives.

Higley also ponders the effect on the alliance of the return of the Democrats to power in the United States. It is quite possible that this will lead to a decline in the political intimacy of the relationship, if the historical precedent of the less ebullient Clinton-Howard relationship is anything to go by. Even if a future Democratic administration does not punish the Howard government for its close relationship to Bush, as Higley suggests it might, the Democrats are likely to be more Atlanticist and multilateralist, and wedded to liberal aspirations for the transformation of international relations through international law and institutions.

Such an approach will sit uncomfortably with the Howard government, with its belief that international relations are too messy and uncertain[9] to be contained in rationalist constructs and with its commitment to hard-headed pragmatism, bilateralism, and traditional realist conceptions of world affairs. Perhaps a period of Democratic ascendancy in Washington will need to await the return of the Labor Party to power in Canberra for the next cyclical high point in political relations, akin to the Clinton-Keating affiliation. Even here, however, O'Connor raises the possibility of a leader from left of the Labor Party seeking to downgrade ties with any U.S. Government, regardless of the party in power.

Public Opinion.

Brendon O'Connor's chapter raises a possible directional, rather than cyclical, change in the politics of the Australian-American relationship. He argues that the heavily publicized intimacy between the Howard government and the internationally unpopular Bush administration, added to the politics of the Australia-U.S. Free Trade Agreement, have driven an increasing and under-reported sense of cultural anxiety among Australians. His close interrogation of a broad range of public opinion data in Australia shows that, on security issues and the alliance with America, Australian attitudes are close to those of the United Kingdom or Israel; but on issues of culture and identity, Australian attitudes are closer to those of the French. Political opponents of the Howard government have cleverly exploited these anxieties by accusing Howard of intending to Americanize Australia's industrial relations laws, and then using those accusations in their seemingly effective campaign against the new "Work Choices" legislation.

O'Connor's analysis suggests the possibility that these two attitudinal trends are linked, that the more dependent Australians feel on the alliance, the more it triggers a countervailing anxiety about the effects of this dependence on their identity and sovereignty. This tension reflects a long entrenched strand of critique in Australia, evident on both the left and right of the political spectrum. Commentators in Australia have voiced self-disgust over Australia's seeming inability to do without powerful allies, and argued that America's influence saps Australia's ability to develop an independent identity.[10] Others have argued that the alliance locks Australia into a militarized posture against a largely benign outside world, mandating high levels of defense spending that are unjustified by the level of threats Australia faces.[11] As Australia entered free trade negotiations with the United States, some commentators portrayed Australia as a guileless chump about to be eviscerated by corporate America, that by getting too close to Washington the Howard government was selling out Australia's real interests.[12] The alleged belligerence of the Bush administration in the international arena aroused old fears about Australia being dragged into conflicts to the detriment of its own well-being. This strain of concern also has a long history. Commentators from the left during the Cold War, mirroring New Zealand, had argued that the alliance implicated Australia in America's imperial ambitions, making it a direct target in any conflict between the superpowers[13] and dragging it into morally compromising covert and enforcement actions in support of U.S. foreign policy.[14]

But, as O'Connor observes, we should be careful about drawing too definite political implications from such public opinion data and elite opinion. Cultural attitudes are notoriously difficult to pin down: the recent outpouring of Australian public grief on the occasion of the death of Crocodile Hunter Steve Irwin shows that Australians more eagerly embrace their own if those Aussie stars also loom large in the eyes of Americans. And the caricatures of Howard as a giddy Americophile go too far. There are clearly elements of the U.S. system he dislikes: its tolerance for gun ownership; its social security and health insurance systems. The case of Mark Latham, who failed in his attempt to install an Australian Labor Party government in 2004, apparently illustrates the limits of how much Australians will tolerate identity anxieties adversely affecting the substance of the Australia-U.S. security relationship. The twinning of cultural anxiety with hard-headed pragmatism on security and alliance questions places Australia much closer to its Southeast Asian neighbors than its cousins in Canada or continental Europe. Arguably, a larger challenge to the relationship arises not from emotionalism but from pragmatism: as Australia builds a relationship with China based on a deepening complementarity of interests, how will this begin to impinge on its pragmatic security relationship with the United States?

Conclusion.

Both Higley's and O'Connor's chapters suggest that coincidences in electoral politics in both allies will contribute to cycles of political intimacy and distance in the Australian-American relationship. The challenge for officials on both sides is to remember that the insulation of alliance dynamics from political pressures or public opinion shifts is not a given. Every effort should be made, in the process of adapting the alliance to the demands of 21st century security, to avoid taking the relationship in directions that corrode the broad public support for it in both countries.

ENDNOTES - CHAPTER 7

1. Arnold Wolfers, *Discord and Collaboration*, Baltimore: The Johns Hopkins Press, 1962, p. 207.

2. Charles Krauthammer, "Standing By Your Side, Mate," *The Australian Financial Review*, June 26, 2006.

3. Peter Edwards, *Permanent Friends? Historical Reflections on the Australian-American Alliance*, Lowy Institute Paper 08, Sydney: Lowy Institute for International Policy, 2005, p. 59.

4. Michael Wesley, "Perspective on Australian Foreign Policy, 2001," *Australian Journal of International Affairs*, Vol. 56, No. 1, April 2002.

5. Quoted in Robert Garran, *True Believer: John Howard, George Bush and the American Alliance*, Sydney: Allen and Unwin, 2004, p. 138.

6. Jacques Almaric, "Purifier les Alliances," *Liberation*, September 17, 2001, p. 4, quoted in Bruno Tertrais, "The Changing Nature of Military Alliances," *Washington Quarterly*, Vol. 27, No. 2, Spring 2004.

7. Australia hosted the inaugural meeting of the U.S.-proposed Proliferation Security Initiative in Brisbane in August 2003; a few weeks earlier it conducted what many in Washington interpreted as a PSI-type enforcement action when ADF forces boarded and seized the North Korean vessel *Pong Su* off the southern coast of Australia.

8. "Bound by Intelligence," *The Australian*, September 3, 2005.

9. John Howard, Address to the Australian Strategic Policy Institute, Sydney, June 18, 2004.

10. See Don Watson, *Rabbit Syndrome: Australia and America,* Quarterly Essay 4, Sydney: Blackinc Books, 2001.

11. Mark Beeson, "Australia's Relationship with the United States: The Case for Greater Independence," *Australian Journal of Political Science*, Vol. 38, No. 3, November 2003, p. 395.

12. Linda Weiss, Elizabeth Thurbon, and John Matthews, *How to Kill a Country: Australia's Devastating Trade Deal with the United States*, Sydney: Allen and Unwin, 2004.

13. Philip Bell and Roger Bell, *Implicated: The United States in Australia*, Melbourne: Oxford University Press, 1993, p. 147.

14. Joseph A Camilleri, *Australian-American Relations: The Web of Dependence*, Melbourne: Macmillan, 1980, pp. 124-126.

CHAPTER 8

THE RELATIONSHIP'S POLITICAL ASPECTS: AN AMERICAN PERSPECTIVE

John Higley

In May 2006 Prime Minister John Howard again visited President George W. Bush in Washington, and again was unnoticed by most Americans. There were a few TV clips of Howard standing with Bush in the Rose Garden and at a joint press conference, a handful of articles in newspapers read by the American political class, and a 15-minute interview of Howard on CNN's Late Edition, which has a small Sunday morning audience. The scant public attention paid to Howard's visit was not a rebuff, however; few foreign leaders visiting Washington catch American eyes, and on this occasion the praise Bush lavished on Howard enabled him to fare better than most. The PM's visit contrasted, nonetheless, with the extensive Australian publicity that attended U.S. Secretary of State Condoleezza Rice's appearance in Sydney and Canberra 2 months earlier. One might infer that the U.S.-Australia relationship has much greater salience to Australia than to the United States. But this would be mistaken; the relationship is of key importance to the United States.

The relationship has been institutionalized and globalized to an unprecedented degree during the Bush-Howard years. Military and intelligence interoperability is close to seamless, and Australia's intended purchases of advanced U.S. weapons systems—Joint Strike Fighters, AWACS aircraft, *Aegis* destroyers, M1A1 tanks—promise to integrate the two defense establishments as never before. The irritant that U.S. intelligence and missile detection installations in Australia long constituted in that country has dissipated. The recent U.S.-Australia free trade agreement (FTA) gives the relationship's economic side a rules-based permanency, so that 55 percent of Australia's direct overseas investment now goes to the United States, numerous Australian companies are established profitably in the American market, and some 70,000 Australians are thereby employed.

The two countries worked closely to reduce agricultural barriers in the abortive Doha round of multilateral trade negotiations; they have jointly initiated an annual dialogue with Japan on Asia-Pacific economic and security issues; they are active in the PO-6 effort to slow global warming; and they cooperate effectively at the United Nations (UN). In the arc of instability to Australia's north, they have a mutual interest in stabilizing East Timor and other island states, aiding victims of natural disasters such as the Sumatra tsunami and Java earthquakes, and providing military and other assistance to the Yudhoyono government in Jakarta. Most dramatically, Australia steadfastly has remained part of the dwindling U.S.-led coalition in Iraq while also contributing to counterinsurgent and reconstruction efforts in Afghanistan.

Washington policymakers assume that Australia cannot play a major world role independent of the United States, and most policymakers in Canberra see Australia as having no credible alternative to its alliance with the United States. By trading loyalty to the Bush administration for privileged access to U.S. foreign and defense policy thinking and to the American market through the FTA, the Howard government has strengthened this reciprocal view. While there is considerable suspicion of Bush administration policies among the Australian public, as Brendon O'Connor documents in Chapter 9, and while the average American's ignorance of Australia is nearly total, most political elites in the two countries hold the relationship in high regard. The concern of many during the 1970s and 1980s that the relationship would be weakened by the passing of the World War II generation is now seen to have been unfounded.

End of story? Perhaps. But it is possible, as Michael Wesley (Chapter 7) has speculated, that the relationship is now at a cyclical high point, and that some deterioration must follow. A change in top political leaders, Bush and Howard, is not far off, and their successors are unlikely to be such close comrades in arms. The warm personal ties between Bush and Howard, formed in the crucible of the September 11, 2001 (9/11), attacks on New York and Washington—which Howard witnessed—will probably not be duplicated. With Democrats having gained control of both houses of Congress following mid-term elections in November 2006, their relations with a continuing Liberal regime in Canberra are likely to be less robust than Republican ties have been. Not a few Democrats will harbor some bitterness toward Canberra for having aided and abetted what they regard as Bush's disastrous war of choice in Iraq. During the run-up to Australia's federal elections in 2007, for that matter, the Liberals may distance themselves from the lame-duck Bush administration in order to avoid being tarred by the sorts of criticisms leveled at Bush and his associates by American critics. Looking further down the road, it is likely that the United States will experience a post-Iraq syndrome, in which Bush's global war on terror will be scaled back as the result of an aversion in the American public to undertakings that risk becoming new Iraqs. The United States probably, in consequence, will be quite reluctant to involve itself militarily in Australia's region. Related to this, the next U.S. administration, regardless of its party coloration, will have to undertake extensive repairs to the American military while coping with severe fiscal constraints. Add, finally, the probability of more abrasive U.S.-Australia trade competitions in foreign markets generated by strong economic lobbies in each country, and it is not hard to see that the relationship's closeness may be peaking about now.

The relationship has a naturalness that will prevent it from withering greatly, however. It is rooted in many cultural, economic, and political affinities; the mutual security interests that drive it are lasting; and there is a long experience of adjusting the relationship to fit changing principals and the governments they lead. Other contributors to this volume examine the mutual security and economic interests that underpin the relationship. My charge is to consider its political aspects from an American perspective.

The Short-Term Outlook.

Changes in the American political scene during the next 2 years are likely to perturb the relationship. President Bush's public approval ratings hover in the 35-40 percent range and may well head toward Vice President Cheney's 20 percent rating. The Iraq quagmire and the trajectory of events in Afghanistan are millstones that hang heavy around the Bush administration's neck; evidence of administration incompetence in several domestic policy domains is substantial; and assorted scandals mainly involving Republican leaders and their lobbyist allies multiply.

With the Democrats in control of both houses of Congress as a result of the November 2006 mid-term elections, how will the relationship be affected? The bilateral security ties at its core will remain unchanged, as will the U.S. strategic guarantee of Australia's security. Australia's access to high-level U.S. intelligence and American defense science and technology will not be reduced in any significant way. To be sure, a whiff of defense protectionism is in the American air, as illustrated by reluctance to allow Britain and Australia sufficient access to Joint Strike Fighter technology to maintain and upgrade the aircraft autonomously once the aircraft are purchased. While President Bush has relaxed U.S. defense disclosure policy to reassure Australia and Britain on this score, the Democrats, having reaped political hay from their attacks on the Bush administration's plan to have Dubai Ports World manage American harbor terminals, may be unwilling to go along with this relaxation.

More concretely and immediately, Democratic ascendancy in Congress will accelerate greatly the exodus of top-level figures from the Bush administration. Donald Rumsfeld has already resigned, and the days of his lieutenants at the Pentagon, who have worked closely with Australian counterparts ever since September 11, 2001 (9/11), are at or near zero. Pressures to replace senior military leaders associated with Rumsfeld and his civilian Pentagon team are already taking effect. The June 2006 resignation of Deputy Secretary of State Robert Zoellick, whose knowledge of Australia was second only to that of his predecessor, Rich Armitage, offered a foretaste of how Bush officials accustomed to working closely with Australians will disappear from high office in Washington. The Australian government's easy access to top U.S.

policymakers will require making new acquaintances, and the relationship's overall atmospherics will need close attention.

Beyond these effects of a Democratic ascendancy, the relationship will have to operate in a politically deadlocked Washington. Congressional committees, newly controlled by Democrats, will unleash a flood of investigations involving televised public hearings and subpoenas of administration officials, and even pay-back impeachment proceedings against President Bush cannot be ruled out. The Democrats will launch a concerted assault on Vice President Cheney and his large and powerful staff, assuming Cheney does not preempt this by resigning for reasons of health. Jockeying by both parties' presidential aspirants in the long run-up to the 2008 presidential election also will contribute to deadlock. Mired in difficulties, Bush administration officials may fail to keep Australia sufficiently informed about impending U.S. actions. Canberra's pique at not being adequately forewarned about the U.S. nuclear deal with India in early 2006 illustrates this possibility.

Despite highly publicized announcements by President Bush and the Democratic congressional leadership that they will work together, indeed that the President welcomes new ideas for the Iraq war, sniping by Democrats at administration initiatives, as well as the Republicans' own deep divisions over Iraq, immigration policy, tax policy, renewing the Bush administration's trade negotiating authority, the Doha round's resumption (if it occurs), etc., dampen prospects for significant congressional accomplishments. Fiscal constraints may further limit administration actions, and Bush's eroding authority also will crimp them. The abandonment of Social Security privatization early in the administration's second term and its inability to gain passage of a new immigration law before the November 2006 mid-term elections signal what a continuing but crippled Republican dominance may entail.

During the Bush administration's waning time in office, trade relations between the United States and Australia are likely to become more strained. Republicans will be tempted to shore up red state voter support for the 2008 elections by clamping down on above-quota imports of Australian beef, lamb, dairy, and other products. For the same political reason, American competition with Australia in foreign wheat and other agricultural markets will sharpen. A straw in the wind is the suspicion of some Australians that the American wheat lobby, with Bush administration connivance, pressured the interim government of Iraq into suspending purchases of Australian wheat on the pretext of punishing the Wheat Board's kickbacks to Saddam Hussein's henchmen during the UN sanctions regime. "So much for the coalition of the willing," a Canberran insider was quoted as saying.[1]

Moreover, renewing egregious subsidies to U.S. agriculture is almost certain to be the price the Bush administration will have to pay in order to gain congressional extension of its fast-track trade negotiating authority, which is due to expire during the first half of 2007. Howls of outrage by Australian agricultural interests and demands for retaliation will follow.

It is self-evident, however, that developments in Iraq and Afghanistan will be the main determinant of American politics during the next 2 years. Plausible scenarios range from bad to horrible. That Iraq and Afghanistan could be transformed into liberal — or at least more or less stable—democracies, as Bush and his associates repeatedly promised (echoed by John Howard), were never serious possibilities. The sine qua non of a liberal or stable democracy is a well-articulated, internally accommodative, and relatively secure political elite.[2] No such democracy has ever emerged without the formation of such an elite, and the odds that one would form in Iraq and/or Afghanistan—or that it could be imposed by occupying forces—have always been negligible. Numerous small and weakly articulated elite groups vie for the leadership of both countries' clashing religious sects, tribes, ethnic groups, and regions. These discordant and disorganized elites had radically different experiences of the Baathist and Taliban regimes, ranging from profitable association to murderous subjugation to forced emigration overseas. Elite groups in both countries distrust and despise each other, and they lack any experience of cooperating peacefully in political matters. In short, it always was unrealistic to believe that post-Saddam and post-Taliban elites in either country could reach the basic accommodation that is a stable democracy's main foundation.

There are, instead, just three realistic scenarios. One is that the splintered elites will establish separate political entities after much bloodshed and population resettlement. Practically speaking, Iraq and Afghanistan will cease to exist. The second is that a faction or narrow coalition of factions, backed by militias in Iraq and warlords in Afghanistan, will create authoritarian regimes, almost certainly with a hard theocratic edge, bearing no more resemblance to a liberal or stable democracy than did the Baathist and Taliban regimes. The third possibility is that unchecked civil wars will be fought until the contending sides, waist-deep in blood, decide they have had enough. There is, I suppose, a fourth scenario: all of the above.

As one or a combination of these grim scenarios unfolds during the next 2 years, how will American politics and, indirectly, the relationship with Australia be affected? The Bush administration now admits that the struggles in Iraq and Afghanistan, especially in Iraq, will be long and hard, so that hopes for early and reasonably satisfactory outcomes are unrealistic. But it insists that the United States must stay the course if global terrorism is to be stopped before it again reaches American shores. The political shelf life of this no doubt sincerely held view is not long-lasting, however. With Democrats controlling both houses of Congress beginning in January 2007, their demands, backed by the power of appropriations, for an early and large troop withdrawal from Iraq will be irresistible.

The severe military manpower costs of the Iraq and Afghanistan occupations—amounting to roughly a battalion each month in dead, wounded, and otherwise incapacitated personnel—will not be sustainable beyond the first half of 2007 without recalling National Guard units to active duty or sending exhausted regular Army and Marine units back for fourth and even fifth combat tours. Moreover, Great Britain, Italy, and Poland have all announced impending Troop reductions or pull-outs in Iraq.[3]

In Afghanistan, the planned drawdown of American troops from 23,000 to 16,000 has had to be abandoned, and it is an open question how long NATO governments can tolerate politically the casualties that are being inflicted on their forces by the resurgent Taliban. Of relevance here is Australia's contribution of a small force to assist the UN reconstruction effort in Afghanistan, accompanied by a special forces unit. It is quite conceivable that casualties suffered by these units, in combination with demands on the Australian Defense Force (ADF) in East Timor and elsewhere in Australia's neighborhood, will require terminating this contribution sooner rather than later.

The Outlook After 2008.

However, my crystal ball for how American politics will affect the relationship after 2008 is as cloudy as anyone's. But I can discern no panic button that will need to be pressed. Despite the divisive Iraq and Afghanistan imbroglios, American political elites still hold to a relatively shared view of U.S. interests and responsibilities, and these include keeping the relationship with Australia in good order. Although the bulk of elites have concluded that the Iraq undertaking was a grievous mistake, few top leaders have broken decisively with the Bush administration's insistence that a precipitous withdrawal would damage U.S. interests even more.

To be sure, unwillingness to condemn the Iraq venture root and branch — Senators Kerry and Feingold have been outspoken exceptions — derives more from an inability to identify a plausible alternative than from a belief that it will ultimately succeed. But on the whole, U.S. political elites recognize that simply scuttling the Iraq effort entails unacceptable risks. They comprehend the predicament that the administration has gotten itself into, and as a result most still pull their political punches. The deep elite cleavage that developed over the Vietnam War has not, at least not yet, been duplicated, however angry most leaders are at Bush and his entourage for having gotten the United States into the Iraq pickle.

The Bush administration's more clearly multilateral foreign policy thrust during its second term contributes to keeping the political elites at least somewhat subdued. Condoleezza Rice, Robert Zoellick (now departed), and Undersecretary of State Nicolas Burns — assisted, one deduces, by Rice ally Stephen Hadley at the National Security Council — have reclaimed from the Pentagon much of the State Department's primacy in foreign policymaking. One indication was the March 2006 revision of the pugnacious 2002 *National Security Strategy*. By detailing U.S. intentions to work closely with Britain, Canada, the European Union, and other allies, the revision had a more multilateral tone, and this tended to reassure political leaders who had been alarmed by the 2002 *Strategy's* brazen unilateralism. In several policy domains — working with European allies to impede Iran's nuclear ambitions and with Asian countries to check North Korea's brandishing of nuclear weapons and missiles; launching and participating in a series of multilateral aid and human rights initiatives in Africa; seeking to integrate China as a stakeholder in the global order — the first Bush administration's unilateralism is now a dead letter in practice, if not yet entirely in rhetoric. Indeed, a striking feature of the second Bush administration's early years — and of continuing political elite circumspection in foreign policy matters — was Rice's exemption from trenchant attacks and criticism. Even here, however, accusations that she was unduly complacent when warned in July 2001, shortly before 9/11, of an impending al-Qai'da attack on the United States have recently put her more squarely in the line of political fire.

Depicting American political elites as being well aware of the dangers that the United States confronts in Iraq and the wider Middle East, and therefore being tacitly united in a search for ways to contain the dangers, is, of course, debatable. Obviously, as

155

the alarm bells set off by Israel's attack on Hezbollah in Lebanon during July-August 2006 dramatically affirmed, the situation throughout the Middle East is extremely volatile. Sectarian civil war rages in Iraq, largely unchecked by U.S.-led coalition forces or by the elected Iraqi government hunkered down in the fortified Green Zone. It remains quite possible that an ignominious U.S. withdrawal from Iraq, and perhaps also from Afghanistan, will be unavoidable. On bad news days, now mostly the rule, images of the Green Zone becoming an American Dien Bien Phu, or a Saigon-like redoubt from which there is only helicopter escape, creep into the mind. Were such an apocalypse to occur, the recriminations about who bore responsibility for it—Republican lions or Democratic foxes—would destroy the political elite's precarious unity in foreign policy matters. That such images of disaster cannot be kept entirely at bay indicates how searing an experience the Iraq war and associated debacles can be for the elites who formulate, and the publics who influence, U.S. foreign policy.

The main question about the U.S.-Australia relationship's vibrancy after 2008 is how this searing experience will shape subsequent U.S. actions. In U.S. foreign policy circles, the neoconservative camp, divided and enfeebled by setbacks in Iraq and Afghanistan, will have been routed, and its shibboleths about using American power to spread democracy and freedom around the world will be ridiculed. The Democratic Party's relatively bellicose wing also will be cowed, with such a leader as Senator Joseph Lieberman having survived only by running on the Independent ticket. Populist nationalists of the Pat Buchanan ilk will crow, seeking to stymie U.S. involvements in international organizations and multilateral undertakings.

Unable to fathom what the expenditure of so much blood and treasure in Iraq and Afghanistan accomplished, American public opinion will oppose further boots-on-the-ground commitments in world trouble spots. And because the damage done to the U.S. military by the Iraq and Afghanistan occupations will take years and hundreds of billions of dollars to repair, the wherewithal for such commitments will be in short supply. One disaffected Army general recently estimated it would take 10-20 years and $60 billion just to repair the damage done before 2006, while a prize-winning economist estimates the Iraq war's long-term cost at well in excess of a trillion dollars.[4] Caspar Weinberger's and Colin Powell's earlier doctrines of employing overwhelming force with a well thought-out exit strategy in any military expedition will be renascent, although the manpower and materiel for their implementation may be unavailable.

These forecasts appear to equate the Iraq and Afghanistan aftermaths with that of the Vietnam War in the 1970s and early 1980s. But the post-Iraq and post-Afghanistan world will differ from the world of that time in important ways. After the Vietnam War, the bipolar Cold War confrontation between the U.S.-led West and the Union of Soviet Socialist Republics (USSR) and its satellites continued to ensure a significant measure of world order for at least a decade. After Iraq and Afghanistan, by contrast, there will be no such order-maintaining camps.

Another difference is that there will be many more failed and failing states in the world than there were 3 decades ago. This is because developments in technologies of production and communication have reduced the capacity of many states to absorb swollen and exceedingly youthful populations in gainful and needed employment. Collapsing or dangerously weak states are the result, and they are proliferating in much of Africa and Oceania, as well as in some of the Caribbean, the Middle East, and South and Southeast Asia. In these areas, as John Keegan has observed, "War is escaping from state control, into the hands of bandits and anarchists."[5] This trend confronts the United States, Australia, and all other Western countries with a host of dangers that range from a tidal wave of migrants desperately seeking Western shelter to a globalization of martyrdom in the form of suicidal but lethal attacks on hated Western bastions of wealth and sacrilege.

How will the U.S.-Australia relationship fare in this ominous world situation? My guess is that it will become less global in pretension and reach. After Iraq and Afghanistan, the United States will be extremely reluctant to risk venturing into new quagmires, as its refusal to answer Liberia's pleas for military help in 2004 and its refusal to deploy even a small force to Darfur in 2006 intimate. Phone calls to Canberra asking Australia to augment U.S. forces in distant lands will no longer occur. Speculation about the eventual emergence of a U.S.- and Europe-led NATO-like force that would police large parts of the globe, and to which Australia, New Zealand, and Japan would make important contributions, strikes me as far-fetched.[6]

The main lesson learned in Iraq and Afghanistan is that, short of recolonization over a long period, for which there is absolutely no U.S. or other Western political and economic support or wherewithal, states that have fallen into the hands of bandits and anarchists cannot be salvaged. As John Mueller concludes in his important book, *The Remnants of War* (2004), "[E]xercises in nation-building that are productive of peace and order—and that ultimately will produce results most likely to be lasting—will have to be primarily accomplished by domestic forces" in the failing states themselves.[7] This view resembles the conclusion that some Australian observers of East Timor's relapse into civil strife and breakdown during 2006 began to reach.

My guess, then, is that the relationship will be altered by disillusionment in both countries with nation-building efforts and by considerable internal political opposition to such efforts. The time when the United States and Australia can act jointly and forcibly to contain or eradicate distant evils is ending. In its thrust, the relationship will again be self-consciously defensive and not significantly proactive. Its military and intelligence sinews will be kept strong, but more as a deterrent than as a solvent of troubles far from American and Australian shores. Meanwhile, the many cultural, economic, and political affinities on which the relationship rests will continue to flourish.

ENDNOTES - CHAPTER 8

1. *Financial Times*, February 14, 2006.

2. John Higley and Michael Burton, *Elite Foundations of Liberal Democracies*, Lanham, MD: Rowman & Littlefield, 2006.

3. Michelle Tan, "Britain reduces troop numbers in Iraq: Italy, Poland pull out forces," *Army Times*, December 11, 2006, p. 11.

4. Joseph E. Stiglitz, "The High Cost of the Iraq War," *Economists' Voice*, The Berkeley Electronic Press, March 2006.

5. John Keegan. "The Threat from Europe." *Spectator*, March 24, 2001, p. 39.

6. Zbigniew Brzezinski, The Christopher J. Makins Lecture to The Atlantic Council of the United States, May 31, 2006, p. 9.

7. John Mueller, *The Remnants of War,* Ithaca, NY: Cornell University Press, 2004, pp. 180-81.

CHAPTER 9

AUSTRALIAN PUBLIC OPINION AND THE AUSTRALIA-U.S. ALLIANCE

Brendon O'Connor

Does America have no better friend than Australia, as Secretary of State Condoleezza Rice has proclaimed?[1] Should Australia's relationship with the United States sensibly be called the "other special relationship," implying that Australia, along with the United Kingdom, is one of America's two most favored allies? Or into the future, will "the mission define the coalition," with Australia's favor depending on its commitment of troops to American-led operations? Reporting on how the Australian people feel about these questions is the central quest of this chapter. It examines the best public opinion data available on the alliance and more broadly on U.S.-Australia relations to gauge the current perceptions and opinions of Australians. I will argue that the data reveal anti-Americanism as a political undercurrent in Australia, but not one that can be utilized yet at the political level. I will illustrate this by examining the anti-American rhetoric vis-à-vis the lack of success of the prominent Australian politician Mark Latham.

In many ways the U.S.-Australia alliance is currently at a high point in its history; and at the broadest security level, this intimacy enjoys strong public support. However, on a number of issues, Australians are clearly uneasy about Australia's closeness to the current Bush administration. Public opinion provides comfort to both pro- and anti-American positions. Although

Australians are unlikely to support a downgrading of the alliance and are just as likely to continue consuming vast quantities of American entertainment, the survey data suggest anxiety about where America's global battles might lead Australia, and what will remain in the future of a genuinely unique Australian culture beyond Australian Rules Football and Dame Edna Everage. It is tempting to see these collective opinions as inchoate and dismiss them as ultimately marginal in the world of foreign and military affairs, which generally has been the preserve of elites. However, there is emerging evidence that public opinion increasingly matters in international affairs.[2] Lastly, public opinion consciously and subconsciously shapes the rhetoric of politicians as they try to connect their actions and intentions with the various currents and undercurrents of their societies.

What do the opinion polls tell us? Before looking at the data in detail, it may be useful to dwell briefly on the manner in which surveys frame their questions. After all, how an opinion poll asks a question has a substantial impact on the answer given. A good example of this is the Lowy Institute Survey titled *Australians Speak 2005*, which asked Australians two questions. The first asked: "How important is our alliance with the United States for Australia's security," to which 45 percent of respondents said "very important" and 27 percent said "fairly important." At the same time, respondents were asked: "Thinking of how much notice Australia takes of the views of the United States in our foreign policy, on the whole do you think we take too much, too little, or the right amount of notice?" to which 68 percent answered "too much" and only 2 percent said "too little."

From this data, it seems fair to claim that most Australians think Australia's alliance with the United

States is important for securing Australia against potential threats, but at the same time most Australians want a foreign policy more independent from the United States. This might be described as wanting your cake and eating it too, and the contradictions in this view are only further muddied by the wording in the question on the importance of the alliance. For example, with the question "How important is our alliance with the United States for Australia's security?" a respondent who answers "important" may not be expressing a preference for a strong alliance in the future, but simply answering that the alliance is important at the present time. Also, the question does not allow the respondent to express a preference for a different type of alliance. This may account for why a majority can say the alliance is important, but that they also want a foreign policy more independent from the United States.

Supporters of the U.S.-Australia alliance allege that a large percentage of Australians endorse Australia's security alliance with the United States and say their claim is supported by opinion polls. This is true in a broad sense, with up to 85 percent of Australians agreeing that the alliance is important for Australia's security.[3] Possibly the best polling data we have on Australian attitudes regarding security is the Australian Electoral Survey (AES), which since its inception in 1993 has questioned voters on the U.S.-Australia alliance. See Figure 1 for election poll responses to the question, "How important do you think the Australian alliance with the United States under the ANZUS [Australian-New Zealand-U.S.] treaty is for protecting Australia's security?"[4]

	Percent
1 Very important	45.3
2 Fairly important	39.2
3 Not very important	12.2
4 Not at all important	3.3
Total	100.0

Figure 1. AES 2004 Election Poll.

The AES question on the alliance's importance is framed in the same leading manner as the Lowy Institute question on the alliance. It seems fair to say, then, that while the alliance is supported by a majority of Australians, ongoing support is probably less than the 84.5 percent shown in Figure 1. For a longitudinal view of Australian public support of the ANZUS alliance, see Figure 2. The AES has expanded its polling more recently to include a separate survey of political candidates. This data, represented in Figures 3 and 4, shows that candidates from the Coalition and the Labor party are strongly supportive of the alliance in a largely bipartisan manner. See Figure 3 for survey results on the question, "How important do you think the Australian alliance with the United States under the ANZUS treaty is for protecting Australia's security?"

See Figure 4 for survey results on the question, "If Australia's security were threatened by some other country, how much trust do you feel Australia can have in the United States to come Australia's defence?"

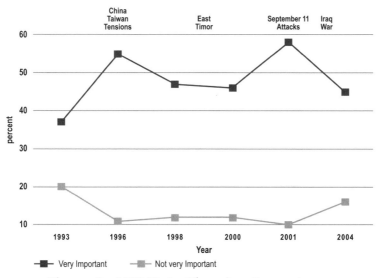

**Figure 2. AES Data Showing Importance
of the ANZUS alliance, 1993-2004
(Percent Holding Opinion).**

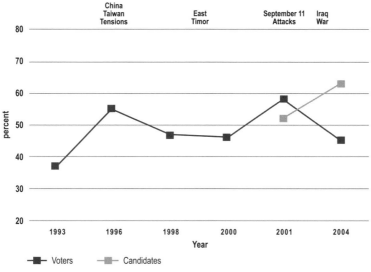

**Figure 3. AES data 1993-2004, Importance
of ANZUS for Protecting Australian Security
(Percent Who Say "Very Important").**

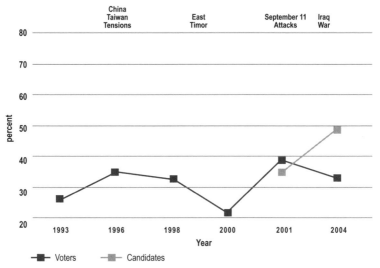

Figure 4. AES Data 1993-2004, Trust in United States
Coming to Australia's Defense.
(Percent Who Say "Great Deal")

Interestingly, in 2001 voters showed marginally stronger support for the alliance than candidates, and they also had greater trust in the United States coming to Australia's aid in a military crisis. However, by 2004 there was a reversal, along with a greater divergence between candidate and voter opinion. This was largely due to 89 percent of Coalition candidates stating that the alliance was very important. This hardening of support for the alliance among Coalition candidates reflected the agreement by their political parties to commit troops to the war in Iraq.

Polls on broader topics relating to how America and Americans are perceived in Australia have produced much more mixed results than the generally very positive attitude to the specific issue of U.S.-Australia security relations discussed thus far. Possibly the contradictory nature of some of this opinion allows it largely to be ignored by Australian politicians. However, results from a survey such as the aforementioned Lowy Institute's *Australians Speak 2005* occasionally ring alarm bells. The survey found that Australians had more negative attitudes toward America than they did toward China, France, Malaysia, or Japan. See Figure 5 for survey responses to the question, "When you think about the following countries, groups or regions of the world, do you have positive or negative feelings about them?"[5]

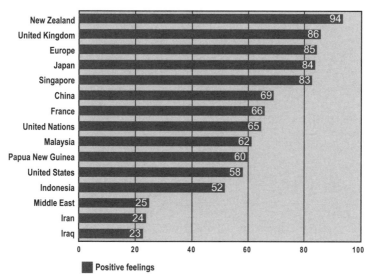

Figure 5. Data From Lowy Institute's
Australians Speak 2005,
Positive Feelings for Various Nations
(Percent Holding Positive Feelings).

These results seem at first quite amazing, with Australians choosing to view nations such as China and Malaysia more positively than their strongest ally of the last 50 years. At the time, some commentators complained about the methodology of the Lowy

Survey, saying that the results were aberrant.[6] However, other surveys, including a 2005 British Broadcasting Company (BBC) poll that included Australians, show similarly negative feelings toward the United States. When Australians were asked in the BBC survey whether U.S. influence in the world was "mainly negative or mainly positive," 60 percent answered "mainly negative," a result similar to the French response. Australians also had responded in a similarly negative fashion when polled on the same question in 2003, reflecting the globally negative attitudes toward the United States following the Bush administration's decision to invade Iraq.[7]

Countervailing evidence can also be found, however: on the eve of the 2004 U.S. Presidential elections, Australians took a more positive attitude toward Bush than did the Canadians, French, Germans, Italians, Japanese, Russians, Spaniards, or Britons. That said, this still equates to only 43 percent of Australians having a somewhat positive or very positive view of Bush.[8] Like most other nations in a 2004 *Globescan/Guardian* survey, Australians said they preferred Kerry over Bush in the 2004 election.

For those looking for further comparative data, the 2003 11-nation BBC/ABC/CBS survey titled "What the World Thinks of America" offers the best sampling on a wide range of topics. The results show Australians to have attitudes on U.S. foreign policy similar to those of the Canadians and Britons. Opinions, although generally critical, are less dismissive than those of the French, Indonesians, or Jordanians. However, when it comes to the influence of Americanization, of American television culture, and of American food on their society, Australians are more critical than Britons and Canadians. In fact, on these issues the Australian numbers are as critical as those of the French; however, it seems fair to assume that the tone and nature of the concerns in Australia is likely to be somewhat different.

The general turn against American foreign policy across the globe, consistently documented by the Pew surveys in recent years, also was reflected in a 2003 BBC survey in which the majority of Australians said they disagreed rather than agreed with American policies on global warming, nuclear proliferation, world poverty, and Israel and Palestine. This may reflect a growing global trend of instinctively not trusting American motives abroad.[9] However, it is significant that in all of these policy arenas, a significant minority of Australians said they "don't know" whether they agree or disagree with American policies. The only area where a majority of Australians agreed with the U.S. response was on "terrorism," support shared by most of the nations surveyed.

On cultural issues and Americanization, the Australian responses make curious reading, seeming to mirror the guilt of habitual cigarette smokers — unlikely to change their behavior any time soon but nevertheless in the dark of the night worrying about its long-term consequences. When asked, "Do you think over time this country is becoming more like America or less like America," 81 percent of Australians answered "more," whereas only 52 percent of Canadians answered "more." When asked, "Do you think that the influence of American consumer products and entertainment in your country is too great," 68 percent of Australians as opposed to 44 percent of Canadians and Britons answered "too great."

It would appear that Australians are becoming increasingly Americanized, though 42 percent of

Australians profess to "dislike" American television (a perusal of primetime television in Australia any given night thus would suggest that a large number of Australian viewers are masochists). Only 21 percent of Canadians said they "dislike" American television. Adding insult to injury, 51 percent of Australians said they "dislike" American food, as opposed to 32 percent of Canadians and 36 percent of Britons. Any American who has witnessed question time in the Australian federal parliament might also find it curious that 63 percent of Australians considered Australia "more cultured than America." Americans also might find it hard to believe that only 1 percent of Australians thought that overall America is a better place to live than their own country. This was the lowest response in the 11-nation survey, with even 7 percent of the French and 15 percent of the Britons believing America to be a better place to live than their own homelands.

These survey results reflect tensions within the Australian identity: Australians consume American culture voraciously, but still seem to have an underlying sense that Australia is ultimately the better place of the two. Like the people of many other nations, Australians see themselves as at least the cultural equal of America and are therefore perplexed by how it is that the United States and its culture have come to hold such attraction around the world.

Nonetheless, while most Australians still want America's protection from security threats abroad, on a more specific level they find it hard to agree with many of the Bush administration's foreign policies, particularly in regard to Iraq. They are not alone in their opinions as even the American public increasingly shares their anxieties about these policies.

As the work of John Zaller[10] and others reminds us, public opinion is fickle, and politicians realize this.

Making voting predictions or policy prescriptions based on the statistics reviewed above would be fraught with risk. The opinions declared are contradictory of some of the other views firmly expressed, suggesting that positions in certain cases may be transitory. In general, Australian opinion reflects the global trend of concern about the direction of recent U.S. foreign policy. However, the cultural anxieties presented here are complex and not easily linked to foreign policymaking. Furthermore, these anxieties may coexist with positive views of the American war on terror and of Australia's military alliance with the United States.

This facility for holding negative views toward the United States while at the same time supporting the alliance is evidenced in the Lowy survey, where a slim majority of those who have a negative opinion of the United States also think Australia's security alliance with the United States is important. However, there are indications from the Lowy survey that Australians already have some tipping point issues that could cause them to rethink support for the alliance. For example, 72 percent of respondents in the survey disagreed with the proposition that "Australia should act in accordance with our security alliance with the United States even if it means following them to war with China over the independence of Taiwan."

The opinions discussed above present challenges for those who want to see a continuing strong political relationship between the United States and Australia. The *Australians Speak 2005* survey is rumored to have worried prominent Australians living in the United States, prompting them to want to see more done about educating Australians about the United States. The recent announcement that the American Australia Association and the Australian government will fund a new American studies center in Australia to the tune of 25 million Australian dollars is an obvious response to these concerns. Whether this center will be successful is hard to tell; some have argued that anti-Americanism is one of the few prejudices that intensifies as the level of one's university education rises. Furthermore, such a venture failed in the 1990s at the University of Sydney.

The Anti-American Challenge.

Could anti-Americanism, or more specifically the alliance, be a significant issue in an Australian federal election? With the two current leaders of the Liberal Party and Australian Labor Party (ALP) at the helm, this seems unlikely: both are strong alliance supporters. However, many ALP branch members and certain individuals and factions within the ALP are skeptical of the alliance generally and deeply concerned at the close relationship Howard has forged with the Bush administration. These critics generally have greater faith in the United Nations and multilateral agreements than the current government, and admire the position taken by the Germans, French, and New Zealanders toward the Bush administration. Open political debate on these questions is much more limited in Australia than in most other western nations, in part because of the overwhelming support the U.S.-Australia alliance enjoys with the leadership of the two major political parties.

However, if a Mark Latham-led ALP government had succeeded in 2004, we may have had a very different relationship between the governments of Australia and America. For a good deal of 2004, the ALP led the Coalition government in opinion polling, with ALP leader Latham's own personal ratings in polls generally very strong. Before becoming leader of the ALP, Latham, in a parliamentary attack on a U.S.-led war in Iraq in February 2003, had described Bush as the "most incompetent and dangerous president in living memory." Latham stated that "President Bush's foreign policy looks more like American imperialism than a well thought-through and resourced strategy to eliminate terrorists." He dismissed Howard as a "yes-man to a flaky and dangerous American president."[11]

These remarks and others by ALP politicians prompted U.S. Ambassador J. Thomas Schieffer to briefly enter the political fray and express his disapproval of the ALP rhetoric.[12] This entry into domestic Australian politics by a foreign diplomat was unfortunate; Schieffer temporarily retreated, but later publicly criticized Latham's 2004 pledge that Australian troops in Iraq would be home by Christmas if Labor won that year's federal election. For his part, Latham, on becoming the leader of the ALP, was quick to praise the U.S.-Australia alliance publicly.[13] However, as his published diaries later revealed, in private he held an extremely negative view of the alliance. Arguably, his decision to withhold his real views from the public reflects the power the alliance ultimately holds in Australian elite politics.

Latham's career is not always easy to make sense of, particularly given his personal style and the resentments he harbored as displayed in their full glory in the *Latham Diaries* published in 2005 after he had quit the federal parliament. Describing Mark Latham to Americans is always interesting, given how critical he was of the Bush administration. On one hand he had much in common with the outsider style of Howard Dean. Latham's temperament also has obvious similarities to Dean's, with Latham having regular "I had a scream"[14] moments. On the other hand, Latham was a great admirer of Richard Nixon, whose portrait hung on his parliamentary office wall and whom he regularly identifies with in the *Latham Diaries*. In sum, Latham was a maverick, but one who deep down identified with what could be called an anti-American position on Australian alliance relations.

To be fair, Latham did not make Iraq or the alliance with the United States a central issue in the ALP's 2004 election campaign; his pledge to have troops home by Christmas was made in April 2004, well before the federal election. This early announcement possibly was timed precisely so it would not be a central issue in the federal election scheduled for later that year. Most of Latham's more inflammatory public remarks about the Bush administration were made before he became leader of the ALP on December 2, 2003.

In 2004, Latham tended to play his political cards more cautiously. After his troop-withdrawal pledge was publicly condemned by President Bush in a joint press conference with John Howard on the White House lawn in June 2004, Latham might have been tempted to adopt a more critical position on the Bush administration and its interference in Australian domestic politics. The risks would have been high, however, in terms of public opinion and how the conservative-dominated Australian print media would have reacted to such a decision. Latham also was criticized by Colin Powell and Richard Armitage, with the latter going so far as to claim that Latham's position on the Iraq war threatened the free trade agreement between the two countries. Armitage also pointedly asked Australians to consider life without the defense shield America provides.[15]

However, as Latham biographer Bernard Lagan contends, ALP polling showed that threatening

Australia's defense alliance with America "would be electoral poison for Latham."[16] It seems that such polls and the counsel of his foreign affairs spokesman dissuaded Latham as opposition leader from criticizing the alliance. However, as Prime Minister, Latham's confessed negativity about the alliance could well have come to the fore.

The public reaction to such negativity, and Latham's general direction as a Prime Minister had he been elected, are both difficult to divine. It is hard to know how much store to place in the *Latham Diaries* because they were written, and probably reconstructed, by a frustrated individual who completely cut his ties with the ALP in 2005 and dramatically abandoned parliament. In his diaries, Latham is extremely critical of his former colleagues, particularly Kim Beazley and Kevin Rudd. Of Rudd, he all but calls him the Maryland candidate with "some missing periods in his [curriculum vitae]."[17] On the alliance more specifically, he is also dismissive. He calls it "the last manifestation of the White Australia mentality. Sacrificing Australian pride and independence...."[18] Without any justification offered, he calculates that "the Americans need us more than we need them" and that New Zealand has the right policy on the United States.[19] These comments would have their supporters within the academy and within segments of the ALP and the electorate in general; however, they are far from being mainstream views, as the polls suggest. At present, such views are voiced in the Australian federal parliament only by the Greens (and maybe a few of the Democrats), but certainly not the current ALP leadership.

However, could they become part of the post-Howard policy response to the U.S.-Australia alliance? This seems possible although not likely. The public seems comfortable enough to hear politicians criticize the Bush administration and the Americanization of Australian public policy and culture, but the data suggest that Australians would be uncomfortable with a politician who seriously jeopardized the alliance.

In summary, Latham's views on the alliance are politically aberrant within elite circles, despite representing the attitudes of a sizable minority of the Australian populace. Concerns about the alliance more generally play into a band of Australian nationalism that is agitating for Australia to find a more independent voice or less pro-American voice. This nationalism is a work in progress, with public discourse and the politicians at the helm making quite significant rhetorical shifts during the evolution from the Keating government to that of Howard. This volatility makes the future shape of Australian nationalism and the role of the alliance within it difficult to predict with confidence. What does seem reasonable to predict, in the short term at least, is that unless Kim Beazley and Kevin Rudd depart from their respective positions as ALP leader and foreign affairs spokesman, skepticism or outright antipathy toward the Australia-American alliance will remain a largely marginalized undercurrent of Australian political life.

ENDNOTES - CHAPTER 9

1. U.S. Secretary of State Rice is fond of telling foreign leaders that "we have no better friend than. . . . See Mark Glassman, "The Best (Almost) of Friends," *New York Times*, May 7, 2006.

2. Andrew Kohut and Bruce Stokes, *America Against the World*, New York, Times Books, 2006.

3. Clive Bean, Ian McAllister, Rachel Gibson, and David Gow, *Australian Election Study*, SSDA Study 1079, 2004.

4. *Ibid.*

5. Lowy Institute, *Australians Speak 2005*, Sydney, 2005.

6. Greg Sheridan, "Public Opinion Is Putty in Academic Hands," *Australian*, March 29, 2005; "Poll-er Opposites," *The Review*, Australia/Israel and Jewish Affairs Council, May, 2005, *www.aijac.org.au/review/2005/30-5/mm30-5.html*.

7. Philip Everts, "Images of the U.S. – Three Theories of Anti-Americanism," European Consortium for Political Research, Joint Sessions of Workshops, Cyprus, 2006, pp. 25, 29; Brendon O'Connor, "What Is Anti-Americanism?" in Brendon O'Connor, ed., *Anti-Americanism* (Vol. 1), Oxford, Greenwood, 2007.

8. *Ibid.*, p. 34.

9. Brendon O'Connor and Martin Griffiths, eds., *The Rise of Anti-Americanism*, London: Routledge, 2006; Brendon O'Connor, ed., *Anti-Americanism*, Four Volumes, Oxford: Greenwood, forthcoming.

10. John Zaller, *The Nature and Origins of Mass Opinion*, Cambridge: Cambridge University Press, 1992.

11. Mark Latham, Address to the House of Representatives, Canberra, February 5, 2003.

12. Maxine McKew, "Tom Schieffer United States Ambassador," *The Bulletin*, February 12, 2003.

13. Ross Peake, "Latham Backs US Alliance," *The Canberra Times*, December 5, 2003.

14. The phrase was used to describe Howard Dean's widely broadcast reaction to his poor showing in the 2004 Iowa caucuses.

15. Bernard Lagan, *Loner*, Sydney: Allen & Unwin, 2005, pp. 88-89.

16. *Ibid.*, p. 89.

17. Mark Latham, *The Latham Diaries*, Melbourne: Melbourne University Press, 2005, pp. 211-212.

18. *Ibid.*, p. 393.

19. *Ibid.*

PANEL IV

ECONOMIC AND BUSINESS ASPECTS
OF THE SPECIAL RELATIONSHIP

CHAPTER 10

PANEL IV CHAIRMAN'S INTRODUCTION

Brendan Taylor

Economic and business factors relate to alliance politics in a number of ways. On the one hand, they often can act as the glue that helps to hold alliance relationships together. A number of studies, for instance, identify a strong correlation between alliance structures and trading patterns.[1] The United States, in particular, has in recent years either negotiated or begun negotiating Free Trade Agreements (FTA) with a number of it close friends and allies in the Asia-Pacific region—including Australia, Singapore, Thailand (with much difficulty), and most recently South Korea— partly as a reward for the support these countries have provided during the so-called Long War. At the same time, however, economic and business factors also can undermine even the closest alliance relationships. There is perhaps no better example of this than the period of severe trade tensions between Washington and Tokyo during the late 1980s and early 1990s, which shook that bilateral security relationship to its very core.[2]

It is somewhat surprising, therefore, that the economic and business aspects of the U.S.-Australia alliance traditionally have been among the least studied and understood dimensions of that relationship. With few exceptions,[3] the Australia-United States Free Trade Agreement (AUSFTA) is the only economic and business-related aspect of the special relationship to have been subjected to serious analytical attention in recent years.[4] This is so notwithstanding the obvious degree of interconnectedness—one might even go so far as to describe it as interdependence—between the economic and business aspects of the special relationship and the range of other political, legal, and strategic dimensions of that relationship considered in this volume. For this reason alone, Leif Rosenberger's and Don Russell's chapters (Chapters 11 and 12, respectively) mark important contributions to the already substantial and still expanding body of work on the U.S.-Australia alliance.

If one accepts the proposition that economic and business factors can impact alliance cohesion negatively, then at least four issues emerge from Rosenberger's and Russell's analyses. First and foremost is the increasing divergence in American and Australian approaches to China's economic rise—a divergence which, interestingly, is evident in Rosenberger's and Russell's contributions to this volume. Although this noticeable gap between Australian optimism and American ambivalence is unlikely to fracture the alliance completely, at least over the short-to-medium term, it can on occasion create disharmony and misunderstanding between Canberra and Washington. During a joint press conference in June 2005, for example, President George W. Bush alluded to differences between the United States and China over issues of values, particularly in relation to freedom of worship, which prompted an immediate reply from Prime Minister John Howard that the Sino-Australian relationship was mature enough to ride through temporary arguments over human rights, and that he remained "unashamed" in developing Australia's economic relations with China.[5] Likewise, Foreign Minister Hon. Alexander Downer's August 2004 comments on the questionable applicability of the Australia-New Zealand-U.S. (ANZUS) treaty to a Taiwan Straits contingency may be seen as a direct manifestation of Canberra's differing perceptions regarding the nature and level of importance assigned to its economic relationship with China.[6]

Second, concerns are beginning to mount in Washington regarding the political and strategic implications of the new commercial relationships that China is forging with traditionally close friends of the United States, including Australia. Washington certainly is attuned to the symbolism of having one of its nearest and dearest allies seduced into the Chinese embrace and to the message this potentially could send to America's other Asia-Pacific security partners. Beyond this symbolic aspect, however, U.S. concerns also pertain to the broader geopolitical ramifications of China's growing energy ties with Australia. Referring specifically to the Sino-Australian relationship, for instance, a widely-cited National Intelligence Council report forecasts that "the relationship between gas suppliers and consumers is likely to be particularly strong because of the restrictions on delivery mechanisms," and that this will have the effect of "reinforc[ing] regional alliances."[7] Because of China's poor proliferation record—and despite assurances to the contrary from the Howard government—Washington is also somewhat uneasy with the recent signing of a nuclear safeguards treaty between Canberra and Beijing, which has paved the way for the export of Australian uranium to China for peaceful purposes.

Third is the sustainability of increased defense expenditures made possible by trade with China. One of the great ironies of this burgeoning Sino-Australian engagement, of course, is the indirect financial contribution it is making toward enabling the most significant upgrading of Australia's defense forces in at least 4 decades. As Rosenberger observes, however, serious questions remain as to the longer-term life expectancy of the associated rise in Australian defense outlays. In addition to this concern, Australia's growing technological dependence upon the United States also promises to have significant financial implications — as the escalating cost of the Joint Strike Fighter (JSF) project already demonstrates.[8]

To be sure, in the absence of its special relationship with the United States, Australia almost certainly would have to spend significantly more than the 1.9 percent of gross domestic product (GDP) that it currently spends for defense. That said, whether Canberra can afford to conceive of its defense requirements indefinitely in the comprehensive manner it presently does — partly in response to the expectations of its American ally — or whether some of those requirements ultimately will have to be underwritten at the expense of others, will become an issue of growing importance in the future of the special relationship.

Fourth, public perceptions of the economic and business aspects of the special relationship do not augur well, particularly on the Australian side. After much initial hype, for instance, Australian news media coverage of the AUSFTA has been predominantly critical.[9] While, as earlier chapters of this volume have shown, rising anti-American sentiment is a complex phenomenon that generally is not attributable to any single causal factor, the negative press coverage of the AUSFTA certainly has done little to assuage the popular perception that Australia has received little in return for its loyalty as shown in the Long War. The simmering political debate in Canberra over whether

Australia should commit to purchasing the JSF in light of unit cost increases and delivery delays likely will add fuel to this fire, particularly in the lead-up to the 2008 deadline by which Canberra is required to reach a final decision.[10]

While it is certainly true that governments during the post-Cold War era have had greater latitude to pursue commercial interests free from the shackles of strategic allegiance, it is still worth recalling here that America's surprisingly resilient network of bilateral alliances in the Asia-Pacific was forged initially through an unusual political bargain wherein Washington offered its junior partners substantial economic benefits in return for asymmetrical security concessions.[11] As Kent Calder concludes, however, a key variable in the continued persistence of this system in general—and for the U.S.-Australia special relationship in particular—is whether there will be "leaders with the vision . . . to look beyond the immediate future to forge a renewed strategic bargain, as their forebears did so ably more than half a century ago."[12]

On the road to that renewed strategic bargain, what steps might usefully be taken to strengthen and sustain the special relationship? Three recommendations of direct relevance to the economic and business dimensions of that relationship are offered:

- Greater time, energy, and resources need to be devoted to studying the economic and business aspects of the special relationship. As noted at the beginning of this chapter, economic and business factors relate to alliance politics in multiple ways. Yet insufficient analytical attention has thus far been given to understanding and explaining the dynamics of these numerous economics-security linkages as they are manifested in the context of the special relationship. If the proposition that economic and business factors can impact negatively upon alliance cohesion is to be taken seriously, then this deficiency requires urgent rectification.

- The precise nature and potential strategic implications of growing Sino-Australian inter-dependence also needs to be studied much more assiduously. Apparently seduced by the attractive commercial and political opportunities presented by China's economic rise, the Howard Government has spent little time (publicly at least) dwelling upon the potentially negative geopolitical implications of China's growing energy ties with Australia. Interestingly, however, Russell's chapter suggests that deepening Sino-Australian interdependence is by no means a one-way street, and that China's growing resource dependence actually might constitute a potential source of leverage for Australia. This novel observation certainly warrants further exploration, if only to address Washington's growing concerns regarding China's deepening commercial ties with close American friends and allies such as Australia.

- Greater sensitivity needs to be shown towards public perceptions of the economic and business aspects of the special relationship, particularly from the American side. The ongoing implementation of the AUSFTA and the progress of the JSF project each threaten to have a corrosive effect on Australian public perceptions of the United States if not handled carefully. As Russell suggests, however, greater efforts also are needed on Australia's part to better understand America's distinctive trade negotiation techniques and to exploit the existing provisions of the AUSFTA in the interests of maximizing its potential benefit to Australia. While, in the final analysis, the pending establishment of a dedicated U.S. Studies Center in Australia certainly will go some way toward realizing greater American sensitivity to the feelings of its ally down under,[13] achievement of greater understanding by Australia will necessitate a shift in its bureaucratic culture which appears—for reasons articulated by Russell—rather unlikely.

ENDNOTES - CHAPTER 10

1. For a review of this literature, see Andrew G. Long and Brett Ashley Leeds, "Trading for Security: Military Alliances and Economic Agreements," *Journal of Peace Research*, Vol. 43, No. 4, 2006, pp. 433-451.

2. For further reading, see Edward J. Lincoln, *Troubled Times: U.S.-Japan Trade Relations in the 1990s*, Washington, DC: Brookings Institution Press, 1999.

3. The most notable being John Ravenhill, "Allies But Not Friends: The Economic Relationship," *Australian Journal of International Affairs*, Vol. 55, No. 2, 2001, pp. 249-259.

4. See, for example, Ann Capling, *All the Way with the USA: Australia, the US and Free Trade*, Sydney: University of New South Wales Press, 2005.

5. Transcript of the Prime Minister The Hon. John Howard MP, Joint Press Conference with The President of the United States of America George W. Bush, The White House, Washington, DC, July 19, 2005.

6. Brendan Taylor, "U.S.-China Relations after September 11: A Long Engagement or Marriage of Convenience?" *Australian Journal of International Affairs*, Vol. 59, No. 2, June 2005, p. 194.

7. National Intelligence Council, *Mapping the Global Future: Report of the National Intelligence Council's 2020 Project*, Washington, DC: U.S. Government Printing Office, 2004, p. 62.

8. John Kerin, "Australia Agrees to Buy US Fighter, Cost Unknown," *Australian Financial Review*, March 31, 2006, p. 30.

9. See, for example, Michael Costello, "Done Like a Dinner on Free Trade Deal," *The Australian*, January 6, 2006, p. 10.

10. For further reading, see Hugh White, "It's the Fighter We Have to Have," *Sydney Morning Herald*, July 19, 2006, p. 11.

11. For further reading, see Kent E. Calder, "Securing Security Through Prosperity: The San Francisco System in Comparative Perspective," *The Pacific Review*, Vol. 17, No. 1, March 2004, pp.135-157.

12. *Ibid.*, p.153.

13. Chris Barrie and Paul Dibb, "Northern Exposure: Why We Also Need to Know Our Friends," *Sydney Morning Herald*, May 26, 2006, p. 11.

CHAPTER 11

THE UNITED STATES AND AUSTRALIA: COMPETING ECONOMIC PERSPECTIVES

Leif Rosenberger

INTRODUCTION

At first glance, the U.S.-Australian alliance has never been stronger.[1] Australia demonstrated its unwavering commitment to the United States immediately after the terrorist attack on September 11, 2001 (9/11), on the World Trade Center in New York City. Australian soldiers are fighting shoulder to shoulder with U.S. military forces in Iraq and Afghanistan. In fact, Australia remains America's most steadfast Asian ally in support of U.S.-led operations in Iraq. U.S. President George W. Bush and Australian Prime Minister John Howard are known to be close personally.[2] On the commercial front, the United States and Australia recently celebrated the first anniversary of the U.S.-Australian free trade agreement (AUSFTA). In addition, American and Australian businessmen have close and extensive ties.[3]

Nevertheless, the United States and Australia are facing some immediate economic challenges and several potentially difficult ones over the horizon that will test the resiliency of the relationship. This chapter explores the nature and extent of these economic and financial challenges. It begins with a look at the contrasting ways the United States and Australia view the economic rise of China. On balance, Washington today views China as more of a commercial threat. In contrast, most Australians view China as a commercial blessing critical to a booming Australian economic performance.

In terms of U.S.-Australian bilateral trade, Australians have reason to view the initial phase of USAFTA as the big buildup for the big letdown. After a year, U.S. merchandise exports were up, Australian exports were down. But even if the costs and benefits could somehow be equalized, I explain in this chapter why the mishmash of bilateral free trade agreements elsewhere actually reduces global free trade, undermines efficient international business models, and is an expensive throwback to the days when each product was built 100 percent in one place. Despite the collapse of the World Trade Organization (WTO) global trade talks, the world needs a coherent global FTA more than ever, rather than a hodgepodge of bilateral FTAs that undercut each other.

While the pervasive Australian view of trade with China is overwhelmingly positive, a few Australians see limits to shared prosperity with China even in the robust energy sector. In addition, a few Australians see China as a commercial threat to at least some of its industries. In this sense, there may be some small convergence among a small segment of Australian businessmen and a larger group of Americans about a perceived Chinese commercial threat.

Interestingly enough, U.S. and Australian responses to China's commercial challenges are strikingly different. Australia, possessing a relatively small economy, chooses to compete with rather than retreat from Chinese commercial products. In contrast, the U.S. superpower is quick to blame China for its huge trade deficit, looks for ways to retaliate, and if need be retreats into protectionism rather than competes with China.

The chapter then looks at the different ways the United States and Australia deal with China in the closely related energy sector. In general, the pervasive Aussie view is that Australia benefits from the shared prosperity generated by trade in China's energy sector, while the United States is more nationalistic and feels threatened by it. But again, a few Australians are discovering there are limits to what Australia can expect to receive from the Chinese market even in the booming resource area, especially when it comes to liquid natural gas (LNG).

Finally, the chapter looks at two potentially difficult issues that could challenge the U.S.-Australian special relationship on down the road. Regarding the first issue, the chapter explores the economic and financial components of Australia's response to the rise of violent extremism. As such extremism erupts in Australia's back yard, Canberra may no longer have the luxury of satisfying rising U.S. expectations for steadfast Australian support in far-flung areas of the world. In addition to *where* Australia chooses to address violent extremism Canberra needs to decide *how* it will deal with the problem. Will Prime Minster Howard keep taking his cue from President Bush, who basically sees the world divided between good and evil? What's the best way to deal with terrorists in Iraq, Afghanistan, or anywhere else?

The Bush administration says the forces of freedom and democracy need to confront terrorism with counterviolence, and they will back down. Many Asian leaders argue that this is the wrong way to deal with violent extremism. They ask different questions: Why are these people so frustrated that they need to resort to violence to change the status quo? What are their grievances? How can we address the social and economic conditions that foster violent extremism and reduce their demand for violence? Australia's view is not the same as America's view. But as to the particular issues on which Australia will take a stand, it remains to be seen.

With regard to the second issue, the chapter looks at the ongoing economic and financial instability in New Zealand. Canberra cares deeply about New Zealand's fate. New Zealand's economic and financial problems could threaten Australia if not handled properly. Frankly, the United States has its hands full trying to dig out of extraordinarily expensive black holes in Iraq, Afghanistan, and now Lebanon. In this sense, the United States and Australia have totally different national interests when it comes to New Zealand. What's arguably vital to Australia's prosperity is tertiary at best to the increasingly embattled and overextended U.S. superpower.

ECONOMIC RISE OF CHINA

In an interview marking his 10th anniversary in office, Prime Minister John Howard highlighted the rising Sino-Australian economic relationship.[4] He said Australia "would be crazy" not to cultivate its economic relationship with China. He added that China was a "huge and valuable market" for Australia. In that same interview, Howard brushed aside American concerns over Sino-Australian ties. He underscored that Australia would "not go overboard" with China. That said, Howard rolled out the red carpet for Chinese officials in Australia. And Beijing did much the same when Howard visited China in late June and early July 2006.

Of course, President Bush also knows how to roll out the red carpet, which he did for Japanese Prime

Minister Koizumi in June 2006. In contrast, Bush's treatment of Chinese President Hu was distinctly muted during his visit in April 2006. Moreover, Michael Green, former NSC Director for Asia, and China expert Bates Gill criticized the Bush-Hu meeting as being form over substance at a time when a serious summit was desperately needed to reconcile divisive U.S.-Chinese issues.[5] Even the form of the meeting was troubled. The Bush administration refused to classify it as a "state" visit, instead calling it a "working lunch." Beijing was justifiably offended, feeling it deserved the kind of political treatment commensurate with its status as a major global economy.

China now has almost $1 trillion in foreign reserves. Most of these Chinese reserves are denominated in U.S. dollar obligations that allow the United States, on such borrowed money, to pursue the wars in Iraq and Afghanistan and the war on terrorists without raising taxes and without any sacrifice for the American consumer. China also is a major trading partner of the United States. Chinese political leaders have every right to ask: Where is the gratitude? And in an administration that carefully choreographs every detail and every person invited to the White House, Hu was subjected to prolonged heckling by a Falun Gong protester at the opening ceremony. Even worse was the introduction of the Chinese national anthem as that of the "Republic of China," the formal name for Taiwan. In short, Hu did not receive the consideration he deserved.

To be fair, Hu did get to meet Bill Gates, Chairman and founder of Microsoft and the richest man in the world. In fact, Hu spent much time with members of the U.S. business community, reflecting China's interest in advancing the already huge U.S.-China commercial relationship. Go into any Wal-Mart, and you will see that the store is flooded with products made in China, a fact now much discussed among U.S. shoppers. In this regard, China will soon overtake Japan as the America's third-biggest export market. U.S. exports to China rose nearly 37 percent in the first 5 months of 2006 from a year earlier.[6] Furthermore, American companies operating in China had another year of strong profits in 2005, with U.S.-affiliated companies enjoying record earnings of $3.2 billion.

That said, corporate America goes out of its way to hide its successes in China. Why hide a U.S. corporate success story? U.S. Undersecretary of Commerce for International Trade Franklin Lavin says the U.S. export strength tends to get "washed out of people's minds" because imports from China are so much larger.[7] The United States reported an $82 billion trade deficit with China for the first 5 months of 2006. The news media are quick to bash China for this imbalance. CNN's Lou Dobbs frequently criticizes U.S. corporations that are allegedly exporting U.S. jobs to China. Given all this negative publicity in the United States about the China link to outsourcing and manufacturing job losses, it makes U.S. corporations unpopular if they talk about doing well in China. Such economic nationalism has taken its toll on U.S. foreign direct investment (FDI) in China, which dropped 22.3 percent in 2005 from $3.9 billion in 2004 to $3 billion in 2005.

In contrast, Australian exports of raw materials to China create jobs in Australia and is thus a political winner. U.S. commercial relations with China, however, is, as we saw above, a political loser. Lou Dobbs would argue that Chinese exports to the United States kill U.S. jobs. While Bill Gates and Microsoft are big enough to ignore Lou Dobbs, most U.S. corporations want to fly under the radar screen and hide their hand in dealing with China. Similarly, Under Secretary Lavin says, "Politically, strong U.S. exports to China are less salient since imports [from China] are so high."[8]

In this regard, the U.S. trade deficit with China is never properly understood in the United States. If we take a broader view, the U.S. trade deficit with all of Asia has not changed much in the past 10 years. The United States used to have large trade deficits with countries like Japan and South Korea. But then China actually did what the U.S. Government asked it to do. China opened its economy up to FDI. Now, the final assembly of products that used to occur in Japan and South Korea is happening in China. It thus stands to reason that the so-called Chinese trade surplus has risen in partial response to this change in final assembly of foreign products in China. Two-thirds of Chinese exports are from foreign-funded or wholly-owned foreign companies based in China. Ninety percent of Chinese high-tech exports are from these foreign companies based in China.[9]

The United States, however, blames the Chinese trade surplus on China pegging its weak currency to the U.S. dollar in order to underprice its exports. The United States argues that the 2.1 percent revaluation of Chinese currency in July 2005 was a drop in the bucket. Senators Charles Schumer and Lindsey Graham threatened to impose a 20-30 percent tariff on all Chinese goods coming into the United States unless China revalues by a similar percentage. The United States threatens to make formal charges of currency manipulation against China if it refuses to enact a bigger revaluation. In contrast, Australia is not about to bite the Chinese hand that buys its exports. Thus, while the Sino-Australian political economy is relatively warm and fuzzy, the U.S.-Chinese political economy is ice cold.

Sino-Australian Shared Prosperity.

Now let's carry further the comparison between the Sino-Australia economic relationship and that of China and the United States. Australia's commodity and service exports to China are booming. In contrast, the United States is losing the economic high ground as a principal trader with Australia. Sino-Australian merchandise trade has skyrocketed 248 percent between 2000 and 2005. In contrast, U.S.-Australian trade has been virtually flat—growing only 13 percent between 2000 and 2005. Five years ago Australia traded with the United States at double the rate with China. Today the situation has precisely reversed itself.[10] From a trade perspective, therefore, China is more important to Australia than is the United States.

China's emergence as the world's manufacturing center largely has been abetted by its trading partner to the south. Australia is supplying much of the iron ore, nonferrous metals, coal, and higher education that fuel China's industrial revolution. In this regard, the economic growth of China and its impact on the world's demand for resources is the single most important factor driving Australia's outstanding export performance. Aussie exports of natural resources to China alone surged by 87 percent to $8.3 billion in 2005, with iron ore a good case in point. The tonnage of Australian exports to China tripled between 2002 and 2005 to 112 million tons. And thanks to China's enormous demand, global prices have surged as well. Prices of Australia's iron ore increased 71 percent in 2005 with a further 19 percent hike in 2006.[11]

Thus the continued economic growth in China provides a vital underpinning for Australia's trade performance and economy. Australia's Reserve Bank

Governor Ian MacFarlane recently stated that in the past 3 years, the value of Australia's trade has increased by around 30 percent. He pinpointed global demand for resources and the rise of China as being the driving factors.[12] The economic effects include strong growth in business investment, rising corporate profits, and an increase in stock prices. The strong demand from China has continued in 2006. In the 10 months prior to April 2006, Australian exports to China soared to a value of 14.5 billion in U.S. dollar equivalents, a 42 percent rise compared to the same period last year.[13] The result is a dilemma for Canberra. It must somehow strike a balance between its increasingly important commercial relationship with China and its long-standing security ties to the United States.

U.S.-Australian Free Trade Agreement (FTA).

To make matters worse for the United States, the Aussies view the greatly ballyhooed USFTA (that went into effect on January 1, 2005) as a big dissappointment.[14] In 2005, Aussie exports to the United States fell by 4.7 percent while U.S. exports to Australia rose by 5.7 percent.[15] But even if the costs and benefits could somehow be evened out, the FTA must be seen in the broader context of the bewildering mishmash of bilateral trade accords that threaten global free trade and efficient international business models. The "Asian noodle bowl" of competing, overlapping bilateral and multilateral trade deals generally hampers rather than facilitates free trade. The Asian Development Bank calculates there are 15 trade and investment initiatives in Asia, all signed since 1998, with a further 20 under negotiation, and at least 16 more proposed.[16] These trade deals divert trade from one country or region to another. Complex clauses, especially those governing rules of origin, create a bureaucratic tangle that sometimes zeros out trade altogether.

Bilateral free trade agreements—like the one between the United States and Australia—are inappropriate and obsolete throwbacks to the old days when a product was built in one factory, under one roof, and in one country, before it was exported and sold in another country. Times have changed, and manufacturing is different these days. Production is now dispersed across different factories in different countries. At each stage of production, parts and materials come from optimized but highly variable locations. Multiple factories in several different countries are used to keep costs down. This process enables more locations worldwide to contribute. Countries get into the game by providing just one or two pieces of the production value chain. Unfortunately, bilateral trade agreements like the AUSFTA tend to be discriminatory, thus distorting and degrading this highly efficient and democratic global business model.

COMPETING THREAT PERCEPTIONS

In contrast to Australia, the realists who dominate China policy in Washington tend to perceive China as both a commercial as well as a military threat. In their eyes, the economic rise of China drives the rise of Chinese military power. They see China's charm offensive and shared prosperity with U.S. allies and friends in Asia as part of an overall Chinese military strategy.[17] At the strategic level, however, this shared prosperity between Australia and other countries in Asia arguably gives Beijing a stake in stability and makes war less likely than when China was not a main actor on the world's trade and economic stage. But if war breaks out between China and Taiwan, China's shared prosperity in the region increases the risk for the United States due to possible denial of access to U.S. bases, transit routes, markets, etc. In August 2004, Australian Foreign Minister Downer publicly told the Chinese in Beijing that Australia was not bound to help the United States defend Taiwan in a China-Taiwan war. Today, 2 years after Downer's comment, Australia's trade with China dwarfs its trade with the United States. Australia will try hard to appease the United States, while bending over backwards not to antagonize China and jeopardize its highly prized economic relationship with that country.

The United States, more than ever, needs access to bases and friendly shores in Australia and other sites in the Asia-Pacific area in the event of a China-Taiwan war because of the widening gap between a rising Chinese defense economy and a falling Taiwan defense economy. China's economy starts by being four to five times larger than Taiwan's economy, and for the past 10 years China's economy has been growing twice as fast as that of Taiwan. According to the Pentagon, China's much larger and faster growing economy has been spending more on defense as a percentage of GDP than Taiwan.

As if that were not bad enough, in January 2006 Taiwan's legislature made its biggest budget cuts in a decade, with the defense budget, which had been growing at only 2.3 percent of GDP, taking the biggest hit. Instead of boosting defense spending to 3 percent of GDP to keep pace with the Chinese military buildup, Taiwan's legislature actually slashed funds for planned arms acquisitions, which already had been delayed for more than a year. At a time when the

China-Taiwan military balance keeps getting worse from a U.S. perspective, Australia and other countries in the region will think twice before they throw away vital commercial ties to a China that is over-matching Taiwan so rapidly.

COMPETING U.S.-AUSTRALIAN ENERGY PERSPECTIVES

Washington also sees China as a threat on the energy front. Such U.S. economic nationalism was visible in 2005 when China National Offshore Oil Corporation (CNOOC), a 70 percent Chinese government-owned company, made a $19.6 billion offer to buy Union Oil Company of California (or UNOCAL), of the U.S. oil and gas group.[18] It was the biggest overseas bid at that time by a Chinese company, the first to trigger a contested takeover battle with Chevron and the first to be made in a politically sensitive strategic sector in the United States.

Most U.S. lawmakers argued that in deciding whether to approve or disapprove, the U.S. Government should evaluate the CNOOC bid on traditional national security grounds. Harboring mental images of CNOOC somehow hoarding Unocal energy for Chinese consumers, they argued that CNOOC threatened U.S. energy security. In the end, the U.S. Congress effectively blocked any Chinese takeover of UNOCAL.

U.S. lawmakers were ill-advised. Their fears are at odds with how the global energy market actually works. For starters, oil is a fungible commodity. For every barrel of oil China might divert for its exclusive use, China would import one less barrel of oil from other sources. Global prices and availability of oil to the United States would remain exactly as before. While denial of access to oil can be used as a military tool in wartime, access depends not on ownership, but on the ability to secure petroleum installations and blockade oil lanes. China is vastly more vulnerable to an oil squeeze than the United States, with the unchallenged U.S. Seventh Fleet commanding the Pacific. A national security issue does exist here, but China would be the one at risk. CNOOC was taking a big commercial risk as well as a strategic risk: If Sino-U.S. hostilities erupted, its proposed U.S. investment would be an early casualty.

U.S. efforts to block PRC takeovers of U.S. companies play into the hands of PRC communist hardliners. They argue that China must prepare for an inevitable confrontation with the United States because it will never permit China to enjoy a peaceful economic flowering. The U.S. needs to undercut that the PRC hardliners' position with evidence to the contrary.

For years the United States criticized Indonesia for its nationalistically-operated oil industry when Jakarta blocked EXXON-Mobil's efforts to buy Indonesian energy assets. Just recently, however, the United States was successful in persuading Indonesia to open its oil reserves to Exxon-Mobil. The United States has a strong interest in persuading countries like Indonesia to open their oil reserves to U.S. investors. It is, therefore, inconsistent for the United States to criticize the Indonesians for nationalism in its oil industry if the United States is similarly nationalistic in blocking foreign investment in the U.S. oil industry. This is the U.S. double standard and hypocrisy at its worst. The United States not only expects to make the rules but also expects to make the exceptions to the rules — China must open its markets to U.S. and foreign investment, but the United States has the right to keep its markets closed to China.

Sino-Australian Energy Ties.

Now let's contrast the U.S.-China tension on the energy front with Sino-Australia energy relations, looking first at nuclear energy. In early April 2006, China and Australia signed a nuclear safeguards treaty, which punctuates an increasingly important economic relationship. The treaty could pave the way for exports of uranium to China for peaceful uses. China is searching for new supplies of uranium as part of its strategy to diversify energy sources, placing less reliance on coal-fired power stations. As part of its New Year economic blueprint, China is committed to reducing air pollution and dependence on coal. By 2020 China hopes to increase by four-fold the amount of nuclear energy it produces. Australian Prime Minister Howard has said that Washington's efforts to curb nuclear enrichment worldwide may even be at odds with the energy requirements of Australia.[19]

In late June 2006, the Prime Ministers of China and Australia, Wen Jiabao and Howard, proudly presided over the arrival in China of the first commercial shipment of liquefied natural gas (LNG). Mr. Howard called the LNG shipment, part of an $18 billion contract guaranteeing supplies for 25 years, the largest single trade deal ever for Australia and "hugely significant" for its resource-dependent export industries. He said it could be the beginning of an enormous additional part of Australia's trade with China.

Limits to Sino-Australian Energy Cooperation.

While Australia's pervasive perception of China as a golden commercial opportunity will no doubt continue, Australia also is learning that there are limits to what it can expect from China, even in the booming resource trade. For example, the red-carpet reception of the LNG tanker in late June 2006 only momentarily masked the disappointment in both China and Australia over how the gas market has stalled in China since the 2002 signing of two contracts with suppliers in Australia such as Australian Woodside Petroleum. China has failed to negotiate any further LNG deals, balking at paying a price higher than that paid in the initial deal. Beijing has pressed Australian for a discounted price on the grounds that China would be an excellent long-term market. Such pressure tactics have been mirrored in other commodity sectors such as iron ore. China wanted to emulate the 2002 deal with Australian Woodside Petroleum for good reason. That contract locked in LNG against an oil price capped at $20-$25 a barrel. Gas exporters, frustrated and annoyed by the Chinese stance, resisted, instead selling most of their available resources to Japan and South Korea, with other supplies earmarked for the United States.

Australia: Beyond Shared Prosperity with China.

While Australia's political culture is enthusiastically accommodative of the shared prosperity with China, the U.S. political culture dwells on China as a commercial threat. But Australia also is becoming aware that China poses a commercial threat to at least some industries. In fact, Canberra finally is developing a plan for responding to the Chinese commercial threat rather than simply basking in an aura of Sino-Australian shared prosperity. Mr. Howard is reviewing policy and developing a new plan to reposition existing industries and bolster support for new sectors. Canberra also is studying how the rise of China now requires an Australian economic strategy that extends beyond the resources boom.[20]

Australian official Ian MacFarlane is soliciting input from Aussie business leaders, a key part of which will come in early 2007 when Australia's business community releases its industry statement. This will be the first such Australian industry projection since "Investing for Growth" (1997), which foreshadowed a $1 billion increase in industry policy funding, including expanded funding for research and development.

Since the last industry statement, Canberra has approached policy issues on a problem-specific basis. As a result, the business community increasingly senses what it views as government drift on policy direction. Businesses claim Canberra is content to just ride the resources boom instead of using its new revenue windfall to strengthen and diversify the economy while preparing a post-boom economic policy.

Canberra's new plan addresses some of these criticisms from the business community, e.g., by seeking to boost productivity in workplaces. Canberra's initiative comes only after the release of a report by the Australian Industry Group stating that up to 30,000 manufacturing jobs could be lost in 2007 due to competitive pressures created by the rise of China. The Industry Group seeks a range of initiatives from Canberra to include tax cuts and export incentives.

While Canberra is starting to see China in a more mixed light, that is, as a commercial threat as well as a commercial opportunity, its response differs from that of the United States. The United States sees a larger and more serious commercial threat, openly blames China and seeks economic sanctions to protect against what it sees as unfair competition. In contrast, Australians are more sanguine and seek ways to boost their competitiveness rather than retreat from China's commercial challenge.

FIGHTING VIOLENT EXTREMISM
AND TERRORISM: WHERE AND HOW?

Another critical issue is Australia's approach to terrorism and violent extremism and the degree to which it meshes with the U.S. approach.[21] As stated earlier, this issue has two economic components. First is the issue of affordability. Australia finds it difficult to underwrite its obligations under the U.S. alliance, making the outlays necessary to meet the rising challenges in the South Pacific and Southeast Asia.[22]

This may seem odd because at first glance. In the first quarter of 2003, Australia's economy grew at its fastest pace in 18 months, and that pace has continued. Strong growth is good news for the defense budget. Australia's defense budget is set to rise 11 percent to $19 million in 2007. Canberra also is committing itself to increases of 3 percent a year from 2008 to 2016. Sustaining such defense spending is financially feasible for Canberra if growth remains strong, tax revenues stay high, and defense budget targets are realistic.

However, Canberra is already concerned about the rising costs of helping regional states in difficulty. Current defense budget projections may not be enough for multiple overseas deployments. With 1,000 troops now deployed in East Timor, the Aussie military/police presence in South Pacific is now at its highest level since World War II. Aussie involvement in the Solomon Islands alone is costing about $ 150 million a year, a relatively large sum to spend on a small nation of just 600,000 people. Australia is in danger of being pulled into regional hotspots for years to come.[23] Violent extremism in weak, failing states in its backyard is on the rise. Aussie stabilization missions in the region are expensive and potentially open-ended.

Can rising U.S. expectations be satisfied while Australia simultaneously is being stretched thin in its own backyard? Can Australia remain shoulder to shoulder with the United States in Iraq and Afghanistan—and perhaps elsewhere—if it cannot afford its primary mission of being a regional sheriff in the South Pacific? Critics in Australia already are questioning procurement of "nonessential equipment to fight nonessential wars" that lack manifest links to Australia's core interests.

Closely related to *where* Australia can afford to confront violent extremism is the question of *how* Australia will choose to respond to violent extremism in the future. Will Australia have situational awareness of the underlying social and economic conditions that foster violent extremism? If so, will Australia have a strong social and economic program to counter such extremism? On July 5, 2006, Australian General Duncan Lewis, Special Advisor on Terrorism to Prime Minister Howard, candidly stated that Australia's approach to terrorism was not in accord with that of the United States. Australian military officer Clay Sutton, assigned to the U.S. Pacific Command, echoes these same sentiments. He adds that differences between the United States and Australia are even more pronounced when it comes to counterinsurgency doctrine and strategy.

These are not academic issues. At the Shangri-La Dialogue of Defense Ministers in Singapore in June 2004, U.S. Secretary of Defense Donald Rumsfeld blasted Asian leaders for being soft on terrorism. These Asian leaders pushed back, accusing the United States of fighting the war on terrorism the wrong way.[24] They argued that the United States was insensitive to the underlying social and economic conditions that give rise to terrorism. Southeast Asian leaders said the U.S. approach was radicalizing Asia's Muslims. A few days earlier, Malaysia's new Prime Minister Abdullah Badawi, a former moderate Islamic teacher, said the United States was breeding a new generation of violent extremists by refusing to acknowledge some of the root causes of terrorism. Abdullah spoke from experience, having successfully used a subtle approach to defeat terrorist disturbances in two states of Malaysia by addressing grievances (such as corruption in the ruling party) and trying to calm rising passions. Armed terrorists were captured without deaths on either side. Similarly, former Singapore Prime Minister Goh called for a more balanced and nuanced U.S. approach. Two years later, following the 2006 Shangri-La Dialogue, Indonesia's Defense Minister also criticized Mr. Rumsfeld for much the same reasons.

As Indian Prime Minister Manmohan Singh has demonstrated, it is both possible and advisable to avoid the false dichotomy between hard line and soft line approaches to countering terrorism. Prime Minister Singh's counterinsurgency strategy combines zero tolerance of terrorism with a robust socio-economic strategy that reduces the tendency toward violence. Singh now identifies Maoists as the single greatest threat to Indian national security, but he admits that the rising Maoist insurgency in India is "directly related to underdevelopment." The aim is to curb pervasive perceptions of social and economic injustice and address legitimate grievances which violent Maoists exploit. Similarly, former U.S. Deputy Secretary of State Richard Armitage says: "Americans have been exporting our fears and our anger, not our vision of opportunity and hope." [25] Similarly, the official 9/11 Commission Report persuasively argues that:

When people lose hope, when societies break down, when countries fragment, the breeding grounds for violent extremism are created. Backward economic policies and repressive political regimes slip into societies that are without hope, where ambition and passions have no constructive outlet.[26]

NEW ZEALAND: COMPETING ECONOMIC PRIORITIES

The United States and Australia have different regional economic and financial priorities. Nowhere is this more apparent than in their attitudes and policies toward New Zealand (NZ). Canberra sees an NZ economy that is closely connected to the vitality of Australia's economy. In this regard, Canberra sees the current NZ economic and financial problems as important to Australia's national interests.[27] In contrast, NZ in U.S. eyes is a small economy of little consequence to the United States or the global economy. It's doubtful that Alan Bollard, the NZ Central Bank chief, gets mentioned much in Washington. After all, he oversees an economy small enough to seem like a rounding error to officials at the U.S. Federal Reserve. Nevertheless, America's new U.S. Federal Reserve Chief Ben Bernanke, who replaced Alan Greenspan, could learn a lot from the economic and financial instability in NZ.[28]

For the past year or so, the NZ Central Bank's overzealous war against inflation has destabilized the economy. Interest rates have remained at 7.25 percent since December 2006, by far the highest in the developed world. Money traders poured hot money into NZ as part of a speculative scheme to profiteer from interest rate differentials. These traders borrowed in low-yielding currencies (like the *YEN*) and "invested" in high-yielding currencies like the NZ dollar, or *KIWI*. A huge capital inflow in 2005 helped propel the *KIWI* to a 23-year high against the U.S. dollar in the process.

This painfully strong NZ dollar over-priced NZ's dairy, meat, and timber exports. By the end of 2005, the deficit in current account (trade deficit in goods and services) ballooned to an alarming 8.9 percent of GDP, the highest NZ ratio in 20 years and double NZ's long-term average. Weak exports also raised the risk of recession in 2006-07. A survey of NZ business leaders showed that the business community was the most pessimistic in 20 years.

Jittery foreign investors faced the prospect of large capital losses if the NZ *KIWI* sharply fell against the *YEN* and other currencies before the bonds denominated in KIWIs matured. Due to significant leverage in the positions of foreign exchange traders, currencies could adjust dramatically. The joy ride for investors would end with a financial crisis and capital losses if NZ was unable to cover its huge deficit in the current account of its balance of payments with footloose hot money. That would trigger a run on the KIWI and a free fall in NZ's foreign exchange rate. That grim scenario happened with the fall of Mexico's *PESO* and Thailand's *BAHT* in the 1990s. In any event, the yield spread of *KIWI* bonds over U.S. bonds was likely to narrow as the U.S. Federal Reserve continued to raise interest rates in 2006. Higher U.S. interest rates potentially undermined the appeal of some money trades to currency speculators.

At one point, the NZ Central Bank took the unusual step of warning foreign investors of the high risks of holding *KIWI*-denominated bonds. Central Bank chief Alan Bollard warned investors about two scenarios. In a soft landing, a decline in NZ's exchange rate could be gradual if domestic spending pressures eased.

But in a hard landing, the *KIWI*'s value could go into an abrupt free fall if global investors reassessed the country's attractiveness as an investment destination and triggered a run on a fundamentally overvalued currency that was killing exports.

Investors are aware that GDP growth slowed from 4.3 percent in 2004 to 2.2 percent in 2005, with the downward momentum moving toward a possible recession in 2006-07. NZ's GDP actually fell 0.1 percent each quarter in the final 3 months of 2005, the worst quarterly economic performance in 5 years. Now the concern was a possible run on the *KIWI*. The NZ dollar slumped to a new 22-month low amid fears of recession. Australians got jittery as the NZ currency started to drag down the Australian dollar. It was not clear was how much lower the two currencies would fall. The joy ride that traders had enjoyed by borrowing lower-yielding currencies and buying high-yielding NZ dollars was running out of steam. This once financially attractive interest rate differential was getting less attractive as interest rates rose in both the United States and Europe. The interest rate advantage was now offset by the falling value of the *KIWI*. On March 26, 2006, Lehman Brothers lowered the boom, recommending selling both the NZ and the Australian currencies. Clearly the financial instability that was hammering NZ also was taking its toll on Australia, which recognized a vital interest in stabilizing this economic and financial turmoil. In contrast, Washington was silent.

The upside of these developments could be an orderly decline in the NZ and Australian currencies, which eventually would boost exports by both countries and require less capital inflow in their balance of payments. But there also is a downside risk of a possible run on NZ currency, with a hard landing

210

and recession possible in NZ. The Wall Street herd mentality also could hurt the Australian economy, which was vulnerable due to a similar high current account deficit.

By June 23, 2006, NZ's deficit in the current account (goods and services) of its balance of payments was the worst in 30 years. Soaring oil prices and consumer demand had driven up the value of imports, and corporations were opting for capital flight to protect financial assets. The current account deficit (9.3 percent of GDP) was the highest since the 1975 oil shock. NZ's current account deficit of 9.3 percent of GDP was now far worse than that seen in Thailand and Mexico, which were both running current account deficits of 8 percent of GDP before their financial crises. Standard and Poors warned that NZ's credit rating could be downgraded due to a high and unsustainable current account deficit. The NZ dollar is now one of worst-performing currencies in the world. It lost more than 10 percent of its value against the U.S. dollar in the first quarter of 2006 alone.

In June 2006, NZ companies anticipated more gloomy reports, with a particularly pessimistic outlook for the third quarter of 2006. That added to signs that NZ's economic growth would be the weakest in 7 years, a consequence of record-high interest rates that were curbing spending. About 39 percent of 559 businesses surveyed in June 2006 expected profits to decline over the following 3 months.[29] Finally, the Central Bank expected that economic growth would slow to 1.4 percent in the year ending on September 30, the weakest pace since June 1999.[30]

In July 1997, the United States turned a blind eye to a faltering Thai economy, arguing that it was a small economy of no consequence to the United States or the global economy. Needless to say, Washington was short-sighted, being caught off-guard by the Asian financial crisis. While it now looks more likely that NZ could fall into a recession rather than a full-blown financial crisis, such a crisis cannot be ruled out. Wellington needs a lot of skill and luck to navigate these troubled waters.

Canberra is deeply concerned about the economic and financial instability in NZ. In contrast, a short-sighted U.S. Government is turning it back on this financial and economic turmoil.

ENDNOTES - CHAPTER 11

1. For excellent background on the U.S.-Australian special relationship, see *Peter Edwards, Permanent Friends?: Historical Reflections on the Australian-American Alliance*, Lowy Institute Paper 08, 2005.

2. See Robert Garran, *True Believer: John Howard, George Bush, and the American Alliance*, Sydney: Allen & Unwin, 2004.

3. See Donald Russell's chap. 12.

4. *FT On-line*, February 28, 2006.

5. See Bates Gill and Michael Green, "Sino-American Relations Need Actions, Not Words," *Financial Times*, April 24, 2006.

6. *Financial Times Online*, July 26, 2006.

7. *Ibid*.

8. *Ibid*.

9. See George J. Gilboy, "The Myth Behind China's Miracle," *Foreign Affairs*, July/August, 2004.

10. Discussions with officials from U.S. Commerce and U.S. Trade Representative (USTR), February and March 2006.

11. *Australian Financial Review (AFR)*, July 6, 2006, p. 11.

12. Australia's Reserve Bank Governor Ian MacFarlane testimony before Australia's federal parliament, February 2006.

13. *AFR*, July 6, 2006.

14. See Linda Weiss, Elizabeth Thurbon, and John Matthews, *How to Kill a Country: Australia's Devastating Trade Deal with the United States,* Sydney: Allen and Unwin, 2004.

15. Discussions with officials from the U.S. Trade Representative office and the U.S. Department of Commerce, March 2006.

16. Florian Gimbel, "ADB Attacks Bilateral Trade Deals," *Financial Times Online,* April 6, 2006.

17. See Milton Osborne, *The Paramount Power: China and the Countries of Southeast Asia,* Lowy Institute Paper 11, 2006.

18. *Financial Times Online,* June 24, 2005.

19. See Rafael Minder, "Howard Says Australia Must Assess Impact of Nuclear Alliance," *Financial Times Online,* July 20, 2006.

20. Discussions with Australian businessmen and government officials, in Brisbane, Canberra, and Sydney, Australia; and Queenstown, New Zealand, June 28–July 22, 2006.

21. See Allen Gyngell and Michael Wesley, *Making Australian Foreign Policy,* Melbourne: Cambridge University Press, 2004.

22. The issue of how much attention Australia should give to Asia is not new. See Paul Keating, *Engagement: Australia Faces the Asia-Pacific,* Sydney: MacMillan, 2000; and William Tow, *Changing Utterly? Australia's International Policy in an Uncertain Age,* Lowy Institute, 2004.

23. See Michael Evans, *The Tyranny of Dissonance: Australia's Strategic Culture and Way of War 1901-2005,* Study paper No. 306, Duntroon, ACT: Land Warfare Studies Center, 2005.

24. See Leif Rosenberger, "Towards a Socio-Economic Struggle against Violent Extremism," Chapter 5 of Kent Hughes Butts and Jeffrey C. Reynolds, eds., *The Struggle against Extremist Ideology: Addressing the Conditions that Foster Terrorism,* Carlisle Barracks: Center for Strategic Leadership, U.S. Army War College, 2005.

25. Richard Armitage, *The 9/11 Commission Report,* p. 377.

26. *Ibid.,* p. 378.

27. Discussions with Australian businessmen and government officials, in Brisbane, Canberra, and Sydney, Australia; and Queenstown, New Zealand.

28. William Pesek, *Bloomberg Online,* July 28, 2006.

29. *Business Survey*, New Zealand Institute of Economic Research, July 11, 2006.

30. *AFR*, July 12, 2006.

CHAPTER 12

ECONOMIC AND BUSINESS ASPECTS: AN AUSTRALIAN PERSPECTIVE

Don Russell

INTRODUCTION

Like many countries, Australia has a complex relationship with the United States. We have the benefit of many shared cultural values, and there exists an easy familiarity at a personal level. But we are still two separate countries with separate national interests and different histories.

From the time of World War II, when Australia first set up a diplomatic mission in Washington separate from the British, security issues have been very important to the totality of the relationship and, notwithstanding the end of the Cold War, this continues today. In part, this is related to the recent focus on the war on terrorism, but the security issues are of longer standing than that and broader in scope.

Australia finds herself in a rapidly changing part of the world where the relationships between countries are evolving in an unpredictable and potentially destabilizing way. There are small countries near to Australia which struggle to function, but there are also large countries like China and India which are changing the balances within our region and the rest of the world because of their size and rapid economic development.

As has been the case with every economic success story in our region, Australia has become a natural supplier of commodities to the new growth economies of China and India. As Japan, Korea, and Taiwan found in the past, in the early stages of export-based economic development, it is important to obtain raw materials at the world's best pricing. This was very much the key to Japan's early success, and other countries in the region have followed its example. Unlike other developed countries that have had to deal with Asian economies at an economic disadvantage, Australia has been an integrated part of Asia's economic success.

Countries now are interrelated economically in a way that makes it difficult to view security issues separate from economic imperatives. Economic integration coupled with deregulation is now seen as the recipe for success. As country after country goes down this path, the old belief that strident nationalism will wilt under the economic forces of self-interest should receive critical scrutiny when considering countries' foreign policy options.

All of this means that to understand the evolving nature of the relationship between the United States and Australia, it is necessary to come to grips with the economic forces at work. This involves not only the two-way economic relationship between the United States and Australia but also their economic relationships with third parties.

THE BILATERAL ECONOMIC RELATIONSHIP

Australia's two-way economic relationship with the United States can be viewed on two levels — the traditional export arrangement and the recent formalization of bilateral free trade. Each will be discussed in turn.

The Traditional Export Relationship.

Australia's traditional export relationship is based on Australia's comparative advantage in the production of agricultural products and natural resources. On the face of it, this should provide Australian industry with attractive market opportunities. The U.S. market is relatively open and attractive to low-cost producers. However, many key Australian exports are covered by quotas and other barriers to trade. Unfortunately, export industries such as wool, sugar, and dairy, where Australia is a highly efficient producer and where there is scope to expand production, are the very industries most heavily protected in the United States.

This keeps Australia's trade negotiators active, but over the years such activity has not produced major gains for Australia. The result has been constant friction and irritation between the two countries. Australians often are shocked over the lack of consideration afforded Australia when it comes to market access for traditional Australian exports and the U.S. willingness to protect its industries in such a blatant way.

Figures 1 and 2 set out the history of Australian exports to the United States broken down by category. As can be seen, the overall export story is far from impressive; over the 17 years leading up to 2005, the average export growth as measured in current prices is only 6.37 percent per annum. Traditional exports (such as wool) have dwindled to virtually nothing. The dominant influence on most of Australia's rural exports to the United States has been the quotas and the fact that the United States tends to manage imports in a way that safeguards the interests of its own rural producers. While U.S. producers have been caught up in rules of the North American Free Trade Asssociation (NAFTA) and the World Trade Organization (WTO)

	Meat	Sugar	Wool	Other Rural	Minerals	Metals	ETMs	Beverages	Other NR	Total
1988	1,005	11	272	204	714	312	825	69	1,033	4,445
1989	901	18	253	205	624	319	1,028	43	1,814	5,205
1990	1,150	20	158	226	785	326	1,324	59	1,755	5,801
1991	1,140	10	157	203	436	307	1,498	58	1,556	5,366
1992	1,187	19	174	259	290	381	1,524	53	1,247	5,134
1993	1,079	21	172	223	267	303	1,870	62	1,070	5,067
1994	808	32	164	206	293	294	1,781	63	1,005	4,645
1995	591	20	188	173	293	233	1,834	77	1,218	4,626
1996	451	155	161	181	341	282	2,120	100	1,186	4,978
1997	639	68	157	250	553	309	2,774	156	1,433	6,339
1998	914	15	125	379	631	1,440	3,095	227	1,650	8,476
1999	998	11	56	420	637	610	3,481	275	1,923	8,411
2000	1,454	23	73	486	1,423	698	4,231	423	2,169	10,980
2001	2,044	27	50	498	1,121	698	5,063	552	1,861	11,914
2002	1,927	27	42	479	1,150	570	5,052	769	1,530	11,546
2003	1,739	16	23	365	676	338	4,039	838	1,421	9,456
2004	1,766	22	22	401	679	495	3,869	897	1,396	9,546
2005	1,636	24	21	433	390	498	3,907	908	1,444	9,260

Figure 1. Merchandise Export Trade with the United States (millions of Australian $).

	Meat	Sugar	Wool	Other Rural	Minerals	Metals	ETMs	Beverages	Other NR	Total
1988	22.6%	0.3%	6.1%	4.6%	16.1%	7.0%	18.6%	1.5%	23.2%	100.0%
1989	17.3%	0.3%	4.9%	3.9%	12.0%	6.1%	19.8%	0.8%	34.9%	100.0%
1990	19.8%	0.3%	2.7%	3.9%	13.5%	5.6%	22.8%	1.0%	30.3%	100.0%
1991	21.2%	0.2%	2.9%	3.8%	8.1%	5.7%	27.9%	1.1%	29.0%	100.0%
1992	23.1%	0.4%	3.4%	5.0%	5.7%	7.4%	29.7%	1.0%	24.3%	100.0%
1993	21.3%	0.4%	3.4%	4.4%	5.3%	6.0%	36.9%	1.2%	21.1%	100.0%
1994	17.4%	0.7%	3.5%	4.4%	6.3%	6.3%	38.3%	1.3%	21.6%	100.0%
1995	12.8%	0.4%	4.1%	3.7%	6.3%	5.0%	39.6%	1.7%	26.3%	100.0%
1996	9.1%	3.1%	3.2%	3.6%	6.9%	5.7%	42.6%	2.0%	23.8%	100.0%
1997	10.1%	1.1%	2.5%	3.9%	8.7%	4.9%	43.8%	2.5%	22.6%	100.0%
1998	10.8%	0.2%	1.5%	4.5%	7.4%	17.0%	36.5%	2.7%	19.5%	100.0%
1999	11.9%	0.1%	0.7%	5.0%	7.6%	7.3%	41.4%	3.3%	22.9%	100.0%
2000	13.2%	0.2%	0.7%	4.4%	13.0%	6.4%	38.5%	3.9%	19.8%	100.0%
2001	17.2%	0.2%	0.4%	4.2%	9.4%	5.9%	42.5%	4.6%	15.6%	100.0%
2002	16.7%	0.2%	0.4%	4.2%	10.0%	4.9%	43.8%	6.7%	13.3%	100.0%
2003	18.4%	0.2%	0.2%	3.9%	7.2%	3.6%	42.7%	8.9%	15.0%	100.0%
2004	18.5%	0.2%	0.2%	4.2%	7.1%	5.2%	40.5%	9.4%	14.6%	100.0%
2005	17.7%	0.3%	0.2%	4.7%	4.2%	5.4%	42.2%	9.8%	15.6%	100.0%

Source: ABS International Trade in Goods & Services 5368.0

Figure 2. Merchandise Export Trade with the United States (percentage of total value).

arrangements, it is rare for Washington to grant a quota increase to Australia if such an increase would hurt domestic U.S. producers.

Australia does have privileged access for beef, and our beef exports are large. However, Australian beef is grass-fed and intended for the hamburger market and thus does not compete directly with U.S. production, which is largely grain-fed. The beef quota is good negotiating coin for the United States — cheap for them, valuable to others. Australia has a number of competitors for access to the U.S. beef quota, with Argentina the main alternative source of supply. Australia therefore is vulnerable to changing political attitudes in Washington when it comes to the allocation of the beef quota. Australia's major gain from the Uruguay Round was an increase in the American beef quota, but Australia always has had to work hard to secure access for its beef, and when access has been secured, Australia has had to work hard to protect it.

Sugar is heavily protected in the United States, and the sugar lobby is well-entrenched. The United States does import sugar, but over the years the sugar quota has been used to further U.S. foreign policy objectives in the Caribbean and Central America.

Some industries such as ship building have no access at all. There is a market for Australian-designed fast ferries, but it is most unlikely that any administration would seek to amend the Jones Act, which restricts U.S. coastal shipping to American-built vessels.

The United States also subsidizes the export of a range of agricultural products, which corrupts international markets and undermines Australia's capacity to export to third countries. This has been an ongoing issue between the two countries, which on occasion has led to pointed disputes. The U.S. Government has some scope to minimize the impact of its subsidy programs by targeting European-subsidized exports, but it is not possible to do this in a way that spares efficient producers like Australia.

Of course, many countries subsidize agricultural exports and protect their local rural producers. Compared to others, the United States does have relatively efficient rural industries. Australia therefore has a strong interest in harnessing the negotiating power of the United States when it comes to multilateral negotiations on agriculture. It is fair to say that without American support, there would be no progress in liberalizing world trade in agriculture and that when the United States wins on agriculture, Australia tends to win too.

The benefits to Australia of American victories on agriculture should not be overstated, as the United States tends to use its negotiating power to support its own rural interests. However, it often is unavoidable that Australia benefits as well as the United States from agricultural trade liberalization, particularly if the negotiations take place in a multilateral context. Australia also is an efficient producer of minerals, metals, and fuels. There is a market for these products in the United States, although Australia tends to be a supplier at the margin, and these exports tend to be volatile. Wine has been a success story (see Figures 1 and 2 under the "Beverages" category), and more sophisticated manufacturing has done well although it has fallen away recently.

The net effect of these changes has been a broadening of the base of Australia's exports to the United States, although rural and commodity-based exports remain important. Figure 3 highlights how trend changes have altered the composition of our exports to the United States.

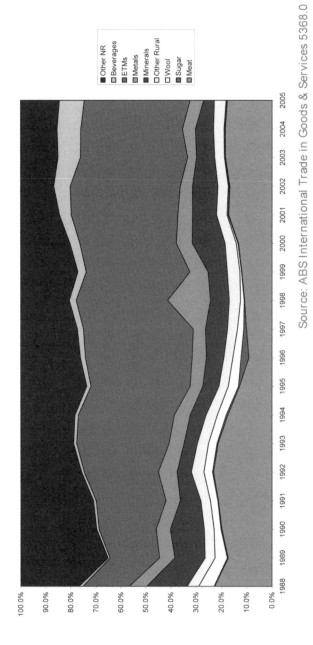

Figure 3. Merchandise Exports to the United States (Percent Share).

Source: ABS International Trade in Goods & Services 5368.0

222

Australia's exports to the United States tend to be priced in U.S. dollars. The sharp depreciation of the Australia dollar ($A) in the earlier part of the decade boosted exports to the United States in $A, but the overall trend is for exports to the United States to decline in relative importance over time. Total exports in nominal terms peaked in 2001 and have been in a declining trend since then.

In 2005 exports to the United States made up only 6.7 percent of total exports, and it is fair to say that the United States has not been a major growth market for Australia. Notwithstanding the recently signed Australia-United States Free Trade Agreement (AUSFTA), this is not likely to change much in the future. The next sections of this chapter will look more closely at the AUSFTA, the growing involvement of Australian companies in the U.S. economy, and the relative U.S. position in Australia's changing trade relationships.

The Australia-United States Free Trade Agreement.

The lack of progress in the current WTO round has created a vacuum that the United States has sought to fill by signing a network of Free Trade Agreements (FTAs) with several countries around the world. The logic of the American position is based on the notion that a FTA allows the United States to bring the full might of its negotiating position to bear on a single country; it also puts indirect pressure on the European Union (EU) to make concessions in the Doha round, as countries steadily make concessions to the United States which may or may not be extended to all countries in some future multilateral agreement.

As the network has become broader, countries have been placed in an invidious position. Either they put their faith in the WTO negotiations and stay out of the U.S.-centric network of agreements or they enter into a separate agreement with Washington and run the risk of paying a price for the privilege with little gain in return. Some countries have responded to this dilemma by seeking to negotiate bilateral FTAs with countries other than the United States.

The United States long has adopted the attitude that countries should be willing to make substantial concessions if they want to sign a FTA with the United States, and this has been the normal practice. U.S. negotiators have become expert at using the intransigence of the American Congress and the importance of the U.S. market to extract concessions from other countries while giving up little, if anything.

Australia came to the AUSFTA negotiations with unusually strong credentials. Australia always has been a good ally of the United States, but our recent close support of U.S. policy, particularly in relation to Iraq, has built up extra credits in Washington. However, even in this environment, the United States gave up very little and made significant gains.

This hard-nosed attitude of American trade negotiators has shocked some Australians, who anticipated that the United States might be less demanding and more supportive of Australian interests. In the end, the United States used the AUSFTA negotiations with Australia as just another opportunity to further its multilateral trade agenda. As has always been the case, working closely with the United States on trade is a two-edged sword; it helps Australia with market access and allows it to influence world policy on agriculture, but it exposes us to intense pressure to accede to the U.S. multilateral agenda.

Australia therefore ended up making concessions on a range of matters that the United States typically pursues whenever it enters into trade negotiations. For example, Australia accepted an extension of copyright protection to 20 years. In the future, Australian users of copyright-protected works will continue to be liable until 70 years after the death of the copyright owner.

As a major net importer of copyright material, Australia traditionally has opposed extending the term of copyright protection because it inevitably will lead to an increased net cost to Australia. It is difficult to estimate the full cost of term extension for all copyrighted works. However, for books alone it has been estimated that the cost to Australia would be on the order of A$800m to A$1.1b in today's dollars.

The United States is a strong supporter of its pharmaceutical industry, and this is reflected in the negotiating position that Washington takes at the multilateral level and with individual countries. By agreeing that the Australian Therapeutic Goods Administration (TGA) must refuse domestic marketing approval to a generic manufacturer where the incumbent patent holder covers the product with a "new use" patent, Australia has made it easier for foreign pharmaceutical companies to "evergreen" patents in Australia that are coming to the end of their lives in the country of origin. The TGA therefore will be required to act as an enforcer of new patent claims against generic competitors even before the merits of the case have been settled in court. This could be quite expensive to Australia, as there are a number of significant patents due to expire in the next few years.

Having strengthened the hand of pharmaceutical companies in Australia relative to generic manufacturers, the United States will find it easier to secure similar provisions in future FTAs that they negotiate with other countries. If enough countries are willing to concede such provisions to the United States on a bilateral basis, it increases the chances that Washington will be able to secure similar provisions at a multilateral level. In the circumstances, however, it is hard to see how Australia could have negotiated a better deal.

We have paid a price for the FTA, but there will be benefits. It is true that the improved market access for Australian beef and dairy is modest and a long way off, and there is a real danger that the United States will renegotiate arrangements if improved market access for Australia creates major problems with American farm interests. But assuming that the phase-in of the quota increases does not create major problems for the United States, Australian rural industries will have secured increased access that the United States could easily have granted to someone else.

The main gain Australia has made with the AUSFTA is that there is now a process in place with reasonably detailed rules covering a wide range of situations. The United States will use these rules and review provisions to further its interests, but a rules-based structure does give Australian exporters to the United States a measure of predictability and a certain freedom from harassment that they did not have in the past. A rules-based system also gives Australia the opportunity to use the same rules to further the interests of Australian industry, assuming of course that Australia is willing and able to use such a system.

Expectations do, however, need to be managed, as some Australians unrealistically expect major net benefits to flow from the AUSFTA. Moreover, Australians should not be surprised when the United States uses every provision of the AUSFTA along with all the WTO processes to further American interests. As the Office of the U.S. Trade Representative (USTR) is fond of saying, "Don't take it personally, we are only playing by the rules."

Australia also should play by the same rules. By law, the USTR must represent the interests of American companies. In Australia, trade policy priorities are very much in the hands of the Department of Foreign Affairs and Trade (DFAT), and inevitably foreign policy and Departmental considerations intrude. In the United States, companies work up their own WTO cases, expecting the USTR to work with them to pursue their interests in Geneva. In Australia, DFAT jealously protects its prerogative to set priorities; an Australian company or industry easily can find its interests traded away for what DFAT views as the broader public interest, or the Department may not pursue a case because of resource constraints. If the Department does take an issue to the WTO, it is uncomfortable with the active participation of the industry and its legal advisers. This could not be more different from the situation in the United States, where American-backed WTO cases utilize the vast resources of the private sector as well as the resources of the U.S. Government. WTO cases in the United States are serious business and are resourced accordingly.

The United States, Canada, and the EU immediately understood that with the establishment of the WTO, the world had changed. There are now effective mechanisms to resolve disputes. There is a Dispute Settlement Body comprised of Panels and a permanent Appeals Body with powers to enforce decisions. The United States, Canada, and the EU have actively used the new processes to further their own interests, and other countries have followed their lead.

DFAT has tended to be less active. The Department is not well-staffed with trade lawyers and appears reluctant to work closely with trade advisers hired by Australian industry.

In September 2001, a Joint Standing Committee of the Parliament Chaired by Senator Helen Coonan recommended the establishment of a separate Trade Advocate Office that would have responsibility for the management of Australia's participation in cases of WTO disputes. The Committee also recommended that this new Office have the capacity to use private sector legal practitioners. A separate Trade Advocate Office has not been established, although DFAT has used the Committee's Report to secure extra resources for the Department itself and to engage in broader community consultation. Unfortunately, DFAT has worked hard to minimize the involvement of private sector legal practitioners in a deliberate strategy to avoid embracing the U.S. approach to trade negotiation.

On the basis of past attitudes, there is a danger that DFAT will be reluctant to use the provisions of the new FTA with the United States in an aggressive way and will cede too much to U.S. trade negotiators and American industries, who doubtless will use every provision of the Agreement to put pressure on Australia to further the interests of U.S. business. Over time, this is likely to compound the sense of disappointment and frustration that many in Australia feel about the AUSFTA.

Australian Investment in the United States.

It would be wrong to conclude from the foregoing that the United States is of diminishing interest to Australian commercial interests. It is true that Australia has been a major beneficiary of Asian growth, Chinese growth in particular, and that the United States has become of declining importance to Australia as an export market. However, despite this reality, Australian companies have never been more committed to the U.S. market, and a large number of highly successful Australian businesses have built strategies that involve a significant presence in the United States. This has taken place outside traditional government-to-government negotiations, but it is where Australia's economic links with the United States are now centered. To the extent that a country's political and foreign policy objectives are in the end driven by economic realities, it is important to keep this in mind.

Many Australian companies now have extensive operations in the United States, and it is commonplace for Australians to work there. Australian companies explicitly focus on the United States when they develop their business strategies. For many companies, a successful American operation is an imperative if the company wishes to be internationally competitive. There have been some spectacular disasters, such as the BHP purchase of Magma Copper in 1996 and the NAB purchase of HomeSide in 1997, but there have also been a growing number of successes. The market is now more wary of Australian companies seeking to expand into the United States through acquisition, but there also is a growing willingness to reward soundly-based business models. There is a realization that success in Australia does not necessarily translate well internationally if the company owes its domestic success to limited competition and protected markets.

This new involvement of Australian business with the U.S. economy has sprung from the deregulated Australian economy of the past 2 decades and is not industry specific. Because it is happening on an economy-wide basis and is not narrowly centered on traditional Australian exports, the importance of the

United States to Australian business arguably is greater than it has ever been.

The importance of America to Australian companies is well reflected in the statistics on investment abroad. Notwithstanding Australia's growing trade relations with Asia and its traditional links with the United Kingdom (UK) and Europe, at the end of 2004, 55 percent of all direct investment abroad was in the United States. Moreover, the trend is, if anything, toward the United States rather than other countries; at the end of 2001 the proportion in the United States was 50 percent. See Figure 4.

	Calendar Year			
	2001	2002	2003	2004
United States of America				
Direct Investment ($ million)	-107,378	-91,464	-102,993	-140,343
Portfolio Investment Assets ($ million)	-81,851	-83,966	-88,598	-106,935
Total ($ million)	-220,635	-206,471	-231,550	-292,116
All Countries				
Direct Investment ($ million)	-214,654	-192,212	-200,977	-254,008
Portfolio Investment Assets ($ million)	-156,028	-161,986	-173,779	-214,424
Total ($ million)	-506,226	-502,663	-539,454	-649,688
US as a proportion of All Countries				
Direct Investment (%)	50.0%	47.6%	51.2%	55.3%
Portfolio Investment Assets (%)	52.5%	51.8%	51.0%	49.9%
Total (%)	43.6%	41.1%	42.9%	45.0%

Source: ABS Cat No. 5352.0 International Investment Position, Australia: Supplementary Country Statistics 2004

Figure 4. Australian Investment Abroad: Level as at December 31.

The companies listed in Figure 5 are examples of Australian businesses that have developed global business models with successful operations in the

United States. The list is not meant to be comprehensive or to suggest that these are attractive stocks.[1] However, the list does provide an indication of the areas where Australian companies have built global businesses successfully and how a presence in the United States has been pivotal to their overall success.

Company	Market Cap 26/6/06	Comment
Aristocrat (ALL)	A$5.9b	World's second largest slot/ gaming machine manufacturer and gaming software developer. Sydney based; 50 percent business in United States, rest in Japan and Australia
Billabong (BBG)	A$3.1b	Self branded surf stores; 48 percent of revenue in North America, 28 percent Australia/ Japan, 24 percent Europe
Fosters (FGL)	A$11.0b	Worldwide alcohol company; 32 percent of revenue from international wine (Beringer Blass)
CSL (CSL)	A$9.4b	No 2 in global plasma products, manufacturing in United States, Europe, and Australia
Cochlear (COH)	A$2.9b	World leader in cochlear implant industry with more than 60 percent world market share
Rinker (RIN)	A$15.6b	One of the world's top 10 heavy building materials groups, 80 percent of earnings in United States, 10,000 employees in United States

Figure 5. Examples of Australian Companies Operating in the United States.

AUSTRALIA'S ECONOMIC RELATIONSHIPS WITH OTHER COUNTRIES

It is useful to look at the U.S.-Australia economic relationship in the context of Australia's relationships with other countries. Figures 6 and 7 set out the details of Australia's merchandise exports broken down by country and broad region. As can be seen, Australian exports are weighted heavily towards Asia, with some 62.3 percent of the total directed to the main Asian markets in 2005. China has been an important growth market in the past 5 years. But despite the growth of China, the overall importance of Asia has changed little over the past 10 years; in 1995, 62.1 percent of Australia's exports went to the main Asian markets.

In fact, China is not the only market for Australian exports that has been growing rapidly. Japan remains a very important growth market for Australian exports, while growth in exports to India overshadows all our major markets. During the period 2003-05, exports to China/Hong Kong grew by 57 percent; but over the same period, exports to Japan, our largest market, grew by 44 percent, and exports to India grew by a staggering 109 percent.

Commodities are the driving force for our exports to Asia, particularly to new markets like China and India. Both of these countries are growing strongly and are dependent on low-cost raw materials to make them internationally competitive. In choosing Australia as a source for raw materials, China and India are following a well-tested strategy pioneered by Japan and followed by Korea and Taiwan. Australia is a highly efficient supplier of high quality raw materials. Moreover, because of the shorter distances involved to Asian destinations, Australia has a cost advantage relative to competitors from South America and Africa.

	USA	EU 25	Japan	Korea	Taiwan	ASEAN	China/HK	India	Other	Total
1988	4445	6396	11488	2021	1468	3461	3280	576	9235	42370
1989	5207	6752	12443	2488	1747	4607	2759	524	10480	47007
1990	5801	6944	13443	2984	1780	5857	2600	642	10840	50891
1991	5367	6572	14821	3366	2330	6661	3436	663	10505	53721
1992	5134	7710	14750	3659	2561	8459	4228	840	11036	58377
1993	5068	7476	15627	4359	2779	8752	5015	922	12741	62739
1994	4645	7246	15991	4707	2849	9648	5472	874	13343	64775
1995	4628	8007	16566	6060	3300	11506	6013	1099	14491	71670
1996	4978	8380	15565	7305	3428	11589	6876	1224	17637	76982
1997	6338	8677	16814	6763	4059	12940	7776	1692	19731	84790
1998	8477	12334	17384	6104	4267	10107	7338	2148	20828	88987
1999	8411	10845	16706	6280	4163	11224	7110	1515	20639	86893
2000	10982	12533	21804	9045	5557	15136	9584	1833	23881	110355
2001	11914	14738	23723	9530	5377	15384	11772	2425	27668	122531
2002	11547	14911	22176	9980	4746	14577	11919	2482	27120	119458
2003	9454	15399	19686	8084	3724	12092	11966	3338	24213	107956
2004	9546	13248	22219	9170	4091	13746	13747	5430	26576	117773
2005	9262	14909	28406	10951	5520	15862	18798	6978	28276	138962

Figure 6. Merchandise Exports by Country (A$m).

	USA	EU 25	Japan	Korea	Taiwan	ASEAN	China/HK	India	Other	Total
1988	10.5%	15.1%	27.1%	4.8%	3.5%	8.2%	7.7%	1.4%	21.8%	100.0%
1989	11.1%	14.4%	26.5%	5.3%	3.7%	9.8%	5.9%	1.1%	22.3%	100.0%
1990	11.4%	13.6%	26.4%	5.9%	3.5%	11.5%	5.1%	1.3%	21.3%	100.0%
1991	10.0%	12.2%	27.6%	6.3%	4.3%	12.4%	6.4%	1.2%	19.6%	100.0%
1992	8.8%	13.2%	25.3%	6.3%	4.4%	14.5%	7.2%	1.4%	18.9%	100.0%
1993	8.1%	11.9%	24.9%	6.9%	4.4%	13.9%	8.0%	1.5%	20.3%	100.0%
1994	7.2%	11.2%	24.7%	7.3%	4.4%	14.9%	8.4%	1.3%	20.6%	100.0%
1995	6.5%	11.2%	23.1%	8.5%	4.6%	16.1%	8.4%	1.5%	20.2%	100.0%
1996	6.5%	10.9%	20.2%	9.5%	4.5%	15.1%	8.9%	1.6%	22.9%	100.0%
1997	7.5%	10.2%	19.8%	8.0%	4.8%	15.3%	9.2%	2.0%	23.3%	100.0%
1998	9.5%	13.9%	19.5%	6.9%	4.8%	11.4%	8.2%	2.4%	23.4%	100.0%
1999	9.7%	12.5%	19.2%	7.2%	4.8%	12.9%	8.2%	1.7%	23.8%	100.0%
2000	10.0%	11.4%	19.8%	8.2%	5.0%	13.7%	8.7%	1.7%	21.6%	100.0%
2001	9.7%	12.0%	19.4%	7.8%	4.4%	12.6%	9.6%	2.0%	22.6%	100.0%
2002	9.7%	12.5%	18.6%	8.4%	4.0%	12.2%	10.0%	2.1%	22.7%	100.0%
2003	8.8%	14.3%	18.2%	7.5%	3.4%	11.2%	11.1%	3.1%	22.4%	100.0%
2004	8.1%	11.2%	18.9%	7.8%	3.5%	11.7%	11.7%	4.6%	22.6%	100.0%
2005	6.7%	10.7%	20.4%	7.9%	4.0%	11.4%	13.5%	5.0%	20.3%	100.0%

Source: ABS International Trade in Goods & Services 5368.0

Figure 7. Merchandise Exports by Country (percentages).

Australia has been a major beneficiary of the surge in commodity prices occurring over recent years, with iron ore and coal being the two major exports for Australia. Together, they currently make up 25 percent of total exports. During 2005, iron ore prices were up 72 percent, hard coking coal 123 percent, soft coking coal 100 percent, and thermal coal 17 percent. The surge in prices has extended well beyond bulk commodities; base metals, aluminum ore, gold, and oil prices have all been dramatically higher.

The rationalization and merger of many commodity companies in the latter part of the 1990s has been an important spur to better returns for commodity companies. However, the major force driving up commodity prices has been surging demand by China. The growing importance of China can be seen in its rising share of Australian exports. In 1995, they accounted for 8.4 percent of Australia's exports; in 2005 this had risen to 13.5 percent.

The growing importance of China also can be seen in the statistics on service credits, which for Australia are largely driven by in-bound tourism. As can be seen from Figure 8, China now accounts for 10.4 percent of total service credits, up from 5.5 percent in 1999. The service credits statistics also show that both the United States and Japan have been declining sources of service credits for Australia. Again, despite the growth of China, the overall importance of Asia for service credits has not changed dramatically; in 2005 the main Asian markets accounted for 39.9 percent of service credits, while in 1999 the figure was 37.3 percent.

The rising economic importance of China thus needs to be kept in perspective. China is very much a price taker when it comes to commodity prices. China may be responsible for current high prices, but since

	USA	EU	Japan	Korea	Taiwan	ASEAN	China/HK	India	Other	Total
1999	4245	5603	3384	564	440	4032	1504	293	7350	27415
2000	5756	6546	3630	752	448	4586	1848	426	8871	32863
2001	4714	6766	3606	994	431	4972	2605	506	9125	33719
2002	4784	6885	3540	946	388	5151	2913	444	9295	34346
2003	4655	7218	3026	1005	391	4742	3052	570	9245	33904
2004	4279	7742	3281	1050	411	4831	3500	676	10019	35789
2005	4431	7733	3132	1232	420	5167	3880	1032	10218	37245

	USA	EU	Japan	Korea	Taiwan	ASEAN	China/HK	India	Other	Total
1999	15.5%	20.4%	12.3%	2.1%	1.6%	14.7%	5.5%	1.1%	26.8%	100.0%
2000	17.5%	19.9%	11.0%	2.3%	1.4%	14.0%	5.6%	1.3%	27.0%	100.0%
2001	14.0%	20.1%	10.7%	2.9%	1.3%	14.7%	7.7%	1.5%	27.1%	100.0%
2002	13.9%	20.0%	10.3%	2.8%	1.1%	15.0%	8.5%	1.3%	27.1%	100.0%
2003	13.7%	21.3%	8.9%	3.0%	1.2%	14.0%	9.0%	1.7%	27.3%	100.0%
2004	12.0%	21.6%	9.2%	2.9%	1.1%	13.5%	9.8%	1.9%	28.0%	100.0%
2005	11.9%	20.8%	8.4%	3.3%	1.1%	13.9%	10.4%	2.8%	27.4%	100.0%

Source ABS 5368.0.55.004

Figure 8. Service Credits by Country (A$m).

the surge in prices, this has not enabled it to use its economic and political standing to extract special cut-rate deals from suppliers like Australia. The recently completed negotiations between BHP Billiton and China's largest steelmaker, Baosteel, are a good indicator of the underlying balances. After much public disquiet from the Chinese, Baosteel eventually agreed to a 19 percent iron ore price increase for 2006-07. This matched the price increases accepted by European and Japanese steel producers.

Having to match the price increases accepted by the Japanese and the Europeans was clearly a shock to the Chinese. The China Iron and Steel Association, which has close links to the Chinese Government and represents the largest Chinese steel producers, has stated that the negotiations involved a "lack of respect for the long-term interests of all parties and showed little interest in fostering a stable, cooperative relationship to achieve common development and a win-win result."[2]

That China is trying to secure for itself a growing share of a limited supply of raw materials enhances the bargaining power of countries like Australia; it certainly does not make Australia or Australian companies beholden to China. It has been estimated that Chinese demand accounted for 40 percent of global demand for iron ore in 2006, up from 14 percent in 2000 (see Figure 9).[3] China has little alternative but to buy raw materials from Australia and match world prices if it wants to continue on a rapid growth path.

Australia has been dependent on Asian growth for almost half a century. Originally that growth was driven by Japan. If anything, Australia's room to maneuver has widened steadily as Taiwan and then Korea expanded. Strong growth in China and India

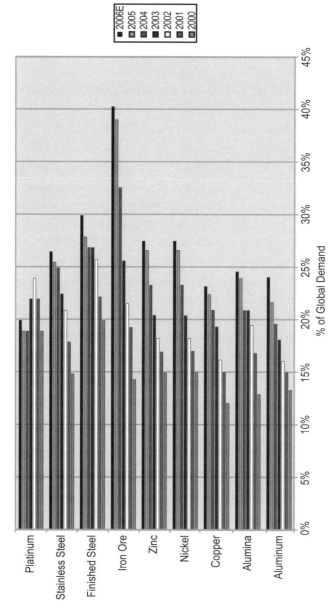

Figure 9. Chinese Demand as a Proportion of Global Demand.

further diversifies Australia's customer base and puts increased competitive pressure on individual buyers.

While the recent experience renegotiating iron ore prices was a sobering one for China, it also is an important guide as to what strong growth in China actually means in terms of China's relations with other countries. The key conclusion for commentators, particularly for commentators who are interested in security issues, is that China's economic growth makes the People's Republic of China (PRC) very dependent on market forces. It depends on securing inputs for its economy and on securing access for its products. Growth is bringing great benefits to the Chinese people, but it also is changing priorities within China and constraining the capacity of the Chinese leadership to behave in ways that are detrimental to the economy. Every year, strong growth brings higher incomes and more wealth, but it also increases the cost of capricious behavior. It is concern about capricious behavior, rather than a larger Chinese economy, that people should focus on.

CONCLUSION

Australia and the United States have had a long and close relationship which dates back to World War II. The relationship has been grounded heavily on mutually agreed security objectives. Initially it was the war in the Pacific, then it was the Cold War, and now it is the war on terror, or the Long War as some have taken to calling it. In particular we Australians currently have a shared interest in maintaining the stability of our region.

Australia-American trade rarely has been at the heart of the relationship, although on occasion disputes over market access for Australian agricultural products have intruded. Over the years, the United States has become of dwindling significance as a market for Australian exports of goods and services. The recently signed AUSFTA is unlikely to reverse this trend to any great extent, although it should bring a useful measure of predictability as it puts in place a rules-based structure to handle disputes. Australia could use the new procedures to its advantage if it is able to assemble the organizational resources necessary to make them work.

The growing involvement of Australian companies in the American economy means that despite the declining importance of the United States as an export market, Australian business has never been more involved with the United States. A large and growing number of Australians work in the United States, and working in the United States is now seen as a normal career move for many Australians. There is therefore a solid and contemporary basis on which to rest the political and security relationship between the two countries.

The recent rapid growth in trade between China and Australia is not a factor undermining the logic of Australia's relationship with the United States, nor is it a factor pulling Australia in a new direction. Just because China is a large and growing market for Australian iron ore and coal, we are not warranted to assume that Australia is becoming an increasingly unreliable ally. China is in the early stages of economic development when commodities are a disproportionately large input to GDP; hence, for the foreseeable future, access to an expanding supply of raw materials is a necessary condition for continued Chinese growth.

While it is galling to Chinese policymakers, China is a patsy when it comes to a willingness to pay high prices for commodities, particularly iron ore and coal. Australia is in no way beholden to China for its access to the Chinese market. If anything, China owes a debt to Australia for satisfying China's growing dependence on raw materials in the same sense that China owes a debt to Middle Eastern countries in the case of oil.

Moreover, Chinese growth does not alter Australia's traditional economic imperatives. For almost half a century, Australia has depended on strong growth in Asia, and this reality has not changed. Indeed, adding China (and India) to the group of countries in Asia with successful economies and thus greater potential as customers, provides Australia with more options rather than less. Thirty-odd years ago, Australia was very dependent on Japan because there were few alternative markets. That is no longer the case. If China does not buy Australian raw materials, there are always markets in Japan, Korea, Taiwan, and India.

Until the last decade, Australia appeared to be facing a long-term decline in trade; every year it seemed that it had to export more commodities to buy the same bundle of imports. With growing world demand for a constrained supply of raw materials, Australia now faces the reverse situation; every year the same supply of raw materials buys an increasing bundle of imports.

But most importantly, Australia's foreign policy for decades has acknowledged the key role that Asian economies play in generating wealth and income for Australians. Successive Australian governments have become highly sophisticated at balancing security ties with the United States on one hand, with the need to maintain the stability of our region on the other. For it is the stability of our region which delivers the cascading wealth of Asian growth.

In the past, Canberra's strong alliance with the United States comported quite comfortably with Australia's close economic and political ties to Asia. Australian foreign policy at its most agile uses the closeness of the U.S.-Australian relationship to magnify Australia's importance to its Asian neighbors; at the same time, the sophistication of its relationships with Asian neighbors makes it a far broader and potentially more useful U.S. partner. But this has required careful management. In recent decades, there has never been a time when a simplistic or heavy-handed approach to the Asia-Pacific region has been in Australia's best interests. A decade ago, conflict between China and the United States would have been as challenging to Australia as it is today. Though China over the past 10 years has developed a growing dependence on Australian raw materials, it would be wrong to conclude that this is a factor pulling us away from the United States. On the contrary, the importance of the American alliance for Australia is as strong as it has ever been.

ENDNOTES - CHAPTER 12

1. West L B Mellon Asset Management could conceivably hold these stocks in portfolios of Australian equities.

2. Steve Wyatt, "Angry China Attacks 'Lack of Respect' in Ore Talks," *Australian Financial Review*, June 24, 2006.

3. Source IISA, WBMS, Brook Hunt, Johnson Matthey, CRU, Deutsche Bank.

PANEL V

SECURITY AND DEFENSE ASPECTS OF THE U.S.-AUSTRALIA SPECIAL RELATIONSHIP

CHAPTER 13

PANEL V CHAIRMAN'S INTRODUCTION

Jeffrey D. McCausland

When one examines the defense relationship between the United States and Australia, the over-arching impression is that it works and is beneficial to both states in pursuing their strategic goals in the past as well as the future. At the end of the day, the important thing is what works. In essence, this is a very pragmatic relationship. To say this might appear to some to be a superficial observation, but it nonetheless is fundamental. For the United States and Australia — like any two sovereign states — the ultimate question is the utility of the relationship. There can be no doubt that this relationship has been and will continue to be extremely useful to both.

Furthermore, if one examines the overall relationship between these two states, to include foreign policy, economics, commerce, politics, and defense, it is the defense relationship that is most routine and imbedded. Australian and American military officers have served together in various theaters and operations. Each attends the other's schools; they share intelligence, military doctrine, and materiel on a regular basis. Australian policymakers even made a request to expand the intelligence relationship between the two countries during meetings in early 2006.[1] In fact, this link is so routine that the greatest danger is for it to become taken for granted, and thus underrated in importance. In politics as well as life, leaders constantly examine, renew, and underscore the value of enduring relationships if they are to prosper. The defense relationship between the United States and Australia is strong, but military and civilian leaders must reevaluate this bond continually in the future. They also must maintain a clear understanding of internal domestic pressures in both states that policy choices generate.

The defense strategy of any nation is a function of three variables—ends, ways, and means. "Ends" are the objectives the state is trying to accomplish. "Ways" are the concepts, doctrines, and ideas the state brings to bear unilaterally or in concert with other nations. "Means" are the resources a state can or is willing to invest in fulfilling its security objectives. This includes people, money, technology, and time. The challenge for the strategist is to seek a balance among these variables. While some might argue that security is fundamental to any state in the international system, this does not mean that the resources available for defense are unlimited. Objectives need to be prioritized, and methods must be settled upon that, through synergies, maximize the probabilities of success. Coalitions, alliances, and bilateral relationships clearly are crucial in this calculation.

There is manifest agreement between Australia and the United States with respect to the broad objectives of the war on terrorists and East Asian security more broadly.

- Defeat those who seek to use terrorism against the United States, Australia, or their allies.

- Prevent the spread of weapons of mass destruction (WMD).

- Wisely manage the emergence of China as a major military and economic power in the region and on the world stage.

Australia has been an important partner for the United States in Afghanistan and Iraq since September 11, 2001 (9/11).[2] Both nations have forces deployed to Iraq, which has become the central military focus, and the road ahead in Iraq will be long and difficult at best. As we move into 2007, there are suggestions that the United States should reduce its forces in Iraq at some unspecified rate. In fact, some observers have characterized this as a debate between "cut and run" and "cut and jog." As this debate continues, and particularly if American forces are reduced, the United States must expect that all of its coalition partners in Iraq (Australia included) will review their own commitments. Furthermore, Afghanistan also will remain a long-term challenge that both nations must be prepared to confront in concert with NATO and other allies.

The "Ends" of Defense Policy.

As Australians evaluate their defense "ends," they of course will consider their bilateral relationship with Indonesia as well as the other states in the so-called arc of instability. Over the longer term, Canberra's regional exertions may become more important to the country than its contributions in Iraq and Afghanistan.

One Australian defense expert observed that "Australia has an Islamic geography." In addition to being the planet's fourth largest country, Indonesia is the largest Islamic country. Large Muslim populations exist in Malaysia and the Philippines as well. Consequently, any suggestion that the so-called Long War is a war of ideologies between the West and Islam presents particular difficulties for Australia as to its relations with its neighbors.

Some in Australia may believe that Americans ignore one of the lessons of the book, *The Tipping Point*, by Malcolm Gladwell.[3] Gladwell underscores the critical importance of context. For example, to assist Americans in understanding Australia's concern about developments in Indonesia, they should visualize the following notional picture: the Mexican population has doubled and continues to grow at a dramatic pace; the Mexican economy is quite weak, and large-scale unemployment in Mexico, particularly among the young, is endemic. To take this imagined scenario a step further, Mexico is now an Islamic state, with several communities committed to instituting Sharia law. By thus vicariously experiencing a broad geographical/political context similar to the one Australia actually finds itself in today, Americans can thus obtain far greater insight and empathy.

Clearly Australian forces as currently configured are stretched. The Australian Army consists of only 26,000 active troops and 17,000 reservists.[4] This force has had as many as 10 ongoing deployments simultaneously in such places as East Timor, Papua New Guinea, the Solomon Islands, Iraq, and Afghanistan. Renewed violence in Timor Leste suggests that a long-term presence by Australian forces in that troubled country will likely be required.[5]

One lesson from these efforts is that any successful campaign to defeat international terrorism must have a military component capable of expeditionary actions. But such a campaign also depends on taking the steps necessary to enhance stability in the target states, which are often beset by complex problems such as economic under-development, burgeoning population growth, AIDS, etc., that create fertile ground for international terrorists fired by religious fervor. One can argue plausibly that the most successful combined military operations by U.S. and Australian forces since 9/11 have been tsunami relief and the assistance provided in Pakistan after the devastating earthquake there.

The United States and Australia also have found common cause in opposing the spread of WMD and long-range missiles. The Proliferation Security Initiative (PSI) is an important manifestation of this common policy goal, with Australia having cooperated in this effort from its initiation in May 2003.[6] This effort has the goal of preventing the shipment of WMD or their components to terrorists or the countries harboring them. Still, the PSI suffers from the absence of any reinforcement of the existing legal authority for states to inspect vessels traveling through their territorial waters or those elsewhere not displaying a national flag or lacking registry.

For the leaders in Washington and Canberra, the primary country of concern in terms of proliferation in Asia is North Korea. Both nations were reminded of the challenge presented by North Korea following its missiles tests in July 2006 and its nuclear test 3 months later. Canberra supported American efforts in the United Nations (UN) to sanction North Korea for its nuclear tests. In addition, Australia announced it was banning North Korea's ships from entering its ports, except in dire emergencies.

With Australia not being part of the six party talks seeking to find a diplomatic solution to the Korean nuclear issue, some Australians might wonder why all the fuss. Part of the answer is that North Korea poses a direct threat to South Korea, a major ally of the United States, as well as to American forces deployed there. But the greatest threat presented by North Korea may be its apparent willingness to proliferate and share

WMD and missile technology with other states as well as terrorist organizations.

Finally, both Australia and the United States realize that the most important geopolitical development in the first half of the 21st century may be the sudden emergence of the People's Republic of China (PRC) as a leading member of the world's power elite. Canberra and Washington understand that they must seek to deal constructively with growing Chinese strength— military, economic, and political—both in the Asia Pacific region and in the world more broadly. In this regard, there is a different view of China in the United States and Australia. This was demonstrated in joint remarks by U.S. Secretary of State Condoleezza Rice and Australian Foreign Minister Alexander Downer in July 2006.[7]

There is a debate in the United States about the future direction of China, with many American leaders construing the emerging China as a potential threat. The U.S. Department of Defense's (DoD) annual report to Congress (2006) describes the expansion and modernization of Chinese military forces in worried terms.[8] In a similar vein, DoD's 2006 *Quadrennial Defense Review* (QDR) observes that "China has the greatest potential to compete militarily with the United States and field disruptive military technologies that could over time offset traditional U.S. military advantages."

The possibility of conflict between the United States and China over Taiwan or some other sensitive issue is cause for major concern in Canberra. From the Australian perspective, there is fear that an American confrontation with the PRC might force the Australians to choose between the Australia-New Zealand-U.S. (ANZUS) alliance and their commercial interests in China and elsewhere in the region.[9] Australian leaders know that other powers in the region would most certainly remain neutral in such a crisis.

As several contributors to this volume have observed, while America tends to see the growth of China as a threat, Australia is more inclined to view it as an opportunity. Consequently, it may be time for leaders in the United States and Australia to enter honest dialogue about the emerging security environment and China's place in it. Washington and Canberra would then be far better positioned to engage China in a constructive, unified manner. The goal would be to persuade Beijing to join the international community – in spirit and in substance – as a partner fully commensurate with its growing size and importance.

The "Ways" of Defense Policy.

The alliance as defined in the ANZUS Treaty is the essential "way" or concept that gives vitality and force to the U.S.-Australian defense relationship. Alliances traditionally have been one method that states employed to enhance their security. They are not expressions of national altruism but rather practical tools of statecraft in pursuit of interests. They must do something. Alliances involve a sharing of resources as well as responsibilities. Historically, they may lose their relevance long before their formal demise. The Southeast Asia Treaty Organization (SEATO), for example, actually "existed" in an international legal sense until 1977, but at some point long before that date, SEATO had lost its relevance.

Article V of the U.S.-Australian defense treaty has been formally invoked only once, and that was in response to 9/11. This confirms not only the continuing importance of ANZUS but also that the alliance is changing. ANZUS, founded in 1951, is nearly as old as the North Atlantic Treaty Organization (NATO). But ANZUS was formed to defend territory that at the time both countries perceived as endangered by a clear external threat. Today, neither country's territory is threatened—at least not in the classical sense of invasion. Consequently, Australia and the United States are bound together to defend common global interests and values. The "threat" is highly contingent, growing out of unforeseeable circumstances of the moment, and when it does loom into view, it may menace one partner more or less than it does the other. This situation creates problems not only for strategists, but also for those leaders who must explain strategy and associated policies to their respective (and frequently skeptical) publics. For example, Australian leaders actively emphasize that the ANZUS Treaty cannot be viewed as directed against any state, particularly China.

Finally, leaders in Washington and Canberra must understand that this will always be an alliance of unequal partners. As one Australian expert observed, in many ways this relationship tends to consume Australia, whereas it will obviously not be of the same moment for the United States. This is not a comment on the importance of the relationship, but rather an acknowledgment of the relative power of the two partners.

The "Means" of Defense Policy.

The 2006 QDR in the United States and the Australian 2000 *Defense White Paper* (with supplements for 2003 and 2005) are critically important in understanding the "means" of defense policy for both states, and the challenges associated with resource allocation. It would appear, however, in light of the emerging security environment that both countries are threatened by a serious strategy/force structure mismatch.

Australia invests only 1.9 percent of its gross domestic product (GDP) on defense, as compared with approximately 4 percent in the United States. For Canberra, this low level of investment is a bone of contention between the so-called Defender-Regionalists vs. the Reformer-Globalists. The Defender-Regionalists tend to be "little Australians or Continentalists" who view the country's defense obligation as being defined by the fixed geography of the Australian continent. For this school, the first if not the only requirement of Australian military forces is to defend the nation from attack and invasion.

The Reformer-Globalists, however, support a broader role for Australian forces in defending national interests, extending the circumference of their potential employment to some distance from Australian shores. This approach obviously calls for a force which is more capable of maritime power projection. Sadly, this debate has focused on roles and missions but has neglected realistic discussion of the size of the Australian defense budget vis-à-vis the missions contemplated. Thus the argument so far appears to be over how to divide the too small pie of acquisition funds available.

For the United States, the QDR described the threats to American security in fairly cogent fashion. The report's emphasis on America's need for allies and renewed partnerships was welcomed in Australia and elsewhere around the world. This was particularly true in the aftermath of the first George W. Bush term that many believed showed a greater emphasis on unilateral action and ad hoc coalitions of the willing. The report also recommended a shift in focus towards the Asia-Pacific region, with a commensurate movement of U.S.

forces to the Pacific, a move welcomed by many in Asia.

Still, while the threat description and concepts as set forth in the QDR seem appropriate, the force structure recommended would reduce the strength of the Army and reserve forces while investing in two new fighter aircraft types, national missile defense, and new naval forces. Some might argue that the 2006 QDR, coupled with the 2006 report on growing Chinese military power, reflects a heightened U.S. concern about China as compared with Iraq and Afghanistan.[10]

In the case of Australia, if it is to continue to "box outside its weight class," tough choices may need to be made to avoid a force structure that will not support its commitments. While some in the United States certainly will contend that the QDR describes a suite of force capabilities ranging from nuclear to heavy conventional to counterinsurgency, Australia cannot match this force, even on a proportionate basis. It is imperative, however, for Australian leaders to convince their public that an increase in defense spending from 1.9 percent of GDP to at least something in excess of 2 percent is required. This increase would need to be accompanied with a careful examination of investment choices.

Australian purchases of the *Hellfire* missile, *Global Hawk* remote-piloted vehicles, *Abrams* tank, and the Joint Strike Fighter (JSF) will enhance interoperability with U.S. forces over the next several years. But real problems may surface as a result of the spiraling cost of certain systems. In this regard, the impending purchase of the JSF may be crucial. For Australia, the purchase of the JSF is the biggest defense project in the nation's history, with costs initially estimated at $10.5 billion for 100 aircraft now having escalated to $16 billion.

In addition, an internal Defense Ministry document suggests that the aircraft may have potential flaws that will reduce its overall effectiveness significantly.[11] In addition, Australian policymakers have threatened to cancel their participation in the project if they are not afforded the same full access to information concerning the plane's stealth technology which has been provided the United Kingdom. Clearly, the United States must do everything it can to support Australia in terms of technology transfers. This is especially true during the ongoing debate over the JSF, with Washington appearing more willing to share information with Great Britain than with Australia.

Developing National Security Strategies.

While ends, ways, and means are the components of strategy, the process whereby leaders determine policy also must be examined. Since 9/11 there is broad agreement that the definition of national security has changed. Natural disasters, pandemics, illegal immigration, etc., have become part of the discussion. American and Australian politicians have discovered that while there may be few votes in individual defense issues, there *are* votes in "national security," and the public pays close attention. In the United States, for example, it was not lost on the citizens of Louisiana that their National Guard brigade was in Baghdad and not New Orleans during the immediate aftermath of Hurricane Katrina.

In the United States, the proliferation of studies — QDR, *National Security Strategy* (NSS), *National Military Strategy* (NMS), Defense Strategy, *Global Repositioning Plan*, etc. — actually may confuse allies about U.S. strategic objectives. Consequently, the next U.S. presidential administration should consider seriously a comprehensive national security review that seeks to better integrate all elements of national power in dealing with the Long War, including in particular the role of allies.

Several Australian experts have pointed out that Canberra is still using a pre-9/11 White Paper with two updates, producing confusing and ambiguous guidance. Australia thus would benefit also from a defense review, an updated Defence White Paper, and a more robust National Security Council structure aimed at better integrating policy. Such improvements in the national security policy processes in both countries might allow a better determination of strategy for the alliance. This might in turn facilitate more forthcoming discussion of combined strategy to deal with the emergence of China and other strategic challenges.

Finally, it is becoming increasingly clear that in the war on terrorists, operations of military forces are only a modest part of the total effort. Consequently, leaders in Canberra and Washington must confront the question of whether their respective governments are organized to confront this emerging reality. Should the alliance collectively and individually focus greater efforts on building police forces that can be deployed to assist in providing stability to failed or failing states? Do our respective ministries of justice, treasury, agriculture, commerce, etc., have a cadre of professionals prepared to deploy, not unlike military forces, to troubled regions?

Conclusions.

Yogi Berra, the quintessential baseball player and philosopher, once observed, "It is hard to predict anything, especially the future." While this sage observation largely remains correct, we should remind ourselves that real leaders *make* the future. The new world of the 21st century that emphasizes the defense of values and interests rather than territory presents Australia and the United States with many new security challenges and a changed environment. An essential element in this new environment is the staggering influence exercised by the international news media. This fact demands that leaders more frequently and clearly communicate with the public in both the United States and Australia.

Defending Australian and American values, interests, and populations unfortunately will demand the expenditure of both blood and treasure. Some in Australia may believe, based on recent experience, that operations against terrorists and insurrectionists can occur without significant casualties. This blithe assumption obviously is not true, as the recent changes in the deployment of Australian forces in Iraq and renewed fighting in Afghanistan clearly indicate.[12]

In the United States, military and civilian leaders have suggested that we may be able to reduce our forces in Iraq significantly by the end of 2007. It is critically important, however, that the American public and our allies around the world not construe any such "success" in Iraq (however it might be defined) as somehow marking an end to the threat of terrorism from radical Islamic groups. Consequently, it is incumbent upon leaders in Washington and Canberra to speak candidly to their respective publics in order to maintain popular support for difficult choices that will need to be made.

To recapitulate, the defense relationship between the United States and Australia is both strong and pragmatic. It is based on many years of cooperation between military forces in peace and war. It is based on both national interests and common values that are embraced strongly by both countries. It truly has been another "special relationship."

In conclusion, let us return to our ever insightful philosopher, Yogi Berra. Yogi was once asked by a sportswriter, "How do you create a world championship team?" At which point Yogi quickly responded, "Get world championship players!" The alliance between the United States and Australia is a championship team. In raising, training, and equipping the military forces that underwrite the alliance, it remains the responsibility of future leaders of both nations to assure that those forces remain of championship caliber. The leaders must maintain and improve this alliance for the benefit of all, never taking it for granted, as the two nations confront the tough challenges that most certainly lie ahead.

ENDNOTES - CHAPTER 13

1. Guy Dinmore, "US Sees Coalitions of the Willing as Best Ally," *Financial Times*, January 5, 2006, p. 5.

2. Donald H. Rumsfeld, "America's Friendship with Asia," *Asian Wall Street Journal*, October 17, 2005, p. 21.

3. Malcolm Gladwell, *The Tipping Point*, New York: Time Warner Book Group, 2000.

4. The International Institute for Strategic Studies, *The Military Balance 2005-2006*, London: Taylor and Francis, Inc, 2005, p. 266.

5. "Turmoil in Timor Leste," *IISS Strategic Comments*, June 2006, pp. 1-2. See also Axel Kukuk, "Australia's Security Policy," *World Security Network Newsletter*, December 2005, pp. 2-7.

6. "The Proliferation Security Initiative (PSI) at a Glance," *Arms Control Association Fact Sheet*, Washington, DC, September 2005.

7. Steven R. Weisman, "Rice and Australian Counterpart Differ About China," *New York Times*, March 17, 2006, p. A8.

8. Department of Defense, "*Annual Report to Congress-Military Power of the People's Republic of China 2006*," Washington, DC, 2006.

9. Paul Dibb, "U.S.-Australian Alliance Relations: An Australian View," *Strategic Forum*, August 2006.

10. Andrew Krepinevich, "The Quadrennial Defense Review," Testimony before the House of Representatives, Committee on Armed Services, September 14, 2005.

11. Michael McKinnon, "Bid to Salvage Fighter Project," *The Weekend Australian*, June 24-25, 2006, p. 1. See also Ross Peake, "Doubts Over Our Planned New Fighter," *The Canberra Times*, July 1, 2006, p. B4.

12. Paul McGeough, "Headlong on the Road to Nowhere," *Sydney Morning Herald*, June 23, 2006, p. 13.

CHAPTER 14

THE UNITED STATES, AUSTRALIA, AND THE SEARCH FOR ORDER IN EAST ASIA AND BEYOND

James J. Przystup

Cold War in origin, the U.S. alliance structure in the years since September 11, 2001 (9/11), has evolved—and continues to evolve—to allow the United States and its alliance partners to address the security threats of the 21st century. The Department of Defense (DoD) 2006 Quadrennial Defense Review (QDR) is a critical document in addressing challenges to international stability and security for the United States and Australia. In operational terms, the alliance structure today is global in scope: North Atlantic Treaty Organization (NATO) forces are deployed in Afghanistan, Japan's Self Defense Force has engaged in a postwar reconstruction mission in Iraq, NATO is opening a security dialogue with Australia and Japan, and Australia's forces are operating in Iraq and again in East Timor. These developments point to a shared recognition among the allies of the global nature of threats to international order posed by terrorism, the proliferation of weapons of mass destruction (WMD), and the uncertain direction of emerging great powers.

Defining the Threat, Shaping the Response: The Quadrennial Defense Review, 2001-2006.

During the Cold War, the nature of the threat to the United States, its allies, and the western world was clear. Anticipating the nature of the post-Soviet world, Secretary of State Lawrence Eagleburger once remarked that the United States would likely miss, not the Soviet Union, but the certainty it provided strategists and defense planners. The 2001 QDR focused on the uncertain nature of threats in the post-9/11 world, accepting surprise as the starting point for defense planning. International terrorism, asymmetric threats, the proliferation of WMD, the diffusion of such capabilities to nonstate actors, and failing states were identified as key security challenges.

The 2001 QDR also addressed the imperative of transforming the U.S. military to allow it to meet the challenges of the post-9/11 security environment. Key concepts involved in transformation were the development of a capabilities–based approach to force planning; the development of joint operating concepts; and the implementation of global force planning. The capabilities-based approach meant that forces no longer would be shaped to deal with a specific adversary in a particular region of the world. Rather, forces would be developed to address how any adversary with access to a wide range of capabilities might fight. Joint operating concepts highlighted networked-linked, dispersed forces, benefiting from speed of decisionmaking and flexibility in planning and execution, and allowing for greater interoperability with allies. Finally, global force planning would allow decisionmakers to manage the integration of forces deployed across the globe to dissuade, deter, or defeat adversaries in various regions.

Over the past 4 years, these concepts have guided the redeployment of U.S. forces in Europe as well as the Asia-Pacific region. On the Korean Peninsula, U.S. forces have pulled back from static defense along the demilitarized zone (DMZ), moving south of the Han

River and to the coast to establish more operationally tenable positions. This has had the effect of increasing flexibility and enhancing deterrence by complicating North Korean planning. The process has been complemented by the recent agreement with Japan to redeploy U.S. forces into and from Japan and to accelerate joint planning to deal with a wide range of security contingencies.

The terms of reference for the 2006 QDR were set out in the *Global Posture Review* (GPR) of August 2004. In short, the GPR spoke to the need to expand the role of allies and build new security partnerships in meeting challenges to international stability and security. At the same time, the GPR called for a reduction of the overseas deployments of U.S. forces in order to reduce tensions with host governments and make security relationships more politically sustainable over time. The GPR emphasized the need for greater operational flexibility and mobility, and for the avoidance of concentration. To this end, it called for the development of readily deployable forces, with the ability to act within and across regions. Released in February, the 2006 QDR does not herald a new beginning; rather, the document represents continuity and is best understood as an exercise in consolidating lessons learned.

Continuity is found in the emphasis on the elements of uncertainty and surprise as the foundation for defense planning. The document continues to underscore the importance of transformation, the need to develop forces that are expeditionary in nature, i.e., that are more mobile, agile, and readily deployable. It continues the call for adjustments in the U.S. global force posture — to move from static defense to the development of surge capabilities. And it continues to emphasize capabilities as opposed to specific adversaries. In this regard, the development of intelligence and surveillance capabilities is highlighted.

At the same time, the global war on terrorists has yielded a number of critical lessons for both the United States and Australia. Among them is the concept of the Long War, a conflict unique in history, that will be waged not against nation-states but simultaneously against nonstate networks in regions across the globe. The Long War is defined as being ideological in nature, with terrorist adversaries attempting to advance "a radical theocratic tyranny."[1] Similarly, Australia's *Defence Update* 2003 recognizes the ideological nature of the conflict, defining the terrorists' objective to be the "roll back" of Western values, engagement, and influence."[2] Likewise, it speaks to the global nature of the threat, making clear that "Australia's security is affected if there are any regions in the world from which terrorists . . . can operate internationally with impunity."[3] Beyond Afghanistan and Iraq, the Long War will be marked by irregular warfare as opposed to conflict among nation-states. Consequently, all U.S. ground forces will be trained for counterinsurgency warfare. The division/corps structure of the Cold War will transition to self-sustaining brigades.

The 2006 QDR, however, recognizes that the struggle against terrorism "cannot be won by military force alone." Accordingly, the United States is focused on helping partners "to police and govern their nations," thus "decreasing the possibility of failed states or ungoverned spaces in which terrorist extremists can more easily operate or take shelter."[4] The document stresses the importance of both military and civilian engagement with U.S. partners, the need to develop greater language skills as well as cultural sensitivity within the U.S. military, and the need for the military to build the capacity to work with police and interior ministries.

In this regard, the 2006 QDR acknowledges the importance of building partnerships and enhancing the capabilities of partners to work together, allowing the United States to act indirectly through others and "shifting from conducting activities ourselves to enabling partners to do more for themselves." Working with partners who possess "greater local knowledge" is viewed as making counterterrorist actions more effective at the tactical and operational levels, while at the same time enhancing U.S. forces' freedom of action at the strategic level.[5]

Australia's *Defence Update* 2005 accepts that global war on terrorists will demand more of American allies and partners. The report notes that in the post-9/11 security environment, the United States is seeking "more flexible options" in the use of its military forces, while expecting its allies to "contribute a greater share of the cost of their own and the region's security." In this regard, *Defence Update* 2005 details Australia's efforts at capacity-building in the Asia-Pacific region, enabling neighboring governments to extend governance and meet the challenges of economic development, internal order, and security.

Beyond its military contributions in Afghanistan and Iraq, Australia's interest, knowledge, and under-standing of its Asia-Pacific neighborhood are key assets relevant to extending governance and denying ungoverned operational space to terrorists. In Southeast Asia, Australia has worked with various governments, Indonesia in particular, to enhance border and maritime security and to strengthen counterterrorist capabilities, including intelligence sharing. In the Southwest Pacific, the Australia-led Regional Assistance Mission has brought stability to the Solomon Islands. Australia also is working with the government of Papua New Guinea (PNG) to professionalize the PNG police force and to enhance overall governance. In East Timor, Australia again has deployed military units to assist in restoring order and to prevent East Timor from becoming a failed state.

Given the globalization of the international security environment and Australia's own national interests, *Defence Updates* 2003 and 2005 recognize the increased likelihood of Australian forces participating in coalition operations beyond its immediate neighborhood. At the same time, the documents note that instability and the lack of governance affecting many states in Southeast Asia and the Southwest Pacific region provide potential breeding grounds for international terrorists. Australia's particular interests in the Asia-Pacific region will require that the Australian Defence Force (ADF) be prepared to respond there as well. The need to balance the demands of coalition operations beyond the Asia-Pacific region with expeditionary deployments closer to home is reflected in Australia's defense debate over force structure and procurement.

The recent deployment of the ADF to East Timor and the decision announced by Prime Minster John Howard on June 22, 2006, of Australia's continuing commitment in Iraqi underscore the global-regional span of Australia's security interests and the multiplicity of the roles and missions demanded of and performed by the ADF.

The QDR and China.

In 2001, the QDR characterized Asia as "gradually emerging as a region susceptible to large-scale military competition." Without naming China, the document raised the possibility that "a military competitor with a formidable resource base will emerge in the region." The 2006 QDR, after acknowledging Russia and India as emerging powers and crossroads states, makes clear that "of the major and emerging powers," China has the greatest potential to compete militarily with the United States and field disruptive military technologies that, over time, could offset U.S. military advantages absent U.S. counter strategies. Obviously, Australia also is keenly interested in the emergence of China, as it has experienced growing economic ties with Beijing. The QDR does encourage China to play a "constructive and peaceful role"; serve as a "partner in addressing common security challenges"; and follow the "path of peaceful economic growth and political liberalization." The hope is that, in so doing, China ultimately will "emerge as a responsible stakeholder and force for the good in the world."

At the same time, the document expresses concern with China's ongoing military modernization, in particular the growth of its strategic arsenal and enhanced power projection capabilities, and its lack of transparency. Accordingly, the QDR calls for a "balanced approach" toward China, one that "seeks cooperation but also creates prudent hedges." In the Pacific, key elements of the QDR's "hedging" strategy include the deployment of an additional carrier to the region, diversification of U.S. basing, strengthened alliance cooperation, and the development of long-range strike capabilities.[6]

The QDR's treatment of China reflects the ongoing policy debate in Washington over the implications of China's rise for U.S. interests in East Asia. In 2004, the Institute for National Strategic Studies (INSS) initiated a study on China and Southeast Asia. In brief, the findings of the study are as follows:

- Southeast Asia increasingly sees China as a partner and market opportunity: the days of the "China threat" are fast receding into history. At the same time, Beijing is effectively leveraging its future potential to increase its influence.

- China's economic dynamism is beginning to restructure economic relations in Southeast Asia. Beijing's free trade agenda is viewed positively as a way to build mutually beneficial economic interdependence.

- Beijing's embrace of multilateralism and across-the-board cooperation, often contrasted with perceived U.S. unilateralism and a narrow focus on fighting terrorism, is winning support in Southeast Asia.

- Although the regional balance of power is considered stable, the balance of influence is perceived as moving in China's direction. At the same time, Southeast Asian governments welcome a continuing U.S. presence in the region as the key to preserving a balance of power and managing China's emergence.

- Southeast Asian governments will seek to avoid any controversy that would involve making a choice between the United States and China.

Within the Bush administration, views of China and China policy more often than not follow the political dictum "where you stand depends on where you sit." In U.S. perceptions, there are many "Chinas" and many China policies competing for primacy.

For example, there is the World Trade Organization (WTO) China, one that is integrating itself into the international trading system, increasingly rules-based in its conduct and open to market-oriented reforms. Over time, it is a China in which, it is hoped, the workings of market forces will create political space between the government/party and the individual, resulting in some form of political liberalization. This is the "good China." There also is the post-9/11 China, the U.S. partner in the global war on terrorists. There is a third China that masquerades as the WTO China, one that, while apparently accepting international rules, is prepared to evade or violate them to secure its ends. A fourth China is the Congressional China—the China that violates human rights, pursues mercantilist policies aimed at controlling markets, manipulates currency, and threatens Taiwan.

A fifth China is former Deputy Secretary of State Robert Zoellick's "stakeholder" China. Zoellick was attempting to assert the State Department's voice and primacy in the China policy debate. Beyond this, his objective was to move China beyond integration into the international economic system to the point of becoming "a responsible international stakeholder," an approach representing an interest-based search for accommodation at the global level. It holds out the possibility that cooperation at the global level can extend back into East Asia. Zoellick was expressing U.S. respect for China's interests in the region—without specifically identifying which of the interests in the United States was to respect and what degree of respect the United States should accord.[7]

Zoellick's China-centric engagement strategy in both its global and regional dimensions marked a departure from the strategy of the 2001-05 Bush administration. Under then Deputy Secretary of State Richard Armitage, U.S. strategy focused on Japan and the U.S.-Japan alliance. Armitage's approach started with the bilateral alliance, grounded on shared values, and worked outward toward the region and the possibility of a mature global partnership. The objective of policy was a strengthened alliance that would enhance stability and security in East Asia and beyond. While rejecting containment as a strategy for China, the unstated direction of the report is toward a hedging strategy. The United States and Japan would work to encourage China's evolution as a responsible regional actor, but, should China move in an opposite direction, it would have to deal with a reinvigorated alliance.[8]

The 2006 *National Security Strategy* combines both "stakeholder" and hedge strategies toward China. It encourages China "to walk the transformative path of peaceful development"; that is, to "continue down the road of reform and openness" and thus meet the "aspirations of the Chinese people for liberty, stability, and prosperity." At the same time, the *National Security Strategy* expresses concern with China's ongoing military modernization and lack of transparency. The document concludes by encouraging China "to make the right strategic choices for its people, while we hedge against other possibilities."[9]

Successful implementation of the hedge strategy will require paying careful attention to the proper balance between the engagement and military elements of the strategy. In the interplay of U.S. global and regional security interests, it also will require a clear choice of priorities in defining the right policy balance between China and Japan. The choices made by the United States with respect to security interests in East Asia also are likely to affect the degree of global cooperation from Tokyo and Beijing.

The Challenge of North Korea and the Korean Peninsula.

For the United States, Australia, and the rest of the Asia-Pacific region, North Korea poses multifaceted challenges. North Korea today is both a declining state, whose implosion could destabilize the Peninsula and large areas of Northeast Asia, and at the same time a continuing military threat to the security of the Republic of Korea (ROK) and to U.S. forces deployed on the Peninsula. North Korea also is a rogue state engaged in a large range of illegal activities ranging from counterfeiting to the production and distribution of illegal substances and the proliferation of weapons of mass destruction (WMD).

It is as a proliferator of WMD that North Korea poses the greatest threat to international security. To deal with the threat of North Korean exports of WMD-facilitative materials, the Bush administration has advanced the Proliferation Security Initiative (PSI). Australia, recognizing the threat posed by failing states, terrorists, and WMD proliferation, has participated in PSI-related exercises from their inception. Japan likewise has participated in and sponsored PSI-related activities. Recently, Japan's Coast Guard organized a multinational exercise aimed at stopping and searching a ship suspected of carrying illegal cargo.

North Korea's pursuit of nuclear weapons underscores the leadership's intense focus on regime survival. An equally important element in Kim Il Sung's survival strategy is North Korea's growing engagement with the South. This engagement provides both economic and political benefits. In terms of economics, the North benefits from shipments of food, fertilizer, and hard-to-track cash transfers from the South. Politically, engagement has served to drive wedges into the ROK-U.S. relationship.

While Seoul's long-term strategic goal remains peaceful unification under its leadership, the reality of North Korea presents it with the immediate, day-to-day challenge of dealing with Pyongyang. In this context, Seoul seeks to promote reconciliation (not necessarily unification); avoid war; avoid collapse in Pyongyang; and prevent a nuclear North Korea. Seoul's focus on reconciliation and avoidance of collapse affects its approach to the nuclear challenge posed by North Korea. The hope in Seoul is that engagement ultimately will dissolve North Korea's security paranoia and lead it to surrender the nuclear program. While the ROK speaks of not tolerating a nuclear North Korea, its engagement strategy actually helps to sustain it. Meanwhile, Seoul and Washington today are involved in a process of transforming the alliance and the U.S presence on the Korean Peninsula so as to enhance the alliance's effectiveness and make it more politically sustainable over time in both countries. Nevertheless, the alliance will have to deal with the evolving political situation both on the Peninsula and in the United States.

On the Peninsula, the election of Kim Dae Jung, the adoption of the Sunshine Policy, and the historic June 2000 Summit in Pyongyang proved to be transformational, at least in the South, with regard to South-North relations. No longer was the North to be viewed as the primary enemy, but rather as a down-on-his-luck elder brother, deserving sympathy — and subsidies — from the South. Kim Jong Il, however, remained just unpredictable and volatile enough to spook the South from risking criticism of the North Korean regime and its practices, including human rights abuses and illegal activities. Once nuclearized, an angry Kim could strike the South at a moment's notice, obliterating 50 years of economic progress and wealth accumulation.

While the Summit proved transformational in the South, North Korea's political and economic system largely remains unchanged. North Korea continues to exploit concerns about the negative consequences of regime collapse to secure a minimalist life support assistance package. With regard to both Kim Dae Jung and now President Roh, North Korea, in a feat of diplomatic jujitsu, has been able to leverage the proclaimed success of the South's engagement policies into a continuing cash cow. Joint meetings are a frequently cited metric that defines the political success of the engagement policy. But to demonstrate success, the Seoul has to pay in the form of economic and financial inducements.

North Korea's ability to capitalize on fears of its own collapse is matched somewhat by South Korea's apprehensions over the stratospheric costs of unification. ROK officials, having studied and restudied the German experience carefully after the end of the Cold War, recognize that costs involved in Korean unification would dwarf those involved in uniting the two Germanies. Keeping the North afloat, while costly, is economically and financially preferable and infinitely less expensive than picking up the bill for unification.

In this regard, China's concern with stability on its borders and apparent determination not to allow North Korea to collapse are crucial factors in prolonging the Kim regime. China's steadfast support for the Democratic People's Republic of Korea (DPRK) has served as a disincentive for Pyongyang to abandon its nuclear program. In Washington, Beijing's reluctance to manage its economic assistance programs so as to move North Korea toward surrender of its nuclear program has raised questions of China's sincerity regarding the stakeholder concept. China's willingness to support the Bush administration's diplomacy on the nuclear challenge likewise is viewed as a test of Beijing's commitment to being a responsible stakeholder.

Ending North Korea's nuclear weapons program and the threat of proliferation from the Peninsula remains the objective of the Six Party talks. Interests in avoiding war and avoiding a nuclear North Korea are shared broadly by the United States, the ROK, China, Japan, and Russia. Interests, however, begin to diverge on avoiding a collapse of the North Korean state, and the priorities attached to the individual interests are ordered differently in the respective capitals.

For Washington, ending North Korea's nuclear program is of primary importance. Of least concern is the collapse of the North Korean state. Indeed, many in Washington would regard the end of North Korea as the only foolproof way to end its nuclear programs. Few tears would be shed over the passing of that long-time thorn in the American side. For Seoul, and Beijing as well, avoiding a nuclear North Korea is important, but the real nightmare scenario is that of implosion and collapse. At the same time, actions that could provoke an unpredictable regime to react in unpredictable ways, including the use of force, likewise are to be avoided. This difference in priorities is reflected in the clearly different tactical approaches to the North and the nuclear issues.

Nevertheless, for the short term, the Six Party process will continue because it serves the political and diplomatic interests of all the governments concerned.

- For China, it allows Beijing to exhibit diplomatic leadership, play a central role in any resolution of the issue, and increase its influence in Seoul.

- For North Korea, the process allows economic aid and assistance from the South to continue to flow, daily deepening South Korea's engagement and daily making it more difficult for Seoul to criticize or pursue a hostile policy toward the North. Meanwhile, Pyongyang continues its nuclear program.

- For the ROK, the process represents another link in its engagement strategy and strengthens the hope that over time North Korea can be persuaded to surrender its nuclear ambitions. And as long as the process continues, it serves to constrain bad behavior on the part of Pyongyang—e.g., more missile launches or nuclear tests.

- For the United States, the process is the best hope of peacefully resolving an issue for which there are no good answers should the process fail. Should the process break down, the Bush administration may find itself having to "do something else," which could be quite unpalatable.

- For Japan, the diplomatic promise offers hope of peaceful resolution, but the continuation of North Korea's nuclear program is a matter of immediate security concern.

The policy question that must addressed is how long the Six Party process can continue without progress on the nuclear issue—what steps should be taken in the event of no progress or, worse, intensification by North

Korea of its missile nuclear weapons development. At this time, there are no apparent answers, but diplomatic divisions on this issue can degrade significantly relations among the United States, the ROK, and China, all to the benefit of Pyongyang. A breakdown in alliance cooperation in Northeast Asia would affect prospects for stability significantly across the Asia-Pacific region.

Concluding Thoughts.

In a soon-to-be-published paper, Bill Tow and Amitav Acharya accurately note that the U.S. security role in East Asia is in the process of historic change. The Cold War hub-and-spokes structure is giving way to less traditional and more nuanced policy approaches to deal with the challenges posed by the global war on terrorists and nontraditional threats and humanitarian contingencies. This evolution of the U.S. alliance structure and security strategy is well reflected in the 2006 QDR, which by self-admission is a document of lessons learned. Among the principal lessons are that the struggle against terrorism cannot be won by military force alone—or even principally; that the United States cannot succeed through its own might or by acting alone; and that success will require rather the building of coalitions and partnerships and reliance on partners with greater local knowledge.

At the same time, long-standing alliance relationships in East Asia should not be thought outmoded. The alliances with Australia, Japan, and the ROK remain the foundation of security in the region and beyond. Together with NATO, the Asian alliances serve as the starting point for whatever coalitions develop in the post-9/11 era. In the words of the 2006

QDR, these relationships will "continue to underpin unified efforts to address 21st century challenges." For example, the United States, the ROK, and Japan provide a foundation for the Six Party talks; the United States, Australia, and Japan strategic dialogue has relevance not only for East Asia but for Iraq, Iran, and the Middle East as well. The nascent NATO, Australia, and Japan strategic dialogue undoubtedly will be global in interest and scope. And of special note, these alliances remain potent inducements for China to move toward responsible stakeholdership, which is in the manifest interest of the Asia-Pacific region and the entire international community.

America's Asian allies may no longer be relying exclusively on Washington. That they are expanding the range of security contacts is both undeniable and, in the context of the 2006 QDR, supportive of post-9/11 international order. In sum, the alliances are evolving and, in doing so, contributing to stability and security in the Asia-Pacific region and beyond.

ENDNOTES - CHAPTER 14

1. U.S. Department of Defense, *Quadrennial Defense Review*, February 6, 2006, p. 1.

2. "Australia's National Security," *A Defence Update* 2003, Commonwealth of Australia, p. 11.

3. *Ibid.* p. 13. Interestingly, the report issued in October 2004 by Japan's Council on Security and Defense Capabilities makes a similar point in addressing the global nature of the threat posed to Japan's security, noting that the objective of Japan's security strategy is "to reduce the chances of threats arising in various parts of the world . . . from reaching Japan or affecting the interests of Japanese expatriates and corporations overseas."

4. QDR 2006, pp. 9, 11.

5. *Ibid.*, pp. 2, 23.

6. *Ibid.*, pp. 29-30.

7. Robert B. Zoellick, "Whither China: From Membership to Responsibility," Remarks to the National Committee on U.S.-China Relations, New York, September 21, 2005.

8. *The United States and Japan: Advancing Toward a Mature Partnership*, Washington, DC: National Defense University, October 2000.

9. The *National Security Strategy of the United States*, 2006, pp. 40-42.

CHAPTER 15

SECURITY AND DEFENSE ASPECTS OF THE SPECIAL RELATIONSHIP: AN AUSTRALIAN PERSPECTIVE

Michael Evans

Alliances are like girls and roses. They last while they last.

— Charles de Gaulle

Since the middle of the 20th century, the Australian-American alliance, based upon shared cultural values, national interest, and a tradition of friendship, has been part of the framework of Australian politics. Although the emphasis and weight given by various Australian governments to the alliance has differed over the past half century, both major political parties, Liberal-National and Labor, have accepted the long-term security and defense benefits of the special relationship with America. In the words of the eminent Australian historian, Peter Edwards, "The Alliance is a political institution in its own right; it may be questioned from time to time by Australians but its existence is seldom challenged."[1] There is no mood in Australia for the kind of insular nationalism that, in the mid-1980s, led New Zealand to disrupt the original Australia-New Zealand-United States (ANZUS) Pact over the issue of American nuclear armed warships visiting its ports.

Because of Australia's bipartisan political consensus over the value of the alliance, the real questions that will shape and define the future of the security relationship with the United States in the early 21st century relate to custodianship of the national interest and alliance management. From the Australian perspective, the key issue regarding the alliance is the level of political skill demonstrated by the Australian government in the daily managing of this bilateral relationship in order that its benefits may be maximized and its costs minimized. This chapter thus concentrates on examining the security and defense aspects of the Australian-American alliance. Four perspectives will be developed. First, the chapter examines how, at the beginning of a new millennium, the health of the alliance is connected intimately to the internal Australian defense debate. Second, we shall explore the implications of a new and different globalized security environment for the workings of an alliance forged at the beginning of the Cold War, in order to assess whether the context for Australian-American cooperation has changed irrevocably in an age of transnational and networked warfare.

Third, this chapter assesses Australia's latitude in developing functional independence when managing the diplomatic, defense, and security dimensions of the alliance over the next decade — particularly as the John Howard government attempts to evolve a global-regional policy seeking to reconcile relations with America with engagement in Asia. Fourth, in an age in which integrated national security policies are rapidly subsuming autonomous defense strategies, the chapter investigates whether Australia's official strategic doctrine as outlined in the 2000 *Defence White Paper* has continued relevance. In this regard, the extent to which the defense component of a national security strategy might be reconfigured to meet the demands of a new era is analyzed.

Defender-Regionalists and Reformer-Globalists: The Alliance and the Australian Defence Debate.

Ever since the al-Qai'da attacks on New York and Washington on September 11, 2001 (9/11), led to Australian participation in the Bush administration's war on terror and to military campaigns in Afghanistan and Iraq, questions of alliance management have assumed a sharper focus in Australian politics. Questions have arisen in Australia over the balance to be struck on such issues as alliance commitment versus national independence; on global allegiance versus regional commitment; and on dependence versus self-reliance.[2] These questions have been magnified and complicated by the fact that the Australian defense and security debate currently is divided into two opposing schools of strategic philosophy: the defender-regionalists and the reformer-globalists.[3]

The defender-regionalists represent a strand of strategic thought that first emerged in the mid-1970s and 1980s in the wake of the controversy over Australia's involvement in the Vietnam War. It is a school of thought closely associated with such figures as Paul Dibb and Hugh White, who formulated the geostrategic doctrine of the defense of Australia. Defender-regionalists believe that Australian defense policy should be governed by the principle of preparing for the most serious contingency, namely, an attack on Australian territory through the "sea-air gap" of the northern island archipelagos. According to this logic, Australia's defense effort should be concerned mainly with the creation of a powerful air and naval arsenal designed to secure the continental approaches. The defender-regionalists tend to be "little Australians" or continentalists, who view the defense instrument as being defined by fixed geographical, rather than fluid policy, imperatives. Moreover, advocates of the defender school emphasize that Australia's security relationship with the United States is based on the 1980s notion of self-reliance in an alliance framework. When it comes to 21st century security, many defender-regionalists tend to believe that 9/11 and the new global security agenda of transnational threats may be transient or exaggerated and is, consequently, far less important than the old regional security agenda of interstate tensions in the Asia-Pacific revolving around such flash points as Kashmir, the Taiwan straits, and North Korea's nuclear ambitions.[4]

The reformer-globalists are a school of thought largely associated with former Defence Minister, Senator Robert Hill. It is a strand of strategic thought that views the 1980s Australian defense policy as a form of unrealistic geographical determinism because it seeks to disconnect defense planning from foreign policy interests. Although it is sometimes erroneously styled an Army school of strategic thought, reformer-globalists tend to be maritimists as opposed to continentalists in their strategic outlook. They believe that Australia's geopolitical identity is that of a trade-dependent maritime state in the Anglo-American liberal tradition. Accordingly, Australia's destiny lies in its history as a liberal democracy and in the web of cultural and trading links that give Australia both its national identity and international purpose. Most reformer-globalists view 9/11 as the seminal event in revealing a new global security agenda dominated by the emergence of networked conflict and by the reality of America's global power. The reformers tend to be influenced by the writings of such theorists as Philip Bobbitt, Robert Cooper, and James Rosenau on the changing character of global order and security. Such concepts as Bobbitt's Long War and the emergent market-state, Cooper's ideas of premodern, modern, and postmodern states, and Rosenau's bifurcation theory of a two-world political universe provide a framework for thinking about strategy in a fluid and post-industrial, globalized world.[5]

For the reformers, the continuities of Australian strategy derived from the Cold War are increasingly insufficient to meet the changes that face Australia in meeting 21st century security requirements. They believe that Australian security policy must embrace both global and regional imperatives, and that the geographical doctrine of Defence of Australia (DOA) is essentially a relic from the Cold War that should be modified in favor of a more outward-looking national security strategy. Such a strategy should embrace regional and global policies, both near and far security commitments, and accommodation for both nonstate and traditional interstate challenges. For the reformer-globalists, Australia has entered a new age of globalization and transnational networks in which national interests need to be upheld by a limited but effective expeditionary capacity that transcends the defense of local geography.[6]

Over the past 5 years, the course of events and commitments to overseas operations in Afghanistan and Iraq have tilted Australian statecraft and security strategy in favor of the reformer-globalists. Yet the ideological supremacy of the reformer-globalists has not yet been translated into concrete change in strategic doctrine. The Australian Defence Force (ADF) is still directed by a pre-9/11 strategic planning document that upholds geostrategic imperatives drawn from the Cold War era, namely, the *Defence 2000* White

Paper.[7] In this respect, it is important to remember that the recent *Defence Updates* of 2003 and 2005 remain essentially meditative statements about the rise of global terrorism, the danger of weapons of mass destruction (WMD), and the threats posed by failed states.[8] Both of the 21st century Australian *Defence Updates* represent intellectual way-stations along the road towards the evolution of new strategic doctrine. The updates are not detailed policy documents; rather, they are attempts to reconcile continuity with change in an era of transition. Not surprisingly, both reviews remain ambiguous and even contradictory in tone — proclaiming simultaneously the arrival of a new security era, yet adhering to the principles of *Defence 2000.*[9]

Indeed, it is difficult to avoid the conclusion that the 2003 and 2005 reviews reflect the gap between the rhetoric of change within the defense establishment and the reality of stasis — at least in terms of endorsed strategic doctrine. In part, the contradictory and ambiguous tone of the two documents can be explained by the divisions in the Australian strategic policy community, which have prevented policy from undertaking a full embrace of the reality of a globalized security environment. It is to this new phenomenon that we now must turn.

Australia, the New Global Security Environment, and the Alliance.

At the beginning of the 21st century, the traditional international system that links sovereignty to Westphalian-style territorial borders has been supplemented by a new globalized security environment. Increasingly, Australia faces a post-industrial world of networks, information technology, and failed states in which violence and threat have become global in nature and can bypass the barriers of national geography.[10] What American theorist Robert Keohane has called "the globalization of informal violence" has occurred. With it, distinctions between civil and international conflict, between internal and external security, and between national and societal security have begun to erode in both time and space.[11] It is important to grasp that the emerging globalized world of the 21st century has not abolished the traditional world order of territorial states; rather, it has superimposed itself upon that older order. In James Rosenau's famous phrase, humanity must now learn to inhabit "two worlds of world politics," the interstate world and the nonstate world. In the new millennium, global security challenge has been recast in terms of a state-centric system and a multicentric system that coexist in a bifurcated world.[12]

The globalization of security, and the bifurcated operating environment it has created, have brought with it three other important changes. The first is a shift in strategic thinking away from a preoccupation with national defense based on borders alone. As nation-states have lost their traditional monopoly over violence, there has been a greater appreciation by advanced states of the phenomenon of networks, interconnectedness, and the potential danger posed by WMD in the use of force. The second change involves the increasing merger of foreign, defense, and domestic policies in advanced countries under the impact of the microelectronic revolution. Third, there is a blending of what were once clearly defined and separate categories of conventional and unconventional warfare into the phenomenon of multidimensional armed conflict. At the beginning of the new millennium, the global diffusion of technology and information networks has created a mosaic of war in which violence and disorder are waged by both state and nonstate forces. Collectively, this complex, bifurcated 21st century security environment places a premium on liberal democracies possessing readiness, speed, and flexibility to meet unexpected challenges through a mixture of expeditionary military forces and an array of homeland security measures.[13]

To what extent has Australia accepted, and responded to, the reality of globalized security and to the two worlds of world politics with their bifurcated interstate and multicentric components? And what has been the impact on the alliance? As will be seen, in some of its key policy actions, the Howard government has departed decisively from the geostrategic doctrine it inherited from the 1980s and has embraced some of the views of the reformer-globalists. The government's approach has been to recognize that Australia's security is interconnected with global security and that the latter is dominated by a single superpower, namely, the United States. As a result, the Howard government has sought over the past decade to reinvent the Australian-American alliance as a deliberate act of policy.[14]

Under a policy of alliance rejuvenation, Australia has been prepared to undertake global as well as regional security responsibilities. Although the policy of reinventing the alliance relationship began in July 1996 with the Sydney statement that sought to relate the Australian-American special relationship to the post-Cold War era, it was given real focus by the attacks on New York and Washington on 9/11. Howard was visiting Washington on that fateful day and witnessed first-hand America's collective trauma and grief. Flying home aboard Air Force Two, on

September 13, the Australian Prime Minister invoked Article IV of the ANZUS Alliance. Not even a writer of thrillers such as Tom Clancy could have foreseen that ANZUS, originally devised as a Cold War pact for the security of the Pacific region in 1951, would be invoked by junior partner Australia following a suicide strike by Middle Eastern fanatics on the continental United States half a century later.[15]

Since 9/11, Australia has joined the United States in combating transnational terrorism and has provided military contingents to meet the crises in Afghanistan and Iraq. Alongside these global commitments to the alliance, the Howard government has sought to confront festering regional strategic issues such as the spread of militant political Islamism into South East Asia, and the governance crisis in Pacific states such as Papua New Guinea, the Solomon Islands, and East Timor. The ongoing Regional Assistance Mission to the Solomons (RAMSI) and the second military intervention mission in East Timor in May 2006 demonstrate Australia's concern for regional stability. Indeed, there has been an acceptance that the U.S.-led global war on terrorists has regional ramifications since it is linked ideologically to the politics of both Indonesia and the Philippines. These linkages have been demonstrated by the rise of *Jemaah Islamiah* and the 2002 Bali and 2004 Jakarta bombing attacks and by the interlocking of global and regional terrorist networks in the southern Philippines.[16]

The aim of Australian security policy therefore has been to prevent what former Minister of Defence Senator Robert Hill described in 2003 as a global arc of terrorism intersecting with a regional sea of instability in the form of failed and weak states in the Asia-Pacific.[17] This global-regional strategy is reflected explicitly in the December 2005 *Defence Update* that states: "The risk of convergence between failing states, terrorism, and the proliferation of WMDs remains a major and continuing threat to international security."[18] In this way, the Howard government has recast Australian thinking about security threats in the 21st century. Over the last 5 years, Howard has upheld the primacy of the alliance as the main bulwark of Australia's security in the new millennium. As the 2005 *Defence Update* puts it:

> The Australian-U.S. Alliance forged during the Cold War remains as relevant and as important as ever. It is based on shared values and interests and remains the cornerstone of our national security. The continued evolution of the alliance to meet new strategic challenges is an enduring strength of the relationship.[19]

In June 2004, only a few months before the general election, much of the Australian Government's thinking since 2001 was summed up in a key speech to the Australian Strategic Policy Institute by the Prime Minister. In this address, Howard dismissed those in the Australian strategic debate who advocated a "narrowly-defined defense doctrine that would circle the wagons and deny Australia a capability to cooperate with allies beyond our shores."[20] The Prime Minister declared that "a geographically cramped, value-free style of realism is dangerously complacent and contrary to Australia's interests." He quoted approvingly the work of such prominent American scholars on the globalization of security as Philip Bobbitt and Joseph Nye. He also expressed scepticism toward the likelihood of conventional attacks upon Australia and announced that Australia would develop an integrated national security strategy in order to promote global and regional security.[21] For Howard, maintaining a global perspective, albeit one that is influenced by regional considerations, "is a measure of our [Australia's] maturity as a nation."[22] Thus, in some key respects, the Howard government has accepted the core arguments of the reformer-globalists, at least in the areas of the primacy of the alliance, the reality of a globalized security environment, and the need for a national security strategy.

Alliance Management and Australia's Functional Principle.

It is no exaggeration to state that in the first decade of the new millennium, the Australian-American alliance is at its strongest since the height of the Vietnam War in the mid-1960s. In an opinion piece in June 2006, *Washington Post* columnist Charles Krauthammer highlighted this reality in noting that "Australia is the only country that has fought with the United States in every one of its major conflicts since 1914, the good and the bad, the winning and the losing."[23] Similarly warm sentiments have been expressed at the highest level within the administration of George W. Bush. For example, in August 2003 Deputy Secretary of State Richard Armitage memorably told the closed-door Australia-America Dialogue Meeting in Melbourne that many Americans viewed Australians as a singularly tough people whose men "shaved with a chainsaw and trimmed their nails with a jackhammer."[24] Although Armitage accepted that Australian and American interests were not always necessarily identical, he argued that historically they usually were highly correlated because of a shared belief in the importance of defending Western liberal democratic values. The special relationship, he noted, was built upon a common perspective and action "forged out of the bones of our fathers and grandfathers and now of the blood of our children."[25]

In May 2003, when Howard visited Bush at the latter's ranch in Crawford, Texas, the American President personally hailed the Australian Prime Minister as "a man of steel" for his support over Iraq.[26] The passage of time since the invasion of Iraq has not diminished official American warmth towards Australia. Three years later, in May 2006, when Howard again visited the United States, the American President described the Australian leader as a "man of conviction" and an "ally, friend, and a good strategic thinker."[27] Yet, historically, Australians and Americans have not always been on such amicable terms. It is worth remembering that President Woodrow Wilson found Prime Minister Billy Hughes so difficult over the territorial settlement at the Paris Peace Talks of 1919 that he described the latter as a "pestiferous varmint."[28] Moreover, in the 1920s and 1930s, Australian-American relations were cool and often marked by difficult trade disputes. Indeed, it was not until World War II that Australians and Americans found common ideological cause in a struggle against totalitarian dictatorship and tyranny.[29]

The point to grasp is that the Australian-American relationship is not static, but dynamic, and it is conditioned by the state of international politics in any given era. In 1951, the alliance began as an instrument of Pacific stability, and its signing was influenced by Japanese rearmament, the onset of the Cold War in general, and of the Korean War in particular. In the 1950s and 1960s the alliance was marked by cooperative military action in Asia using forward deployments of U.S. and Australian forces in Korea and Vietnam. In the 1970s and 1980s, the emphasis within the alliance switched towards greater Australian self-reliance along with technical and intelligence cooperation. In particular, the Australian-U.S. Joint Defence Facilities at Nurrungar and Pine Gap became important installations in America's nuclear targeting regime. In the post-Cold War era of the 1990s, cooperation on information age weaponry in the form of the Revolution in Military Affairs and the rise of networked warfare became significant features of alliance activity. In 1996, the joint Australian-American Sydney Statement described the alliance as a major contribution to the development of a stable regional security environment that promoted democracy, human rights, and economic prosperity.[30]

In the early 21st century in the wake of 9/11, the alliance has evolved yet again, encompassing cooperation in the upholding of both regional and global order. From the U.S. strategic perspective, the alliance has become a multidimensional instrument, with both the U.S. *National Security Strategy* and the *Quadrennial Defense Review* of 2006 viewing Australia as a global ally.[31] From the Australian perspective, America's focus on multidimensionality means that America is a more active and demanding ally. How has the Howard government reacted to this evolution? Some figures in Australian politics, notably former Opposition Leader Mark Latham and former Liberal Prime Minister Malcolm Fraser, have attacked Howard as being too subservient to, and compliant with, U.S. policies. Other critics have argued that the United States is now a revolutionary superpower committed to unilateralism and have implied that Howard has sacrificed Australian engagement in Asia on the altar of the alliance.[32]

The reality is very different. While there has been increased strategic interdependence with the United

States, Howard clearly has rejected the idea that Australia faces a choice between the American alliance on the one hand and Asian engagement on the other. Rather, he has become a master of functionalism who believes that the two approaches can, and should, be managed adroitly as the strategic essence of Australian statecraft. Indeed, the Howard years have witnessed a great deal of policy subtlety based on a functional principle that seeks to define a synthesis between Australia's Asian geography and its Western history. A particular brand of Australian functionalism that pivots on the alliance now represents the essence of Howard's statecraft.

The Prime Minister has sought to synthesize national interest, alliance military commitment, and international responsibility, and has embodied a sophisticated equation of power, influence, capacity, and responsibility—a policy mixture that is poorly understood by many Australian commentators. Indeed, Howard, who came to office in March 1996 largely as a result of his grasp of domestic politics, has developed over the last decade into the most significant Liberal leader on foreign and security policy since Robert Menzies. Howard's journey from untried novice to experienced practitioner of diplomatic-military affairs represents one of the most remarkable transitions in recent Australian political history.[33]

Howard, ever the student of political history, has recognized that Australia will never be able to achieve an equality of status in the alliance through a functionalism based on strategic or military weight. After all, the United States accounts for 43 percent of world military spending, with Australia accounting for a mere 1 percent. In boxing terms, the United States is a heavyweight Smoking Joe Frazier, while Australia is a middleweight Les Darcy. Nonetheless, if the alliance cannot be an equal partnership, the Howard government has sought to cast every Australian strategic commitment in the light of national political purpose.

For instance, the military commitment to Iraq in March 2003 involved 2,000 Australian military personnel, some 2 percent of the Coalition's military forces. Yet, at the same time, alongside the United States and United Kingdom, Australia's deployment also represented 33 percent of the coalition of the willing's political commitment. For Australia, the commitment to Iraq represented a functionalism based on careful military diplomacy. It was a military diplomacy that employed niche military forces of world-class caliber in order to maximize Canberra's political and strategic influence with the Americans. Moreover, in the 2003 Iraq commitment, the ADF contingent's independent command, force autonomy, and an exit strategy were all well-defined by Canberra at the outset of the mission.[34]

Australia's functional approach to the alliance is concerned with what the great diplomatic scholar Arnold Wolfers once described as the goals of foreign policy in today's milieu in which nations "are out not to defend or increase possessions they hold to the exclusion of others, but aim instead at shaping conditions beyond their national boundaries."[35] Australia has two overarching milieu goals in the age of globalized security—namely, balancing the demands of the alliance with America against security and trade engagement in Asia. As Howard put it in a major speech at the Lowy Institute for International Policy in Sydney in March 2005, Australian security policy must reflect the country's unique East-West intersection of history, geography, culture, and economic opportunity. The choice facing the country is not between Western history and Eastern geography or between globalism and regionalism. Rather, the task is to create a balanced alignment in national security policy.[36] Howard's approach to the security dilemma posed by Australia's geography and history has been to create an *additive* rather than an *alternative* dialectic — an aggregate calculus that absorbs the cultural legacy of history and respects geography, but does not make geography destiny.

It is, then, what might be called the milieu goals of global-regional integration that underpin contemporary Australian defense and security policies. For Australia, American power is the foundation stone of strategic stability in the Asia-Pacific and is seen as fundamental to integrating the United States into the security architecture of the region. The Howard government has declared openly that the Asia-Pacific in the 21st century will be the decisive arena of global politics. As Howard has put it, "History will have no bigger stadium this century than the Pacific Rim."[37] It is in this region that Rosenau's "two worlds of world politics" intermingle in the most combustible manner. Great power dynamics merge with new transnational threats; strong states mix with weak polities; rapid globalization proceeds, but against a tapestry of unique and ancient cultures; and traditional concerns over sovereignty collide with nascent regionalism. Moreover, the world's greatest strategic imponderables are found in the Asia-Pacific. The region is home to eight of the world's ten largest armies and to three of the world's most dangerous interstate flashpoints: the Taiwan Strait, the Korean peninsula, and Kashmir.

At the other end of the conflict spectrum, in no area outside of the Middle East are transnational, substate threats and Islamic terrorism more dangerous than in parts of Asia. This is especially true in Southeast Asia, where major security concerns exist in Indonesia, the Philippines, and Thailand. Thus, there has been increased security cooperation between Australia and Indonesia, as well as cooperative intervention by Australia in the Solomon Islands, Papua New Guinea, and East Timor. In Howard's vision of global-regional security, Australia becomes an advocate of a strategic partnership between the three great Pacific democracies — the United States, Japan, and Australia — through the agency of the new Trilateral Security Dialogue.[38] Thus, Canberra has supported Japanese Prime Minister Junichiro Koizumi's outward security policy and the gradual modernization of the Japanese Self Defence Force. For instance, the decision to send an Australian cavalry regiment to al-Muthanna province in southern Iraq to protect Japanese construction troops is a classic illustration of the interweaving of Australian global-regional security policy. The al-Muthana deployment has as much to do with supporting Japan's outward security policy as it does with bolstering the U.S. alliance. It also was the employment of aspects of what might be called Australia's additive dialectic of alliance with America and engagement with Asia that saw Australia accepted as a member of the inaugural East Asia Summit in late 2005.[39]

However, Australia's functionalism and its simultaneous policy of deepening security relations with both the United States and the Asia-Pacific face the sternest challenge over China. If China's rise translates itself into strategic rivalry with the United States, then the activity of Beijing will become a dagger that strikes at the heart of the geographical-historical intersection that currently shapes Australian policy. To date, the

Howard government has chosen to deemphasize the potential strategic repercussions of China's economic development. As the Prime Minister put it in August 2004, while America has no more reliable ally than Australia, Canberra has "a separate strong growing relationship with China, and it is not in Australia's interests for there to be conflict between America and China."[40] Against the reality that Australia's trade with China has quadrupled in a decade, Howard has rejected the view of China as a kind of Oriental version of a pre-World War I Germany that relentlessly has begun a march to seal its place in the sun. Instead, he has warned that "to see China's rise as a zero-sum game is overly pessimistic, intellectually misguided, and potentially dangerous."[41] In Canberra, the preference is to view China as the Middle Kingdom of "Market Leninism," construing its emergence in an optimistic light. As Howard told Chinese Premier Wen Jibao in April 2006, China's economic expansion and outward moves were positive developments. Australia thus did "not see any merit at all in any policy of containment towards China."[42] The Prime Minister went on to uphold the closeness of the Australian-American relationship and its foundation in history and shared values. He noted, however, that:

> the strength and the depth of that [Australian-American] relationship in no way affects or will it affect, the capacity of Australia to interact with and form a close and lasting partnership and friendship with China. I take the optimistic view . . . of relations between the United States and China. I do not subscribe to the school to which some belong of an inevitable breakdown leading to potential conflict.[43]

Yet there are, have been, and will continue to be inevitable strains in the Australian policy approach.

Foreign Minister Alexander Downer's August 2004 statement concerning Taiwan that implied Australian neutrality in the case of a Sino-American security crisis represents one example of the strain involved in balancing Washington and Beijing. Moreover, Canberra's lack of opposition towards the lifting of the European Union's arms embargo on China alongside a rather tepid response over Beijing's passing of a new Taiwan Anti-Secession Law, illustrates the potential for China to become a running sore in the affairs of the Australian-American alliance.[44]

Much of the future of the alliance may depend on the prospects of China becoming a responsible stakeholder in the regional-global status quo, a strategic partner rather than a strategic competitor. Thus, regarding China, it is unclear whether Australians will remain, in American eyes, Bush's men of steel or whether they will become once again Wilson's pestiferous varmints. Something of the American attitude can be gauged by Armitage's blunt expectations of Australia expressed in 1999. In the event of an Sino-American armed clash over Taiwan, he stated, "We would expect you Australians to bleed for us in the event of such a war."[45] On another occasion, Armitage observed that "if Washington found itself in conflict in China over Taiwan, it would expect Australia's support. If it didn't get that support, it would mean the end of the U.S.-Australia alliance."[46]

The great irony of Australia's dual-pronged pro-alliance and regional-centric security strategy is that while the alliance is at a historical high tide, this tide has risen under the shadow of an ascending Chinese dragon with an insatiable appetite for Australian raw materials. Australia's dual policy requires a balance between alliance loyalty to the United States and pragmatic self-interest vis-à-vis China. In this sense, a careful examination of Australian functionalism reveals an approach to defense and security that increasingly is *refined* rather than *defined* by alliance considerations. Whether such a subtle balance can survive a future Sino-American security crisis is one of the great unknowns of Australian politics. It is far from clear that Australia will be able to achieve what one leading scholar has called "discriminate engagement" with Washington and Beijing without paying the ultimate price of "strategic entrapment."[47]

Defense Posture and Australian National Security.

How has Australia's rejuvenated approach to the alliance and its global-regional approach to security policy translated into military capability and strategic doctrine? In terms of military capability, it is easier to judge. Simply given America's lead in military technology, alliance considerations are vital factors in Australian force development. Indeed, interoperability, combined training, and intelligence exchange remain at the military heart of the Australian-American special relationship. Under the 2003 *Defence Capability Plan*, some A$50 billion is allocated to equip the ADF for 21st century warfare. Modernization embraces missile defense, maintenance of Joint Defence Facilities, cooperation in the development of the Joint Strike Fighter, and purchases of American military assets such as *Abrams* tanks and *Hellfire* missiles. The planned acquisition of the *Global Hawk* unmanned aerial vehicle (UAV) and of the long-range Joint Air to Surface Standoff Missile (JASSM) — a self-guided land-attack stealth cruise missile — further demonstrate the vitality of the Australian-U.S. special relationship in defense terms.[48]

The most striking change in recent capability development is the modernization of the Australian Army to meet increased global-regional requirements. After a quarter of a century as the Cinderella service, the Australian Army is now being recast from a light infantry force into a larger, medium weight mechanized force through a 10-year A$1.8 billion program known as the Hardened and Networked Army (HNA). Army reform is designed to give the government more and better options both within the alliance and for coalition operations within the region. In tandem with the HNA is the planned purchase of aerial warfare destroyers and amphibious ships for the Navy that will, in turn, give the ADF a greater expeditionary focus and capability.[49]

Doctrinally, however, there has been considerable disagreement and ambiguity with regard to defense policy. Despite 9/11 and its dramatic aftermath, Australia's official defense posture remains governed theoretically by the geostrategy embodied in the December 2000 *Defence White Paper*. As noted earlier, despite the publication of the 2003 and 2005 *Defence Updates* reflecting the reality of a globalized security environment, the principles of the 2000 White Paper have yet to be formally superseded. Indeed, the 2003 *Foreign Affairs White Paper* and the 2004 *Prime Ministerial Statement on Counter-Terrorism* that posit global challenges in many ways are more indicative of policy change and may imply the declining utility of an independent defense strategy to the present coalition government.[50]

In the strategic policy debate, there has been no doctrinal resolution of the disagreement between the reformer-globalists and the defender-regionalists. The former school believes that the ADF is most likely to have to fight on complex terrain in joint full-spectrum operations that may involve sustained close combat. The latter school believes that it is better to structure the ADF to fight a traditional air-sea battle. To describe the differences in shorthand, it might be said that the reform school believes that the future of war for the ADF is probably a littoral version of the 2004 battle of Fallujah in the Sunni Triangle or an East Timor with a land, sea, and air fight.

The defender school, on the other hand, believes that the future of war for the ADF is the 1942 battle of the Bismarck Sea *redux* with a force structure conditioned, in the words of Paul Dibb, by the "the iron discipline" of strategic geography.[51] These views highlight that the real difference between the reformers and the defenders is at root a philosophical one related to differing visions of the future of armed conflict. The defender-regionalists retain an air-dominant, continentalist view of strategy drawn from the late Cold War, while the reformer-globalists believe the real challenge in an age of globalization is one of joint, global-regional maritime-style operations in highly complex conditions that are likely to require a larger and more capable army.

The importance of the outcome of this philosophical debate has been highlighted by Major General Jim Molan, Deputy Chief of Staff for Operations in Iraq in 2004-05 under U.S. General George Casey, and currently Adviser to the Vice Chief of the ADF on Joint Warfighting. Molan has warned that, with the exception of its special forces, the Australian military has not been tested in combat since the 1970s. Accordingly, if the ADF is to develop into a capable, joint 21st century warfighting force, it must learn rapidly from the experiences of its larger American ally. In Molan's view,

American warfighting skill remains the benchmark for the "world's best military practice," and the ADF must adapt itself for a future in which "sophisticated joint operations involving sustained close combat" may become the military norm.[52]

At the higher policy level, the intellectual uncertainty with regard to Australia's defense posture needs to be resolved not by a new Defence White Paper but by an articulated National Security Strategy. The reason a National Security Strategy is required is that Canberra needs to reconcile U.S. global strategy and Australian regionalism and balance their interface within a coherent strategic framework. Without such a conceptual framework, the role of the alliance cannot be integrated properly in an overarching security posture, nor can the future roles of the ADF be analyzed and refined properly.

Any new defense policy must be designed to reflect the regional-global nexus that now defines Australia's foreign policy. Australian strategic doctrine should be maritime (offshore and expeditionary) rather than continental (defense of local geography) in character and should have three components. First, the force structure of the ADF should be reconfigured for expeditionary littoral operations in the northern archipelagos and the South Pacific. In effect, the ADF of the 21st century needs to resemble a smaller version of the U.S. Marine Corps — a force of great operational and tactical versatility. Second, based on this maritime force structure, there needs to be a clear recognition that global out-of-area operations by the ADF are central to the task of upholding Australia's security interests. Third, there needs to be an integrated focus on sovereignty protection and homeland security as opposed to an unrealistic doctrine of geographical defense. Australia's security and defense policymakers need to remember Dutch-American geopolitician Nicholas Spykman's famous dictum: "The geography of a country is rather the material for, than the cause of, its policy."[53]

Conclusion.

In January 2006, former New South Wales Labor Premier Bob Carr observed that the strength of the Australian-American alliance may have reached a historical high tide, and that such a situation is "as good as it gets."[54] It certainly is true that, halfway through the first decade of the 21st century, the alliance remains an indispensable strategic asset to Canberra that has added not only to Australia's national security, but also to its strategic weight and capability edge within the Asia-Pacific region. The alliance gives Canberra access and influence in Washington and the capitals of Asia out of all proportion to Australia's size as a middle power.

Howard's view of the Australian-American alliance is that of a sheet anchor that permits policy synthesis between Western history and Eastern geography. In the new millennium, the alliance has evolved into a global-regional instrument to meet the challenges of bifurcated nonstate and interstate worlds. In consequence, Australia has developed a multifaceted security outlook—one that is at once globally attuned, regionally focused, and alliance-oriented. For Australian policymakers, the great political challenge is twofold. First, they must ensure that the electorate continues to appreciate the strategic significance of the alliance. Second, they continuously must seek to curb the growth of any regional tensions that might escalate into a sudden-death confrontation between America and China over the issue of Taiwan. On the military front, the great challenge for policymakers will be to keep the ADF functional and interoperable with the huge U.S. military without sacrificing Australian interests, all within the constraints of an affordable defense budget.

Over the next decade, Australia's strategic outlook will reflect the pursuit of milieu goals, while emphasizing functionalism and refining an additive dialectic between America and Asia. It will require a thoughtful synthesis of national security requirements — one that embraces history, political purpose, geopolitics, military power, force readiness, economics, logistics, and diplomacy. Such a policy synthesis will demand great skills in statecraft and a cold-blooded recognition that such a balance is contingent on Australia not having to choose between America and China, between history and geography, or between liberal values and burgeoning trade. This is a challenge worthy of a Metternich or a Bismarck, and it remains to be seen whether Howard's successors will be capable of mastering such a complex diplomatic and security balancing act.

Finally, if there is a necessity for making a choice in Australian foreign and defense policy, it should be remembered that in every war and security crisis since its foundation in 1901, Australia repeatedly has chosen to defend its heritage of Western liberal democratic values. As Foreign Minister Downer has recently argued, the defense of liberal democratic values remains an enduring aim of Australian foreign policy. "Australia," observes Downer, "continues to be a significant force for the spread of freedom and democracy. We have fought wars for these values in the past; we continue to fight for them now."[55] Ultimately, then, while economic relations are of significant moment, cultural beliefs remain binding because they determine identity and meaning. The great historical lesson of Australian statecraft is the principle that liberal democratic values have always dominated policy. Such values are inherent in the Australian-American alliance and are likely to provide the essential foundation for the "other special relationship" as it confronts the strategic uncertainties of the early 21st century.

ENDNOTES - CHAPTER 15

1. Peter Edwards, *Permanent Friends? Historical Reflections on the Australian-American Alliance*, Sydney: Lowy Institute for International Policy, Paper 08, 2005, p. 2.

2. For recent analyses of the alliance, see Edwards, *Permanent Friends? Historical Reflections on the Australian-American Alliance*; Rod Lyon and William T. Tow, *The Future of the Australian-US Security Relationship*, Carlisle Barracks, PA: U.S. Army War College, Strategic Studies Institute, December 2003; Commonwealth of Australia, *Australia's Defence Relations with the United States: Issues Paper*, Canberra: Joint Standing Committee on Foreign Affairs, Defence and Trade, March 2005; Paul Dibb, "US-Australian Alliance Relations: An Australian View," *Strategic Forum*, No. 216, Washington, DC: Institute for National Strategic Studies, National Defense University, August 2005, pp. 1-6; Christopher Hubbard, *Australia and US Military Cooperation: Fighting Common Enemies*, Burlington, VT: Ashgate Publishing Limited, 2005; and Greg Sheridan, *The Partnership: The Inside Story of the US-Australian Alliance under Bush and Howard*, Sydney: New South, 2006.

3. For a useful analysis of the current Australian defense and security debate, see Christian Hirst, "Reformers and Defenders: Perceptions of Change in Australian Defence Strategy since 11 September 2001," *Australian Army Journal*, Summer 2005-06, Vol. 3, No. 1, pp. 77-93.

4. For the views of the defender-regionalists, see the case of Hugh White and Paul Dibb, to the Australian Parliament's Joint Standing Committee on Foreign Affairs, Defence and Trade, Inquiry into Australia's Defence Relations with the United States on April 2, 2004, available at *www.aph.gov.au/house/committee/jfadt/usrelations*. See also Hugh White, "Old, New or Both?

Australia's Security Agendas at the Start of the New Century," in Derek McDougall and Peter Shearman, eds., *Australian Security After 9/11: New and Old Agendas*, Aldershot: Ashgate Publishing Limited, 2006, pp. 13-28; and Paul Dibb, "Is Strategic Geography Relevant to Australia's Current Defence Policy?" *Australian Journal of International Affairs*, June 2006, Vol. 60, No. 2, pp. 247-264.

5. The reformer-globalist position has been well-articulated by Senator Robert Hill in a number of key speeches, especially "Beyond the White Paper: Strategic Directions for Defence," June 18, 2002; "The Changing Security Environment," January 24, 2004, available at *www.minister.defense.gov.au/HillSpeechtpl.cfm*; and Robert Hill, "Australia's Defence and Security: Challenges and Opportunities at the Start of the 21st Century," in *Global Forces 2005: Proceedings of the ASPI Conference, Day 1 – Global Strategy*, Canberra: Australian Strategic Policy Institute, April 2006, pp. 7-11. See also Allan Gyngell, "Australia's Emerging Global Role," *Current History*, March 2005, pp. 99-104.

6. See, for example, Alan Dupont, "Transformation or Stagnation? Rethinking Australia's Defence," *Australian Journal of International Affairs*, Vol. 57, No. 1, April 2003, pp. 55-76; Michael Evans, *The Tyranny of Dissonance: Australia's Strategic Culture and Way of War, 1901-2005*, Canberra: Land Warfare Studies Centre Study Paper No. 306, February 2005, pp. 66-104; and Paul Monk, "The World Has Changed—What Do We Do Now? *Quadrant*, September 2005, pp. 35-40.

7. Commonwealth of Australia, *Defence 2000: Our Future Defence Force*, Canberra: Defence Publishing Service, 2000.

8. Commonwealth of Australia, *Australia's National Security: A Defence Update 2003*, Canberra: Department of Defence, 2003; and *Australia's National Security: A Defence Update 2005*, Canberra: Department of Defence, 2005.

9. See *Australia's National Security: A Defence Update 2003*, pp. 5-12; and *Australia's National Security: A Defence Update 2005*, pp. 1-4.

10. For a discussion, see Evans, pp. 88-95.

11. Robert O. Keohane, "The Globalization of Informal Violence: Theories of World Politics and the 'Liberalism of Fear,'" in Craig Calhoun, Paul Price, and Ashley Timmer, eds., *Understanding September 11*, New York: The Free Press, 2002, p. 80.

12. James N. Rosenau, *Turbulence in World Politics: A Theory of Change and Continuity*, Princeton: Princeton University Press, 1990, pp. 249-253.

13. For discussion of aspects of these changes, see *New World Coming: American Security in the 21st Century, Supporting Research and Analysis*, Phase 1 Report on the Emerging Global Security Environment for the First Quarter of the 21st Century, Washington, DC: U.S. Commission on National Security/21st Century, September 15, 1999; Mary Kaldor, *New and Old Wars: Organised Violence in a Global Era*, Cambridge: Polity Press, 1999; Philip Bobbitt, *The Shield of Achilles: War, Peace and the Course of History*, New York: Alfred A. Knopf, 2002, especially chapters 10-12 and 24-26; Robert Cooper, *The Breaking of Nations: Order and Chaos in the Twenty-first Century*, London: Atlantic Books, 2003; Colin S. Gray, *Another Bloody Century: Future Warfare*, London: Weidenfeld & Nicolson, 2005; and Isabelle Duyvesteyn and Jan Angstrong, eds., *Rethinking the Nature of War*, Abingdon: Frank Cass, 2005.

14. Edwards, *Permanent Friends? Historical Reflections on the Australian-American Alliance*, pp. 43-46.

15. For the impact of the September 11 attacks on the Howard government, see Sheridan, pp. 35-39.

16. For an outline of Australian military activity, see Department of Defence, *Winning in Peace, Winning in War: The Australian Defence Force's Contribution to the Global Security Environment*, Canberra: Defence Publishing Service, 2004.

17. Geoffrey Barker, "Hill Sees "Arc of Terrorism," *Australian Financial Review*, October 10, 2003.

18. *Australia's National Security: A Defence Update 2005*, p. 4.

19. *Ibid*, p. 13.

20. Transcript of the Prime Minister, The Hon. John Howard, MP, "Address to the Australian Strategic Policy Institute, Westin Hotel, Sydney, June 18, 2004, available at *www.pm.gov.au/news/speeches/speech921.html*.

21. *Ibid*.

22. Tom Allard, "PM Claims New Strategic Maturity," *Sydney Morning Herald*, March 8, 2005.

23. Charles Krauthammer, "Why I Love Australia," *Washington Post*, June 23, 2006.

24. For the text of Armitage's address to the 2003 Australia-U.S. Dialogue, see "Bound to Stick Together," *The Weekend Australian*, August 16-17, 2003.

25. *Ibid.*

26. Summary of U.S. President's News Conference in *The Australian*, May 4, 2003.

27. "Transcript of the Prime Minister, The Hon. John Howard, MP, "Joint Press Conference with the President of the United States of America, George W, Bush, East Room, The White House, May 16, 2006," available at *www.pm.gov.au/news.interviews/ Interview1940.html*.

28. Quoted in Rupert Darwall, "John Howard's Australia," *Policy Review*, August/September 2005, p. 58.

29. See P. G. Edwards, ed., *Australia Through American Eyes, 1935-1945: Observations by American Diplomats*, St Lucia: University of Queensland Press, 1979.

30. For good assessments of continuity and change in the alliance since its inception, see Edwards, *Permanent Friends? Historical Reflections on the Australian-American Alliance*, chapters 2-4; and Hubbard, *Australia and US Military Cooperation: Fighting Common Enemies*, chapter 4.

31. President of the United States, *The National Security Strategy of the United States of America*, Washington, DC: The White House, March 2006, p. 40; Department of Defense, *Quadrennial Defense Review Report*, Washington, DC: U.S. Government Printing Office, February 2006, p. 7.

32. See Mark Latham, *The Latham Diaries*, Melbourne: Melbourne University Press, 2005, p. 393, where the alliance is described as "the last manifestation of the White Australia policy"; and Malcolm Fraser, "An Australian Critique," *Australian Journal of International Affairs*, Vol. 55, No. 2, July 2001, pp. 225-34. See also the views of Owen Harries, "Don't Get Too Close to the US," *The Australian*, February 17, 2004; and *Benign or Imperial? Reflections on American Hegemony*, Sydney: ABC Books, 2004.

33. For example, Nick Cater, ed., *The Howard Factor: A Decade That Changed the Nation*, Melbourne: Melbourne University Press, 2006, deals mainly with domestic issues.

34. For an outline, see Department of Defence, *The War in Iraq: ADF Operations in the Middle East in 2003*, Canberra: Defence Publishing Service, 2003.

35. Arnold Wolfers, *Discord and Collaboration: Essays on International Politics,* Baltimore: The Johns Hopkins Press, 1962, pp. 67-80.

36. Transcript of the Prime Minister, The Hon. John Howard, MP, "Speech to the Lowy Institute for International Policy, Sydney: March 31, 2005, available at *www.pm.gov.au/news/speeches/speech1290.html.*

37. *Ibid.*

38. *Ibid.* See also Anna Searle and Ippei Kamae, "Anchoring Trilateralism: Can Australia-Japan-US Security Relations Work?" *Australian Journal of International Affairs,* Vol. 58, No. 4, December 2004, pp. 464-78.

39. For the background to Australia's admission to the East Asian Summit, see Patrick Walters, "Asian Juggernaut," *The Weekend Australian,* December 10-11, 2005.

40. Quoted in Dana Dillon and John J. Tkacik Jr., "China's Quest for Asia," *Policy Review,* December 2005/January 2006, p. 37.

41. Transcript of the Prime Minister, The Hon. John Howard, MP, "Address to the Asia Society Lunch, New York, September 12, 2005, available at *www.pm.gov.au/news/speeches/speech1560. html.*

42. Transcript of the Prime Minister, The Hon. John Howard, MP, "Address to the Luncheon in Honour of His Excellency Mr. Wen Jiabao, Premier of the State Council, People's Republic of China, Parliament House, Canberra, April 3. 2006, available at *www.pm.gov.au/news/speeches/speech1855.html.*

43. *Ibid.*

44. See Ross Terrill, *Riding the Wave: The Rise of China and Options for Australian Policy,* Canberra: Australian Strategic Policy Institute, March 2006, chapter 4.

45. Cited by Paul Dibb in evidence to the Joint Standing Committee on Foreign Affairs , Defence and Trade, Inquiry into Australia's Defence Relations with the United States on April 2, 2004, available at *www.aph.gov.au/house/committee/jfadt/usrelations/tor.htm.*

46. Quoted in Edwards, *Permanent Friends? Historical Reflections on the Australian-American Alliance,* p. 45.

47. William T. Tow, "Sino-American Relations and the 'Australian Factor': Inflated Expectations or Discriminate Engagement?" *Australian Journal of International Affairs*, Vol. 59, No. 4, December 2005, pp. 451-68.

48. See Gregor Ferguson, Daniel Cotterill, and Tom Muir, "Top 23 Projects 2004," in *The Cost of Defence: ASPI Defence Budget Brief, 2005-2006*, Canberra: Australian Strategic Policy Institute, May 2005, pp. 150-89.

49. Department of Defence, *The Hardened and Networked Army*, December 2005, available at *www.defense.gov.au/army/hnawelcome_62693.html*.

50. Commonwealth of Australia, *Advancing the National Interest: Australia's Foreign and Trade Policy* White Paper, Canberra: Department of Foreign Affairs and Trade, 2003; *Protecting Australia Against Terrorism: Australia's National Counter Terrorism Policy and Arrangements*, Canberra: Department of the Prime Minister and Cabinet, 2004.

51. Dibb, "Is Strategic Geography Relevant to Australia's Current Defence Policy?" p. 263.

52. Major General Jim Molan, "Fighting Joint," unpublished draft paper 2006, pp. 1-10. I am grateful to Major General Molan for permission to quote from this paper. Some of these views also are contained in Major General Jim Molan, *Operations in the Land of the Two Rivers*, Canberra: Command Paper 6, Australian Defence College, 2006, pp. 7-11.

53. Nicholas J. Spykman, "Geography and Foreign Policy, 1," *American Political Science Review*, Vol. 32, No. 1, February 1938, p. 30.

54. Geoff Elliot, "US Alliance 'As Good as it Gets,'" *The Australian*, January 20, 2006.

55. Alexander Downer, "Carry On the Battle to Conquer Tyranny," *The Australian*, June 13, 2006.

CONCLUSION

CHAPTER 16

THE FUTURE OF THE U.S.-AUSTRALIA ALLIANCE: ADAPTING TO NEW CHALLENGES?

James A. Schear

What does the future hold for Australian-American relations? A spirit of cautious optimism pervades this volume of essays. After more than half a century, the alliance has proved remarkably resilient. It has survived periods of turbulence, most notably during and after the Indochina conflict, as well as the buffeting effects of economic tensions and domestic political swings on each side. Since the Cold War's demise and, especially, after the September 11, 2001 (9/11), attacks and the Bali bombings, both countries have hung together more often than not on high-stakes issues. Shared character traits help to reinforce this solidarity. While Australian and American social mores are by no means identical, we still share so much in common — immigrant origins, democratic values, a (nearly) common language, and an admirable disdain for aristocratic pomposity — that the rest of the world could be forgiven for assuming our relationship always will be close. And that assumption may well prove accurate — perhaps.

Yet, an equally plausible view — evident throughout this volume — is that complacency is never advisable when it comes to managing complex alliance relationships, even among kindred spirits. Ultimately, alliances cannot afford to stand still; like sharks, they need to move forward in order to breathe. Even its most dewy-eyed supporters would concede that the U.S.-Australia alliance can prosper only so long as both sides firmly believe that what they are getting out of the relationship equals or exceeds what they are putting into it.

Such pragmatism is especially apt as we look toward the end of this turbulent decade. The latter-day political intimacy enjoyed by Canberra and Washington—due mainly to the close relationship between Prime Minister John Howard and President George W. Bush—has been genuine, but it could well recede when new leaderships in each country come to the fore. Moreover, as several chapters in this volume have argued, changes in the larger geo-political landscape, particularly in the Asia-Pacific region, are likely to test the relationship no matter how well our leaders get along.

The looming test for the alliance, in short, is how it will adapt in the face of cross-cutting pressures. Will the pressures generated by a changing global environment tend to act more like a glue that holds the U.S.-Australia alliance together or a solvent that erodes its foundations? In his Panel IV Introduction, Brendan Taylor framed economic factors in terms of their adhesive or erosive effects, and this metaphor can be applied more broadly. In either case, the quality of adaptability is going to be vital: most obviously, it can help to moderate divergent pressures, but it can help ensure that converging pressures will produce effective policy and joint action. For without effective action, solidarity by itself does not buy much. As British historian A. J. P. Taylor once quipped about Prime Minister Herbert Asquith: He was "unshakable as a rock and, like a rock, incapable of movement!"[1]

Context Matters Greatly.

Security relationships usually are not products of benign circumstances, and the U.S.-Australia alliance is

314

no exception. It was forged in the darkest moments of World War II. By 1942, international order effectively had collapsed. Nazi Germany occupied much of continental Europe. Imperial Japanese forces were pressing down upon Southeast Asia and the western Pacific. Singapore had fallen. British and American forces were falling back in retreat. Northern Australia was under attack. The future looked incredibly bleak; there was no sense of inevitable victory.[2] To be sure, the wartime generation that endured those traumas was no more clairvoyant than we are today. That their worst fears proved short-lived, mercifully, prompts one to wonder whether optimism in today's volatile context might be unwise.

Naïve optimism surely is unwarranted. One can see looming challenges at every level of international society, especially in greater Eurasia where the drama of rising and rebounding powers is being played out. At the center of this vast expanse is Russia, which has faltered on its path toward democratic governance while rebounding economically on its strength as a global energy supplier. The challenge facing Russia is not so much internal dissent—if anything, Vladimir Putin fulfills a national thirst for strong leadership. Rather, it is the increasing potential for confrontation with neighbors along its vast periphery, most especially Georgia and Ukraine, coupled with a desire to play on a wider global stage—most notably in the Middle East, the Persian Gulf, and East Asia—where its involvement decidedly has been mixed.

In striking contrast to the Russian situation, India's upward path seems more assured, buoyed by its post-Cold War economic opening and its own democratic traditions. Along with sustaining its own socio-economic development and managing tensions within

315

its large and diverse population, New Delhi's biggest test internationally lies in whether it can press forward with Pakistan to achieve a *modus vivendi* over Kashmir, while avoiding entangling involvements in and around other parts of the subcontinent and southwest Asia.

What then about China? Its rise is surely the central event of the early 21st century. Yet China remains very much a work in progress. The country's sustained economic growth and its generally cooperative diplomatic posture internationally belies an ongoing military buildup and rising social discontent at home, the latter generating tensions that may prove hard to manage, especially in economic down-turns, unless more responsive, accountable — and ultimately democratic — governance takes root over the long run.

The concerns expressed in this volume regarding China's potential for driving wedges between Washington and Canberra should not be taken lightly. Clearly, the People's Republic of China's thriving internal market has been a huge boon for Australian exporters, especially on the natural resource side. Over time, Beijing's expanding ties with neighbors throughout the East Asian community are bound to constrain those who would attempt to isolate China or confront it militarily, either over Taiwan or, more generally, as its power and influence grow in the coming years. One can scarcely miss the greatly increased sensitivity throughout much of the region to any posture that could be construed as a policy of anti-Chinese confrontation.

That said, geo-politics abhors systemic imbalance. Let's face it: something resembling a modern-day Chinese-centric vassal state network is just not something that Australia or most regional actors want to see emerging in East Asia. Consequently, a

U.S. posture that prudently hedges against possible Chinese aggressiveness, maintains a military balance, sustains its bilateral alliances, supports inclusive multilateralism while actively pursuing cooperation with Beijing on a range of international problems both near (e.g., North Korea) and far (e.g., Iran, Darfur), is going to be welcomed by most of China's neighbors for its counterbalancing effects. And despite U.S. distractions elsewhere, one can argue plausibly that this is the present overall trajectory of American strategy in the region.

To invoke the earlier metaphor, a rising China— even a peacefully rising one—provides more glue than solvent to our alliance structure. The adaptive challenge will be to keep the hedging and cooperative tracks of the strategy in balance, and, above all, to deflect any suggestion that U.S. policy is bent upon unwarranted confrontation.

So far as the U.S.-Australia connection is concerned, the overall pattern of great power relations is, on balance, good news. Why? Because unlike previous eras, no emerging great power aspires to overturn the existing global order, which has generated unparalleled prosperity among its stakeholders.[3] All of the great powers, along with the larger community of modern, well-governed states, have a huge stake in a globalizing economy. This is not to say geo-politics will be free from jostling, rivalry, or hostility in the face of American preeminence. Furthermore, "powder-keg" situations (to borrow Andrew Scobell's apt label in Chapter 5) in places like the Taiwan Strait or North Korea could, if triggered, wreak enormous damage. But no aspiring great power could remain immune from damage inflicted by its own capricious acts; and none has an ideological disposition that would blind it to these realities. Moreover, while one can point to haunting parallels with the globalizing world system devastated by World War I,[4] great power relations today are not fettered by the kind of rigidly opposed, interlocking alliance structures that drove millions to their deaths in a disastrous sequence of events that began with two shots fired by a tragically lucky Serb assassin on a Sarajevo side street in June 1914.[5]

Looming Threats?

What about other possible threats to stability? One, quite clearly, is the ongoing proliferation of weapons of mass destruction (WMD), either in the hands of rogue regimes like Iran and North Korea or of currently stable countries that could suffer political upheavals in the future. There is also the problem of increased radicalization apparent throughout the Muslim world and its diaspora, inflating the sails of Islamist jihadi groups which are vying against more moderate constituencies for the hearts and minds of the Islamic *umma*.[6]

To these challenges I would add a third category: a cohort of state and state-like entities that perceive existent threats and whose reactions could embroil outside powers in regional confrontations. The list here is a diverse one: Pakistan (vis-à-vis India); Israel (vis-à-vis Iran, Syria, or Palestinian Islamists); Taiwan (vis-à-vis you-know-who); Georgia (vis-à-vis Russia); the Kurdish areas of Iraq (vis-à-vis all their neighbors); and even North Korea (vis-à-vis the United States). None of these chronically fragile situations are likely to escalate to the kind of horrific conflagration that ushered in World War I; but the risk of worldwide reverberations from much smaller regional crises cannot be discounted, especially if WMD is in the mix.

It is essential that alliance partners strive toward a common perspective on these problems—a task easier said than done. Consider the WMD issue: the U.S.-led invasion of Iraq of 2003, in which Australia participated, was driven in large measure by fears that an oil-rich tyrant with a history of aggression against his neighbors and citizens would use his WMD capability, once fully developed, to deter outside powers from attempting to thwart his aggressive designs. Making the world safe for conventional aggression is clearly one motive for WMD proliferation. There is also the proliferation-for-profit motive, either via official state channels or via murky private transactions (e.g., the A. Q. Khan case in Pakistan). Arguably, North Korea presents the classic third party transfer problem—if Pyongyang comes to view its stock of WMD materials as just another illicit commodity that can be sold to any would-be buyer with enough cash. Finally, there are motivations that focus on empowering nonstate actors with WMD, as extended deterrence against retaliatory interference with aggressive acts elsewhere by the state providing the WMD. Israeli analysts often point to this nightmare scenario when considering future Iranian patronage of nonstate clients like Hezbollah, which array themselves as front line fighters against the Israeli Defense Forces.[7]

Similar proxy problems bedevil assessments of transnational terrorism. No issue has loomed larger for the Bush administration and the Howard government than effectively countering terrorism. And yet the campaign to suppress the most threatening variant of this phenomenon—al-Qai'da and affiliated groups— has brought the United States and its allies face to face with a broader range of militancy in the Muslim world that blurs traditional lines between political radicalism, insurgency, and terrorism.

There are, for example, Shiite groups which have communally-based political organizations supported by armed militia loyalists—the Mahdi Army in Iraq or Hezbollah in Lebanon. A rekindled neo-Taliban organization fighting Afghan and North Atlantic Treaty Organization (NATO) forces in southeastern Afghanistan is a Sunni variant of a nationally-focused Islamist group, but with an ideological commitment to armed struggle against foreigners. Meanwhile, former Baath Party loyalists attacking U.S. forces and the fledgling Iraqi national government definitely are not Islamists but rather Sunnis who have benefited from (and occasionally fight with) foreign jihadi fighters and suicide bombers bent upon attacking Western "infidels" and fomenting sectarian conflict with Shiite "apostates." Closer to Australia, Jemaah Islamiyah (JI) has served as al-Qai'da's eastern front in Southeast Asia, promoting a regional Sunni Islamist agenda through terrorist attacks aimed at foreigners and non-Muslim communities in the Indonesian archipelago and beyond.

What kinds of glue or solvent pressures do these WMD-proliferation and transnational threats pose for our alliance? Terrorism can be a very corrosive issue among allies and partners. Even when allies agree on the magnitude and character of a particular threat, they may dispute the underlying causal factors at work or the optimal methods for combating the scourge. Judging by appearances, the United States and Australia have not stumbled across these kinds of disputes, certainly not to the degree seen in U.S. relations with its continental European allies. Australians and Americans know they are targets and, tragically, have the casualities to show for it—a sense of danger that conjures up the old Franklinesque adage: "We must all hang together, or most assuredly we shall all hang separately."[8] Both

320

countries also share (as do other allies, to be sure) an abiding concern about so-called threat convergence — those "perfect storm" scenarios in which terrorist networks, WMD proliferation, state weakness, and criminal syndicates might feed off each other in malign ways.

The real test for alliance adaptation is whether both sides can keep their counterterrorism strategies in close alignment. Enhanced homeland security and more aggressive proliferation control measures (such as the Proliferation Security Initiative [PSI]) are essential elements and not much in dispute. Somewhat more challenging is the management of integrated civil-military operations within the Islamic world, which attempt to strike a balance between "kinetic" missions (aimed at capturing or killing terrorist or insurgent actors) and capacity-building operations (aimed at winning the trust and confidence of local populations and thereby driving a wedge between them and violent actors in their midst). This is the classic counterinsurgency task — something with which U.S. and Australian special operations forces are well-acquainted but which, even in auspicious circumstances, requires patience, effective cross-cultural communication, and capable local partners in whom one can repose trust.

What is controversial about counterinsurgency is not how to do it but when to launch it, as well as the place and utility of state-building, regime change, and democracy promotion more generally within the realm of counterterrorism endeavors. Operation IRAQI FREEDOM, especially, has taught some hard lessons regarding what outside interveners reasonably can expect to accomplish when trying to stabilize a large, fractious (even if wealthy) country which has no legacy of inclusive governance in living memory and (as yet) no history of chronic civil war. While John Higley's dark forecast of U.S. post-Iraq retrenchment (Chapter 8) almost certainly is too pessimistic, there can be little doubt of deep American public consternation (and allied angst) over future state-building projects when the pathway into them is perceived to be a war by choice. Ironically, Canberra's involvement in state-building activity may be less domestically contentious given that in most cases these activities are a function of promoting stability within Australia's regional neighborhood.

Minding the Asymmetrical Gaps.

All of the challenges sketched out above would be daunting enough if the United States and Australia were allies of equal strategic weight. That we are not is often assumed to throw yet another layer of anxiety on top of an already complex relationship. On the Australian side, familiar questions abound: Will U.S. global assertiveness embroil Canberra in distant conflicts and demand more commitment than a country of 20 million citizens can possibly muster? Will future Australian leaders be tarred as stooges or poodles for acquiescing to ill-advised American expeditions? Will the alliance be more of a millstone weighing down Australia than a national asset to be preserved?

These are all fair questions, to be sure. Given its preeminence, America is bound to be a polarizing force — attracting some, repelling others. While U.S. policies, in particular the war on terrorists, no doubt have aggravated the problem, the trend towards greater polarization already was apparent in the 1990s. U.S. leaders wearily have grown accustomed to attracting criticism whenever Washington decides to throw its strategic weight around (as in Iraq) or refrains from doing so (as in Darfur).[9] And for some of America's allies, the imperative of strategic protection has become far less important than it was in the Cold War era, while the domestic political hazards of becoming embroiled in America's behavior have grown. Bottom-line: It is just plain tough to be an ally of the United States in today's unipolar world.

Australia is not immune from these problems. At the same time, there are several mitigating factors at work in the U.S.-Australia context. The oft-cited tension between a global versus regional focus of alliance-based cooperation is far less a problem for Australia than it is for the NATO allies. Many of the problems that Americans regard as global in character — namely, terrorism and transnational threats — for Australia are problems of its immediate neighborhood. "Thinking globally and acting locally" is a label that works well as a policy stance for Australia. It provides Canberra with latitude to organize its priorities in a fashion that meets both sides' concerns, while also helping to foster realistic U.S. expectations regarding what a country of its relatively small (demographic) size and resource base can contribute on the global stage.[10] It is also worth noting that Australia's alliance bona fides benefit greatly from the fact that it is not any state's presumptive rival within the region; consequently, it can burnish its credentials as both a bridge-builder and a nonthreatening security partner with others in the region, including not only countries in transition such as Indonesia but also U.S. allies such as Japan and the Republic of Korea.

For the United States, the greatest challenge in sustaining alliance relationships is to keep its power in a broad strategic perspective. Not long ago, U.S. commentator Charles Krauthammer observed that "Australia's geographic and historical isolation has bred a wisdom about the structure of peace." Australia understands "that peace and prosperity . . . are maintained by power—once the power of the British empire, now the power of the United States"; and that American retreat or defeat . . . would be catastrophic for Australia and for the world."[11] That is an enticing argument for American ears, but it begs the obvious question: How should American power be used? What counts as an adroit use of power when the purpose is not merely defense of the homeland or an ally but the maintenance of systemic stability?

To wield power without getting blinded by it is no easy matter. The methods of mobilizing and, especially, projecting vast amounts of power can be so all-consuming that we lose sight of the larger objective, which, as Frederick Kagan reminds us, is ultimately persuasion.[12] Power comes in many forms—military, diplomatic, economic, and informational—and it can be applied for various tasks—to destroy or construct, to deter, coerce, dissuade, or entice. But in the end, when the task at hand is maintaining global stability, what counts most is one's ability to utilize power *persuasively*. That is to say, to maneuver an enemy, competitor, partner, or, yes, even on occasion an ally into a posture that you, they, and other stakeholders regard as acceptable relative to all other plausible outcomes.

That is not to say all actors on the global stage are ultimately susceptible to persuasion—some, clearly, are not. But that there are irreconcilables only serves to reinforce the essential validity of the argument, for their goal is also to persuade, and ours must be to negate and preempt their ability to do so by proffering a more attractive vision. That is a tall order, one that requires good knowledge of what others value and how to adapt our methods to the task of influencing their choices. Success, however, demands no less.

ENDNOTES - CHAPTER 16

1. A. J. P. Taylor, *English History: 1914-1945*, London: Penguin Books, 1970, p. 41.

2. For a more detailed portrait, see Thomas Schieffer, "An Alliance of Shared Commitment," *Defender*, Spring 2004, pp. 13-15.

3. See Fareed Zakaria, "It's the Economy, Mr. President," *Washington Post*, November 20, 2006, p. A17.

4. See Niall Ferguson, "Sinking Globalization," *Foreign Affairs*, March/April 2005.

5. Gavrilo Princip, a diminutive, sickly Serb former student and member of a secret Serb society, had gone into a cafe for a sandwich after thinking he missed his chance to get a shot off at the Austrian Archduke, Franz Ferdinand, who was visiting Sarajevo. As fate would have it, the Archduke's car took a wrong turn by the cafe and had to back up the street in order to turn around. Princip was waiting.

6. For an expanded discussion on this point, see chapter by Joseph McMillan and Christopher Cavoli, "Defeating Transnational Terrorism," in Stephen J. Flanagan and James A. Schear, eds., *Strategic Challenges: America's Global Security Agenda*, Washington: Potomac Books, forthcoming.

7. See commentary by Gerald Steinberg in Judith S. Yaphe, and Charles D. Lutes, *Reassessing the Implications of a Nuclear-Armed Iran*, McNair Paper #69, Washington, DC: Institute for National Strategic Studies, National Defense University, 2005, pp. 75-76.

8. Attributed to Benjamin Franklin at the signing of the American Declaration of Independence, July 4, 1776.

9. See Robert Kagan, "Anti-Americanism's Deep Roots," *Washington Post*, June 19, 2006.

10. For more on this theme, see Paul Dibb, "U.S.-Australia Alliance Relations: An Australian View," *Strategic Forum #216*, Washington, DC: Institute for National Strategic Studies, August 2005, pp. 2.

11. Charles Krauthammer, "Why I Love Australia," *Washington Post*, June 23, 2006, p. A25.

12. See Frederick W. Kagan, "Power and Persuasion, *The Wilson Quarterly*, Vol. 29, No. 3, Summer 2005, pp. 57-65.

ABOUT THE CONTRIBUTORS

ROBERT AYSON is Director of Studies, Graduate Studies in Strategy and Defence, the Australian National University. His publications include *Strategy and Security in the Asia-Pacific* (coeditor, with Desmond Ball; Allen and Unwin, 2006). His areas of research interest include strategic concepts, nuclear proliferation, Asia-Pacific security, and Australian and New Zealand defense and security issues.

MICHAEL EVANS is a fellow at the Australian Defence College in Canberra. During 2002-05, he served as head of the Army's think tank, the Land Warfare Studies Centre at the Royal Military College in Duntroon. He has been a research fellow in the Department of War Studies at King's College, University of London, and at the University of York, and serves on the editorial boards of two leading journals in the field of security affairs. His extensive writings on strategic affairs and contemporary military operations include *The Tyranny of Dissonance: Australia's Strategic Culture and Way of War, 1901-2005* (Canberra, 2005). Dr. Evans received his Ph.D. from Western Australia.

THE HONORABLE BILL HAYDEN is the former Governor-General of Australia (1989-96). He was elected to the House of Representatives in 1961 and held his seat in Parliament until his retirement in 1988. He was a member of the Opposition Shadow Ministry from 1976 until 1983 and Leader of the Australian Labor Party from December 1977 until February 1983. During the Hawke government, Mr. Hayden served as Minister for Foreign Affairs in 1983 and Minister for Foreign Affairs and Trade during 1987-88. He holds a Bachelor of Economics degree from the University of Queensland.

JOHN HIGLEY holds the Jack S. Blanton Chair in Australian Studies and directs the Center for Australian and New Zealand Studies at the University of Texas at Austin, where he also has been chair of the Government Department. During 1976-84, he was a senior research fellow in sociology at the Australian National University. His research interests include domestic, foreign, and trade policy issues relating to Australia and the United States, as well as the comparative study of political elites. Mr. Higley's most recent book, coauthored with Michael Burton, is *Elite Foundations of Liberal Democracy* (Rowman & Littlefield, 2006).

JOHN C. HULSMAN is a former senior research fellow at the Heritage Foundation and a member of the Council on Foreign Relations, as well as a contributing editor to *National Interest*. He advises congressional leaders from both parties on foreign policy issues and makes regular appearances on ABC, CBS, Fox News, CNN, MSNBC, PBS, and BBC. His most recent book (with Anatol Lieven) is titled *Ethical Realism* (Pantheon, 2006). Dr. Hulsman holds a Ph.D. in International Relations from the University of St. Andrews in Scotland.

PAUL KELLY is editor-at-large of *The Australian*. He was previously editor-in-chief of *The Australian* (1991-96). He has published extensively on Australian and international issues and is a frequent commentator on television. In 2001 he presented the five-part television documentary on Australian history and character titled *"100 Years-The Australian Story."* Mr. Kelly is a fellow of the Australian Academy of Social Sciences and a participant in the Australia-America Dialogue. In 2002 he served as a visiting fellow at the Kennedy School of Government and a visiting lecturer at the Weatherhead Center for International Affairs at Harvard University.

Mr. Kelly holds a Doctor of Letters from the University of Melbourne.

JEFFREY D. MCCAUSLAND is a Clarke Forum Fellow and contributing professor in the Department of International Studies at Dickinson College, Carlisle, PA. He is also a senior fellow at the Carnegie Council on Ethics in International Affairs in New York as well as director of national security affairs for the Buchanan, Ingersoll, and Rooney law firm in Washington, DC. Dr. McCausland's past positions include Dean of the U.S. Army War College, member of the National Security Council Staff, and Professor of Leadership at the U.S. Naval Academy. He also serves as a national security consultant to CBS television and radio. Dr. McCausland is a retired colonel in the U.S. Army and holds a Ph.D. in International Relations from the Fletcher School of Law and Diplomacy.

BRENDON O'CONNOR is a senior lecturer at the School of Politics and Public Policy, Griffith University. He is a recipient of a Fulbright Fellowship in support of his ongoing research on anti-Americanism, and organized a Fulbright symposium on this topic at Griffith in July 2006. His publications include a four-volume series titled *Anti-Americanism,* which he is editing for Greenwood Press (forthcoming) and a coedited book, *The Rise of Anti-Americanism,* published by Routledge (2005).

JAMES J. PRZYSTUP is a senior research fellow at the Institute for National Strategic Studies of the National Defense University, Washington, DC. He has worked on the staff of the U.S. House of Representatives Subcommittee on Asian and Pacific Affairs and on the Policy Planning Staff of the U.S. Department of State. He also served from 1994 to 1998 as director of the Asian

Studies Center of the Heritage Foundation. Dr. Przystup is a specialist in Asian security issues, and has a Ph.D. in Diplomatic History from the University of Chicago.

LEIF ROSENBERGER has been the economic advisor at the U.S. Pacific Command (PACOM) since 1998 and is a broadly acknowledged expert on Asian national economies. He is the primary author of *Asia Pacific Economic Update 2005*. Before going to PACOM, Dr. Rosenberger was Professor of Economics and held the General Douglas MacArthur Academic Chair of Research at the U.S. Army War College. He currently teaches international finance and trade in the Executive MBA program at the University of Hawaii. He also has served on the faculties of Harvard University and Dickinson College.

DON RUSSELL is an executive director with West LB Mellon Asset Management in Australia. During 1985-93 and again in 1996, he was the principal adviser to the Honorable Paul Keating during his time as Treasurer and as Prime Minister. During 1993-95, he served as Australia's Ambassador to the United States. Dr. Russell holds a Ph.D. from the London School of Economics and Political Science.

JAMES A. SCHEAR is director of research at the Institute for National Strategic Studies (INSS) of the National Defense University, Washington, DC. He has held research appointments at Harvard University, the Brookings Institution, and the Carnegie Endowment for International Peace. Prior to joining INSS, Dr. Schear served as Deputy Assistant Secretary of Defense for Peacekeeping and Humanitarian Affairs (1997-2001). In 1999 he was awarded the Secretary of Defense Medal for Outstanding Public Service for his efforts during the Kosovo crisis. In 2006, he served as an advisor to the bipartisan Iraq Study Group cochaired by former Secretary of State James Baker III and former Congressman Lee H. Hamilton. Dr. Schear holds a Ph.D. in International Relations from the London School of Economics and Political Science.

ANDREW SCOBELL is Research Professor of National Security Affairs at the Strategic Studies Institute (SSI) of the U.S. Army War College. He is also an Adjunct Professor of Political Science at Dickinson College, Carlisle, PA. Dr. Scobell has written and lectured extensively on Asia-Pacific security. Among his most recent works is his edited volume (with Larry Wortzel) titled *Shaping China's Security Environment: The Role of the People's Liberation Army* (U.S. Army War College, October 2006). Dr. Scobell taught at the University of Louisville and Rutgers University before joining SSI in 1999. He holds a Ph.D. in Political Science from Columbia University.

DOUGLAS T. STUART is the first holder of the J. William and Helen D. Stuart Chair in International Studies at Dickinson College, Carlisle, PA. He is also an Adjunct Professor at the U.S. Army War College. Dr. Stuart has written extensively on U.S. national security policy, NATO politics, and Asia-Pacific security. He is the author of *Phalanx: A History of the 1947 National Security Act* (Princeton University Press, forthcoming). He is a former NATO Fellow, and a guest scholar at the Brookings Institution, the U.S. State Department, the International Institute for Strategic Studies, and the Elliott School of George Washington University. Professor Stuart received his Ph.D. in International Relations from the University of Southern California.

BRENDAN TAYLOR is a lecturer in graduate studies in the Strategy and Defence program at the Australian National University. He is a specialist on Northeast Asian security, American foreign policy, economic statecraft, and alliance politics. His recent publications include an edited book on the changing nature of Australia's Asia-Pacific security relationships, published by Routledge (forthcoming), and "US-China Relations After September 11: A Long Engagement or Marriage of Convenience?" in the June 2005 issue of the *Australian Journal of International Affairs*. Dr. Taylor received a Ph.D. from the Australian National University.

WILLIAM T. TOW is a professor in the Department of International Relations at the Australian National University. His research interests include alliance politics, U.S. security policy in the Asia-Pacific, and Australian security issues. He is the editor of the *Australian Journal of International Affairs*, and has held teaching and research appointments at numerous universities, including the University of Queensland, Griffith University, the University of Southern California, and Stanford University. He also has served as a visiting research associate at the International Institute for Strategic Studies, and as a member of the Foreign Affairs Council and the National Board of Directors of the Australian Fulbright Commission.

MICHAEL WESLEY is director of the Griffith Asia Institute at Griffith University. Prior to taking this position he was the Assistant Director-General for Transnational Issues at the Office of National Assessments. His research interests include Asia-Pacific politics and security, UN peacekeeping, Australian foreign policy, and regional organizations. His recent publications include *Making Australian Foreign Policy* (coauthored with Allan Gyngell,

2003). Professor Wesley is the research convenor of the Australian Institute of International Affairs, a member of the Australian Member Committee of the Council for Security Cooperation in the Asia-Pacific, and a member of the Australian Research Council's College of Experts. Professor Wesley holds a Ph.D. in International Relations from the University of St. Andrews in Scotland.